FEMINIST THEATERS
IN THE U.S.A.

In *Feminist Theaters in the U.S.A.* Charlotte Canning takes an in-depth look at the growth of grassroots feminist theater in the United States of America from 1969 to the mid-1980s. These women were no longer content with portraying women's experiences created from a male imagination, being relegated to a few isolated positions in theater organizations, or continually seeing their labor erased from theater history. Instead, inspired by the strength of the "women's lib" movement, they formed theater groups of their own across the country. Charlotte Canning, by interviewing over thirty women who were part of this movement, reveals their influences and their influence, their methods, their history, and their reception from audiences and critics. These women offer a first-hand account of the excitement, struggles, and innovations of this significant dynamic era.

Feminist Theaters in the U.S.A. not only provides a historical survey but also achieves a fine balance between critique and celebration. Canning reveals a history which enriches, empowers and challenges modern-day feminist theater practitioners, theater historians, and students.

Charlotte Canning is Assistant Professor in the Department of Theater and Dance at the University of Texas at Austin. She has published a wide variety of articles about feminism and theater history.

GENDER IN PERFORMANCE
General editors: Susan Bassnett and Tracy C. Davis

The *Gender in Performance* series reflects the dynamic and innovative work by feminists across the disciplines. Exploring both historical and contemporary theatre the series seeks to understand performance both as a cultural and a political phenomenon.

Also available:
CONTEMPORARY FEMINIST THEATRES
To each her own
Lizbeth Goodman

ACTRESSES AS WORKING WOMEN
Their social identity in Victorian culture
Tracy C. Davis

AS SHE LIKES IT
Shakespeare's unruly women
Penny Gay

FEMINIST THEATERS IN THE U.S.A.

Staging women's experience

Charlotte Canning

London and New York

First published 1996
by Routledge
11 New Fetter Lane, London EC4P 4EE

Transferred to Digital Printing 2004

Simultaneously published in the USA and Canada
by Routledge
29 West 35th Street, New York, NY 10001

© 1996 Charlotte Canning

Typeset in Bembo by
Ponting–Green Publishing Services, Chesham, Bucks

British Library Cataloguing in Publication Data
A catalogue record for this book is available from
the British Library.

Library of Congress Cataloguing in Publication Data
A catalogue record for this book has been requested

ISBN 0–415–09804–1 (hbk)
ISBN 0–415–09805–x (pbk)

Then it was August 26, 1970, and a march was called to commemorate the Nineteenth Amendment to the Constitution, the establishing of women's right to vote. . . . As we approached, what we saw took our breath away. Women everywhere – thousands and thousands of women. . . . [W]hat a sight the avenue was, women filling all the spaces, banishing the cars, the honking, the men. How we gazed upon each other. With what amazement and pleasure we talked and laughed and wept as we flooded that capacious boulevard. And with what confidence we lured the hesitant from the sidelines. How they fell into the arms of the river that we became that day, we women of all shapes, sizes, and ages marveling at each other.

(Eunice Lipton)

A gap thus exists between the event and our knowledge of it. We must turn to documents, artifacts, and reports in order to identify and construct the event. But even the best kinds of written and material evidence . . . are not the event; they are only the records of the past that still remain in the present. They are traces, footprints in the sand. Their meanings are potential rather than received . . . because the identity of the event depends in part on how it was constituted as a separate occurrence in the documentation itself. That is, someone else, before the historian, has already given meaning to the event in the process of designating and repeating it.

(Thomas Postlewait)

In a threatening world presence-through-memory can provoke a spirit of resistance among the threatened. Knowing this, many powerless groups . . . have grittily and richly kept their history visible and audible to and for themselves.

(Catherine Stimpson)

CONTENTS

ILLUSTRATIONS

ACKNOWLEDGEMENTS

A book like this cannot be written without the support of colleagues, friends, and family but it definitely could not have been written without the women I interviewed. Their generosity made much of what is in these pages possible. When my enthusiasm flagged theirs was strong; when I needed to continue conversations beyond the interviews by flooding them with letters and phone calls, they responded willingly. They shared their thoughts, experiences, and lives with me and I am grateful for this. The sense of feminist community I document in this book still exists and I was the fortunate beneficiary.

My work was begun at one university and finished at another. At the University of Washington I would like to thank Barry Witham, Shirley Yee, and Laurie Sears. Liz Fugate and the School of Drama Library provided me with invaluable material as did the Sophia Smith Collection at Smith College, the Billy Rose Collection at New York Public Library at Lincoln Center and the Women's Collection at Northwestern University. At the University of Texas at Austin, Oscar Brockett, Ann Daly, Sharon Grady, Lynn Miller, Joni Jones, Elizabeth Richmond-Garza, Sharon Vasquez, and David Mark Cohen have provided friendship, support, and encouragement. A Special Research Grant from the University Research Institute at the University of Texas enabled me to hire an assistant, Judy Sebesta, whose excellent work helped me to complete the manuscript. I would also like to acknowledge Maria Beach, James Harley, and David Thompson who were my assistants while I was writing.

There are many other colleagues throughout the profession who expressed interest in and excitement about my work but there were some without whose support this work would not have been finished. Janelle Reinelt and W. B. Worthen read and responded to

ACKNOWLEDGEMENTS

some of this work. Katrin Seig, Jill Dolan, and many of the other women in the Women and Theater Program of the Association for Theater in Higher Education provided intellectual and political support, as well as friendship. I especially want to acknowledge Esther Beth Sullivan. Her work and friendship have been models for me and without them this work would be much less than it is. I am grateful to Sue-Ellen Case for my training in feminist theory and theater and for her friendship.

I also want to acknowledge Tracy Davis and Talia Rodgers who edited this book. Their insights and information were invaluable. Particularly, Tracy Davis' close readings strengthened and improved my work immeasurably.

My extended family of Cannings, Hills, and Schwentkers, especially Andrew Canning, also played a huge role in my ability to write this book. I want to thank them for their patience, as well as their excitement and interest. I particularly want to single out Fritz Schwentker who has been extraordinary throughout. While carrying on with his own work he devoted time and energy to mine and in doing so provided me with more than he can imagine.

Ruby Rochetto deserves special thanks for supplying the cover illustration.

much of the instability described here has to do with the processes of constructing history, I think some of it is intrinsic to feminism.

Feminism and its past have a fraught relationship and my work was caught between two contradictory but coexistent trajectories that have emerged from feminism. One trajectory was shaped by the activities of early feminist histories and early scholarly works, recuperating and retrieving women's labor erased by the operations of theater history. This task has been mentioned by feminist historians as one of the primary duties of the scholar, to provide women with a history, demonstrating that their past is rich and varied by establishing precedents of women working successfully and innovatively in the cultural arena. Theater books such as Karen Malpede's 1983 *Women in Theater: Compassion and Hope* or the 1983 edition of Helen Krich Chinoy and Linda Walsh Jenkins' *Women in American Theater* operated in this vein. This kind of knowledge is empowering and signals to women that they are working within a tradition that supports and legitimates their work. As Nancy Rhodes describes above, knowing their history and their predecessors has given women the confidence denied them by the dominant discourse. The second trajectory is a more critical tradition that evaluates the women's and feminist contributions without feeling the same need to celebrate them or to refrain from commenting negatively on the contributions of early feminism. Works that moved along those lines, for example, are Jill Dolan's 1988 *The Feminist Spectator as Critic* or Sue-Ellen Case's 1989 article "Toward a Butch–Femme Aesthetic." Scholarly and theatrical activity has come to focus strongly on the investigation of the differences of race, class, sexual preference, age, and location, often castigating the feminism of the 1970s for its emphasis on the similarities of women, their experiences, and their struggles.

The contradiction between celebration and critique comes from the very fabric of feminism in the U.S.A. From the beginning of the Second Wave in the mid-1960s through to the present, feminism has been torn between embracing all women as sisters and potential feminists, and rejecting the efforts of earlier women. When feminist groups began to organize they dismissed outright the efforts of women earlier in the century as bourgeois, reformist, and counter-revolutionary.[2] While aware of these efforts, it was necessary, in order to gain credibility within radical circles, for them to take revolutionary China and the Civil Rights movement as their models rather than reaching back into women's history to the Seneca Falls

Declaration, the suffrage movement, or the various women's organizations of the late nineteenth and early twentieth centuries.

One of the first large public actions coordinated by many of the Women's Movement organizations took place as part of the Counter-Inaugural March on Washington D.C. in 1969. Designed to "give back the vote," the march protested women's oppression in a supposedly democratic society. The women organizing the march, including Shulamith Firestone and Barbara Mehrhof, invited Alice Paul, an early twentieth-century activist, leader of the suffragist movement, and the founder of the National Women's Party, to join them in the march and participate in the planned activities. "As . . . someone who had endured jail for the . . . cause, Paul was not interested in repudiating suffrage. Indeed, when . . . asked . . . to join them onstage in burning their voter registration cards, Paul reportedly 'hit the ceiling.'"[3] The anecdote could stand in as a metaphor for the relationship of feminism and history – the history is present but the relationships of the current moments and the past moments are complex, contradictory, and conflicting. As Sally Banes says in her study of 1960s' avant-garde performance, "to make a clean break from even a despised past is impossible."[4] Firestone and Mehrhof could not have had the vote to "give back" as a symbol of women's second-class status in the U.S.A. without the previous labors of Paul and others, yet the idea of giving it back was a direct affront to the women who had labored so hard to get it. The paradoxical relationship of feminism and history is well illustrated by this example. Suffrage, at the time, was crucial to women's ability to affect change but by the 1960s it was obvious that the vote was an insufficient tool to bring that change about. "Giving it back" was both a powerful symbol for, and a deep insult to, feminists.

The emphasis of personal experience over traditions and accumulated knowledge was a hallmark of the New Left, and the feminist movement also embraced it: "Action/experience was to take precedence over history and memory."[5] Feminism has continued the tradition of repudiating what happened previously in history in favor of a valorization of the present moment as more productive and radical ground for change. Writing a history of feminist activities is always contradictory, as it must in some way go against the material under consideration.

One of the ways feminism's conflicted relationship with its history is expressed is in feminism's constant state of change and the vigorous debate over that change. Since it was re-established in the 1960s as a major political movement, feminists have argued over what feminism means, who feminists are, and how to achieve what they want to achieve. Charlotte Bunch described the first national meeting of women involved in "women's liberation."

> Over two hundred women from groups in some twenty cities came to talk about women's liberation at a YMCA camp outside Chicago at Thanksgiving 1968. Snow and wind raged outside as verbal battles raged within. Arguments flew between groups defined as feminists and leftists, between advocates of reform versus revolution, between those labelled "politicos" and "life-stylists," whose focus was more personal.[6]

It is evident from her description that part of what inspires debate is the labels that attempt to differentiate among various kinds of feminism. Besides the "politicos" and "life-stylists" mentioned above, in 1974 Jessie Bernard identified "liberation-oriented women" and "rights oriented feminists" as the two "branches of the feminist movement."[7] Judith Hole and Ellen Levine in their 1971 book identify politicos as well as the "rights" and "liberation" branches as types of feminists.[8] Many of the labels were intended merely to identify different activities, although they could also be used to indicate preference as Alice Echols does in her 1989 book where she describes how cultural feminism diluted and undercut the more far-reaching work of the radical feminists.

In a move that influenced many feminist scholars in the U.S.A., especially those in theater, British feminist Michelene Wandor identified "three major tendencies" within feminism.[9] Wandor's three types were eventually adapted to the particulars of the situation in the U.S.A., but her major points were unchallenged. The three kinds of feminisms were radical (sometimes referred to as cultural in the U.S.A.), bourgeois (liberal), and socialist (materialist).[10] Briefly, radical/cultural feminism proposes that there are unalterable differences between men and women and that those differences are two separate cultures. Wandor identifies it as a "dualist analysis of social structures divided simply along gender lines."[11] Women are often celebrated as superior to men and that superiority must be celebrated and preserved. Bourgeois/liberal feminism emphasizes working with already existing structures to place women on equal footing with men. It stresses increased opportunities, more roles for women, including women playwrights in a season or jobs for women in non-traditional fields such as technical direction, but, as Wandor describes, it "accepts the status quo."[12] Socialist/materialist feminism places gender in the context of material and social conditions, and sees gender as a discursive construction. Gender distinctions are not reified as natural, as in cultural feminism, or simple discrimination, as in liberal feminism, but produced through a complex nexus of economics, culture, history, and other forces. Wandor also comments that it allows for divisions among women, recognizing that "there are times and issues over which solidarity between women can cut across class or cultural barriers, but it also recognizes the importance of struggles based on class . . . and that women can have important differences among themselves."[13] Even this brief and simplified summary demonstrates how productive the distinctions are and were, allowing women to identify different ways to be a feminist and explaining to some extent from where the disagreements and divisions among feminists might emerge. Perhaps inevitably these categories became rigid and qualitative. Ignoring what Sue-Ellen Case had written on the subject in 1988 when she encouraged people to see the competing theories not as a series of unalterable choices but as "tactics to be employed when they were useful," liberal, cultural, and material feminisms were often used as mutually exclusive categories, so if one were a cultural feminist one could not be a materialist feminist and so on.[14]

The work of feminist theater groups was often placed under the heading "cultural" feminist as differentiating it from liberal or materialist feminist, characterizing it as the necessary labor of pioneers who paved the way but had operated under naive or simple views of women and feminism. This work tended to be gathered under a single heading – cultural feminist theater or women's theater, indicating that it was all very similar, though I found the exact opposite to be the case. The groups in question turned out to be diverse in their politics, productions, and processes. A variety of positions on race, sexuality, and theory that were erased from a general perspective were, on the contrary, as crucially at issue when the work was done as they were when this work was written. That is not to deny differences or developments, but it is to say that the differences and developments were in part possible because of what preceded them. The issue was the position of the past within feminism. As the identification of the intersection of feminism and

5

theater is a fairly recent one it was often discussed ahistorically.[15] The widespread identification of the three feminisms mentioned above – cultural, liberal, and material – led me to a study of the groups examined in this book but ultimately they were insufficient to account for and differentiate among the work the groups produced. As Jill Dolan notes in the introduction to *Presence and Desire*,

> now that the sifting and distinguishing work has been accomplished and productively employed, feminist theater criticism and theory can move beyond the binaries of materialist and radical thought and practice, to look vigorously at how they can be combined and thought in tandem to create an even more vital critical method and creative practice.[16]

While Dolan drops liberal out of her consideration her summary situates this book productively. *Feminist Theaters in the U.S.A.: Staging Women's Experience* straddles both sides. While conceived of within the taxonomies, in realization it moved beyond them and yet the influence of both the taxonomies and their rejection can be perceived in these pages.

Grappling with these contradictions, while initially paralyzing, ultimately proved to be empowering. Rather than seeing them as negative, I instead saw that they offered proof of the dynamism and power of feminism. Many of the women interviewed for this work no longer do feminist theater the way they had done in the past, but all of them felt they had participated in something of immense importance and value. Joan Scott, in a debate with historian Linda Gordon over the use of poststructuralist theory in women's history, writes that "it is in the nature of feminism to disturb the ground it stands on," noting that the presence of difficult and frustrating contradictions do not signal "decline or disarray, but the vitality of this critical moment."[17] This work moves among different models of feminist critical and historical practice, making visible the achievements of women from an earlier moment in time, while including their biases, assumptions, and flaws.

Maintaining the tensions between history and feminism, celebration and critique, and change and stability greatly influenced the organization of this book. This book is not a strict chronology that offers a linear narrative of a specific set of feminist theater groups. Rather, it addresses the theater as a historical movement, by looking at the circumstances of its emergence, its position within feminist politics, its position within feminist communities of women, as well as its theatrical production and reception in the specific context of the U.S.A. The book participates in the feminist emphasis on personal subjective experience and memory over the collective historical memory by working primarily from interviews with the participants of the movement but it emerges from the later tradition within feminist scholarship that takes a more critical than celebratory approach. While all the women in the groups discussed here had positive experiences and did work that they still hold in high regard, at the same time they all remembered the challenges, difficulties and problems that their work entailed. The intention, then, is to be critical without losing sight of celebration, acknowledging that most theater experiences are usually both. In that vein *Feminist Theaters in the U.S.A.: Staging Women's Experience* also attempts to construct a possible collective memory by considering various groups in a single book. The women interviewed were chosen with an eye toward identifying voices and groups that have not received much critical or historical attention. For example, I did not interview anyone from At the Foot of the Mountain (AFOM) as I believe that, of all the feminist theaters, AFOM has received a great deal of attention – there have been dissertations, articles, and sections of books devoted to them – while many other groups included here have received little or no mention at all. AFOM is discussed because it was an important group but limited interview time and resources went to adding to rather than duplicating the information already available. Included also are some individuals whose work is clearly related to the themes, emphases, and interests of the theater groups. The primary focus is on work done by the theater groups but I endeavored to account flexibly for work that is related in a variety of ways.

The book is organized into six chapters plus an introduction and conclusion. Chapter one, "Writing the History of Feminist Theater Groups," examines the possibilities of constructing a history of the theater groups by delineating the notions of women's experience that shaped the theaters' work. Experience as a category of history is examined in light of the interviews I conducted and previous critical and historical works on the subject. The chapter proposes three categories for discussing the theater groups emerging from the subjects emphasized in the interviews and books and from the need to balance recuperation with critique.

"Feminism, Theater, and Radical Politics: Intersecting at Experience," the second chapter, establishes a grounding and genealogy for the work of the groups. It offers three possible contexts for viewing the theaters: the radical politics of the New Left, the larger feminist movement, and the experimental theaters in which many of the women gained their early training. The discussion also further articulates the notions of experience so crucial to feminist theater. Included are brief examinations of four experimental theaters to provide a more specific picture of the work that influenced women as they founded their own theaters. There is no single context appropriate for the work examined here and by offering multiple sources I hope the possibilities for different politics and practices of the groups become clearer.

The third chapter, "Collectivity and Collaboration," is an examination of the ways in which the groups were organized, of their working and creative practices, and of how they grappled with the differences of race and sexuality. The chapter concludes with the chronological histories of four groups to provide some possible realizations of the ideas discussed in the previous chapters. The four narratives provide a crucial illustration of the ways in which groups, although categorized together, can be examined as contiguous and entirely separate.

Chapters four, five and six concentrate on production and reception. Starting from the idea, as proposed by Michèle Barrett, that there is something that can be identified as a "feminist event," I examine what was onstage and how the audience reacted as ways to identify the "feminist event." This notion is predicated on an unstable relationship, that of the performers and the audience, and can be added to the list of "tensions" identified here in the introduction. Chapter four, "Representing Community and Experience: Plays About Mothers and Daughters," looks at one subject that came directly from concerns and focuses within the feminist community. Moving from definitions of community and ritual, a form that was intended to express those definitions, the chapter looks at specific plays as evidence of the importance of the mother/daughter dyad to feminism and the ritual/communal forms developed to represent it.

Another aspect of the relationship of experience and theater is explored in chapter five. "Representing the Patriarchy and Experience: Plays About Violence Against Women" works as an example of how feminist communities dealt with negative experiences that were imposed by the patriarchy, as opposed to those that were positively shaped by feminist revisions of culture, politics, and

8

relationships. In contrast to the mother/daughter bond, which was seen as a good experience devalued by the patriarchy, violence was viewed as a bad experience imposed on women, thus defining the experience as necessarily patriarchal rather than feminist.

The final chapter, "The Community as Audience," looks at the specific ways the community/theater relationship was played out by the audiences. The immediate and overwhelming responses of the audience formed a significant part of the experiences of feminist theaters. After a discussion of how the performer/spectator dynamic changed in the 1960s and 1970s, the chapter demonstrates how the altered dynamic was crucial for the theaters' investment in a reciprocal community relationship. This is followed by a brief conclusion that discusses the different reasons for the dissolution of many of the groups and the influence and impact of the groups on later feminist theater work.

Between 1969 and 1986 there was an explosion of feminist theater activity in the U.S.A. For the first time in history women had an enormous collective impact on theater. No longer content with portraying women's experiences created from a male imagination, being relegated to a few isolated positions in theater organizations, or continually seeing their labor erased from theater history, women, inspired by the growing feminist movement, formed theater groups across the country that were heterogeneous in size, repertory, organization, and politics. These groups were truly grassroots in nature – they were shaped with attention to local concerns and there were no national or celebrity figures setting agendas. This book offers one possible history of that activity. As Joan Mankin wrote to me in a letter discussing our somewhat different interpretations of parts of Lilith's history: "Of course everyone has her own ideas about what the focus of a book on feminist theater should be."[18] I hope there will be more books to follow that offer some of those other ideas. I also hope that women in theater never again find themselves in the position Nancy Rhodes did in the mid-1970s, as she described in the epigraph, unsure if there is a history of women and theater and disempowered by the absence of that knowledge. When her research turned up a history of women in theater she asked herself, "these were women doing these things and why can't I do them also?"[19] As her experience points out, a history, no matter how contradictory or problematic, is a crucial component of power, accomplishment, and change.[20]

1

WRITING THE HISTORY OF FEMINIST THEATER GROUPS

It's All Right to Be Woman Theater (founded 1969, New York City) defined their theater as a vehicle for the exploration of the experience of women together. "Whereas theater has been to date, a combining of specialists, the essence of our theater is to convey the collective experience."[1] The group stressed that the inspiration for creation is women's everyday lives, their dreams, feelings, and thoughts. "Making theater out of these private parts of ourselves is one way we are trying everyday to take our own experiences seriously."[2] When Karen Malpede asked them if, by basing their theater on their own life experience, they were assuming the audience's "personal but as yet unconfronted" experiences to be the same as their own, they replied: "What we're doing is confronting our own experience. . . . Because women have never really taken themselves seriously."[3]

IARTBW was focused almost solely on the celebratory side of experience. In the course of their only show, *It's All Right to Be Woman*, in which the specific content changed from performance to performance but the general outline remained the same, they had sketches about drug abuse, homophobia, and rape but the performance was primarily oriented toward making women feel good about their lives. They always began with the entire company singing together and accompanying themselves on simple instruments as they sat in a circle. The song was one they had composed, setting the poem, "A Chant for My Sisters," to music.[4]

> its all right to be woman
> dishwasher, big belly, sore back
> swollen ankles . . .

> its all right to be woman
> coquette
>   seductress
>   conniving bitch
> its all right to be woman
> chant for my sisters
> strong before me
> harriet sojourner emma and rosa
> harriet sojourner emma and rosa. . . .[5]

The show ended with the performers chanting in a circle. "As the chant ends, the audience joins the performers dancing and clapping, finally forming a circle of solidarity."[6] Theater that presented women's experience with a message of support and celebration was relatively unknown in 1969 and it is not difficult to see why it had a strong impact on its audiences.

The representation of personal experience as theater resonated clearly and inspirationally for many women. Karen Malpede, of New Cycle Theater, found it difficult to explain the impact that a 1971 performance by IARTBW had on her. The effect began even before the performance:

> I had never been in a room with three hundred women before and it was the most exhilarating experience . . . My first experience of it was total disorientation – okay, where's the focus? Where's the great man? Where do you look? And in two seconds, it all happened really fast, I was thrown back into myself.[7]

Clare Coss' memory of seeing the group for the first time was similar to Malpede's.

> I think the name really tells us what it meant to all of us . . . it's all right to be a woman! I just went to one performance . . . and I remember feeling totally affirmed as a woman, that it was the first time I had really seen a positive image of a woman onstage that made me think this is what my life is about. . . . They didn't wear costumes, dressed in everyday clothes, that was something impressive to us at the time. What it was was just speaking from their own experiences. . . . It was an important rite of passage . . . to be given permission, to be given validation of a feminist vision.[8]

Both Coss and Malpede describe moments of discovery without precedent in their lives. Neither of them could find an analogy for the experience, but both knew right away what it was they saw onstage: their own image and experience as they had come to understand them through feminism. The lack of conventional artifice, the everyday clothes instead of costumes, the improvisations around actual dreams of actual women, and the rejection of a traditional performance space were unsettling and exhilarating. By rejecting the standard conventions of theater, IARTBW gave women something both familiar and entirely new. Roberta Sklar of the Women's Experimental Theater saw:

> theater, however crude the methods were, however lacking in theater training and history, what I saw was the content very specifically generated from the female experience, not only the female experience but the specific experience of the people who were performing it. It was dovetailing the general female experience with the individual.[9]

The sense that there were connections among women emerging from shared experience was so far-reaching and so profound that twenty years later each of these women could describe the moment when she clearly and forcefully realized the implications of a performance by IARTBW.

While Malpede, Coss, and Sklar were not "average" audience members, in that they were all theater practitioners who would go on to create feminist theater, the most interesting feature of their descriptions of their memories of the theater group is the simultaneous connections they made between the performance and their individual lives, and the performance and their community. Each woman felt personally affected, saying "I was thrown back into myself" or "I remember feeling totally affirmed as a woman." But each woman also grasped the larger possibilities and significances that went beyond their own responses. What they described is remarkably similar to the process of consciousness-raising, looking to one's own life as the inspiration for political action. Their reactions clearly articulate the connections between feminist theater and experience, as well as the importance attached to that experience by the theaters and audiences.

IARTBW is one example of the way women had begun by 1969 to use theater to represent feminist interpretations of their lives derived from their experiences within the women's movement and

12

feminism. In 1970 Charlotte Bunch noted about this phenomenon: "Increasingly important are women's liberation plays, like *How to Make a Woman* produced in Boston. . . . These startle women into a new awareness of their situation and introduce them to the movement for liberation."[10] Identifying itself as "feminist theater," the newly established grassroots performance tradition was unprecedented in its absence of leading figures, central tenets, or model groups. By the mid-1980s most of these groups were no longer in operation. Most of their members had moved on to other theater ventures, a few abandoned theater altogether. Feminist theater took different forms, few women worked together in companies. But for at least fifteen years there was a dynamic political theater movement that spread across the U.S.A. Despite its prevalence, few works are devoted to it. That is changing, but as people write about this movement they discover, as I did, that the project demands not just attention to the subject at hand, but attention to the way the subject is identified, understood, and presented. It was not enough simply to interview participants and research publications, I also had to come to a critical understanding of how and why women told their stories, and my place in their narratives. I recognized that history is a form of memory and a history of feminist theater groups would be in many ways the history of the participants' memories of feminist theater groups. The published sources were also products of their moments in history and their places of production. Using them meant making critical moves similar to the ones I made as I interpreted the texts of the interviews. The resulting chapter tries to come to terms with these complex demands by framing the interviews, research, and writing as highly interested and theoretical enterprises. By starting with three women's memories of being witnesses to the kind of work they would all later go on to do, I hope to point out the instability and tenuousness of history as well as the passions the theaters have and continue to elicit.

INTERVIEWS AS HISTORY

How to position women's stories, in this case interviews, and the relationship of the historian to the history, specifically the interviewer to the person interviewed, is often at issue in feminist history. The history that follows is based on oral history interviews conducted up to twenty years after the events took place. The specific methodological choices that were made about this history were based on several sources including the changing and contradictory discourse of women's history since 1969, techniques and theories of oral history, and the specifics of the interviews themselves.

Debates occur constantly about how and why one does history, what makes feminist history feminist, and what controls the relationship of celebration to critique. The earliest attempts to theorize and offer a specifically feminist view of history were produced by the women in the New Women's History movement in the 1970s to early 1980s. Women, including Linda Gordon, Gerda Lerner, Paula Giddings, Carroll Smith-Rosenberg, and Joan Kelly, wrote histories of previously ignored topics such as the history of women and birth control, women and the family, and women and work, which they surmised were as formative for earlier generations of women as for themselves and their peers in the women's movement. These were subjects that had not been considered legitimate historical investigations by the historical establishment. "We were not trained to study women, nor had we thought to do so until the women's movement transformed our lives and our consciousness."[11] Women historians and women theater practitioners responded similarly by seeking to combine their feminist politics with their work.

Given this basis in the political reinterpretation of personal experience current in feminism it is not surprising that Gerda Lerner, as she theorized the components of a specifically "women's" history, wrote "[h]istory must include an account of the female experience over time and should include the development of feminist consciousness as an essential aspect of women's past."[12] What Lerner and others were calling for in history is that which Malpede, Coss, and Sklar had experienced while watching IARTBW, a connection between their own lived experiences and the women's experiences being explored onstage. Carroll Smith-Rosenberg points out that women's history was, to a great extent, dictated by the concerns and needs of the grassroots political movement that was and is the basis for feminism. The political movement and the historical project were intertwined; each providing the other with inspiration and information, "the focus of women's history followed contemporary concerns."[13] The New Women's History movement in academia empowered the political movement of feminism in two ways: by providing information about women and their experiences that had been erased, and by allowing women to re-examine themselves and their work in a new and liberating context. The grassroots feminist movement and community provided historians with the impetus and support to explore aligned concerns.

The more feminist historians delved into the category of experience, the less experience was simply the impetus for choosing certain stories and the more it became the defining category for telling those stories. Concentration on the lives of women pointed up the inadequacies of existing modes of creating history. Smith-Rosenberg documented her own changing methodology: "By returning to traditional male historical sources . . . I had begun to see women, not as they had experienced themselves, but as men had depicted them." She goes on: "I ceased to search in men's writings for clues to women's experiences. Rather, I . . . recommended the search for women's own words."[14] Thus it was believed that, with the introduction of women's "words" or experiences, the problems of re-defining history would be largely solved, that what had been created through the erasure of women would be abolished with their presence. These investigations correspond to what Sue-Ellen Case called "initial explorations" in theater that concentrated on creating a "basic vocabulary" and a general map of feminism's overall project.[15]

New Women's History made radical suggestions about the alteration of the field of history. The women who participated in the movement challenged traditional history to understand periodization as the organization of value and meaning, to add gender as a distinct category in historical investigations, and to critique constantly the definition of what constitutes evidence. However, this way of doing history was challenged by the growing interest in poststructuralist theories. The theories of Michel Foucault, Jacques Derrida, and many others brought new ideas and conceptions of history to bear on feminist history. Historians, such as Joan Scott or Denise Riley, began to use deconstruction and other theoretical models to reconfigure historical methodology and further grapple with the category of experience. Indeed, experience had become a paradoxical category for feminists: necessary but problematic. Poststructuralism took the same account of experience as New Women's History but explored its constitution of meaning for the political agenda of feminism. "Theory must be able to address women's experience by showing where it comes from and how it relates to material social practices and the power relations which structure them."[16] Poststructural feminist historians began with a

15

critique of the New Women's History model; acknowledging its importance and then widening the field to investigate ways of making histories that sought more radical solutions to the question of women's experience.

Joan Scott used poststructuralist theory in *Gender and the Politics of History* to examine the construction of gender and how that construction in turn constructs the meaning of experience. In her view, an untheorized interpretation of experience serves to reinforce norms and hegemonic interests rather than challenging them. Thus, women's histories "written from this position, and the politics that follow from it, end up endorsing the ideas of unalterable sexual difference that are used to justify discrimination."[17] Scott began from the premise that gender, and the experience and identity derived from it, is a construct placed within the intersecting discourses of politics, sexuality, history, race, and class.

> Experience is not seen as the objective circumstances that condition identity; identity is not an objectively determined sense of self defined by needs and interests; politics is not the collective coming to consciousness of similarly situated individual subjects. Rather politics is the process by which plays of power and knowledge constitute identity and experience. Identities and experiences are variable phenomena in this view, discursively organized in particular contexts or configurations.[18]

This configuration contrasts with Smith-Rosenberg's assertion that by using "women's words" she could present experience as the women themselves understood it. The stability assumed in experience is gone, reconfigured as something which changes constantly.

The shift depicted here was not a seamless replacement of one set of methodologies with another. Rather it was the addition of one set of theories to another. The value of poststructuralist theory was hotly debated by feminist historians, as Claudia Koonz wrote about Joan Scott's book:

> her [Scott's] theoretical work begins not with experience, a notion she considers so specious that she often encloses the word in quotation marks. ... The message seems clear: *Cherchez la femme* and leave real women on the side.[19]

16

Koonz expressed a very real sense of outrage at Scott's deconstruction of one of the foundations of feminist thought. This harsh attack on Scott certainly bears out Chris Weedon's assertion that the "meaning of experience is perhaps the most crucial site of political struggle over meaning."[20] Scott's focus, unlike the more stable focus of New Women's History-based critiques, concentrated on understanding and dismantling the effects of gender, rather than reinforcing them. Experience was not used as factual proof of women's difference from men but instead was positioned as material that demonstrated the way politics, identity, and experience shape one another to reveal the "silent and hidden operations of gender."[21] More recently Joan Hoff wrote that history influenced by poststructuralist theories has served to isolate women's history in the U.S.A. from other countries and that "because it uses far less confrontational language [it] . . . is also far less politically oriented, less concerned with describing and bettering the plight of women."[22] Hoff and Koonz are examples of scholars who see the use of poststructuralist theory as an abandonment of the bases of feminist history. However, there are useful methods to be adapted from each of these approaches.

Using the methodologies suggested by New Women's History, the interviews for this book would have been positioned as women's words giving unmediated stories of their work on theater groups. Women's testimonies of their experiences would carry a great deal of weight in the overall work. Working from theories inflected by poststructuralist theories, the interviews would work as interpreted accounts of what women constructed as their experiences in the moment of telling. There would be no assumption that the accounts are simply true; instead it would be assumed that they are versions created to suit the moment, the interviewer, and the situation. Oral history theories offer a way to follow both contradictory trajectories – to see interviews both as true and as impressions of occurrences, to use them as stable accounts of events and as subjective and conflicting memories. Combined with the feminist history methodologies outlined above, oral history makes this history of feminist theater groups possible because there is very little information about the groups in any traditional historical works.[23]

Historians regard oral recollections as overt interpretations of events rather than as records of them. Paul Thompson in *The Voice of the Past* writes that experience is a transformative category that gives "new dimension[s]" to existing history.[24] In his view, oral

17

histories, interviews, and accounts of personal experience are rarely used to validate the status quo, but instead are a "challenge to the accepted myths of history, and the authoritarian judgement inherent in its tradition. It provides a means for a radical transformation of the social meaning of history."[25] This method of historicizing offers a "voice" to those forced into silence by the processes of history more interested in and shaped by the concerns of the dominant discourses. Thompson's sense of these materials as oppositional is confirmed by Susan Armitage who, like Thompson, understands the possibilities of oral history as revolutionary, or at least resistant. Her model is derived from the engaged perspective of feminism, responsible and accountable to a specific social and political movement. She intentionally looks to women and their experiences as a vehicle for change.

> The very act of focusing on women and asking them "to speak for themselves" is a challenge to traditional male-centered history. We, the interviewers, make that challenge explicit by articulating the values we find in our interviews, and by locating them in a historical context.[26]

For Armitage, experience exists not only in the story that the interviewee has to tell, but also in the method the interviewer uses to bring the material to the attention of the public. The interviewer and the interviewee construct a collective historical subject together that offers a challenge to hegemonic interests. Because oral histories, she argues, rely heavily on interviews and emerge from shared labor and energy, the histories are consciously created through collaboration. This activity Armitage and others view as feminist.

Interviews provide more than a narrative of the events in question, they also present a complex picture of women's personal articulations of their artistic, political, and social positions. The interview "provides a picture of how a woman understands her self in her world, where and how she places value, and what particular meanings she attaches to her actions and locations in the world."[27] Telling personal stories not only supplies experiences as history, but also offers evidence about the complex processes surrounding the construction of meaning both by the interviewer, in the questions asked and the focused topics, and by the interviewee, in the answers given and the alternative topics offered. Experience emerges through a multi-leveled process: internal interpretation, reinterpretation in the intervening years as the historical moment changes, and choices made to cast the narrative appropriately for the interviewer. Concomitant with the narrative created by the interviewee, the interviewer's own interpretation plays a vital role in the construction of the oral history. Within oral history the historian generally enters the community as a stranger and asks for stories and experiences in order to interpret them and assign meaning to them. In this way, she inevitably becomes part of the story. Thus, determining the importance of orally received experience requires theoretical and historical operations as rigorous as those applied to written sources.

In "Doing Oral History" Renato Rosaldo describes this facet of oral history and the dangers of utopian or untheorized notions of the possibilities of experience. Rosaldo is fully aware that interviews do not contain facts but perceptions about the past shaped by the present. Oral histories are "texts to be read."[28] Interviews function as dual operations of a simultaneous past and present because they are culturally mediated texts offering a "past" in the present and are stories and attitudes about the present as well as the past. History and experience are not constants, past and present bear shifting relations to one another.

> Doing oral history involves telling stories about stories people tell about themselves. Method in this discipline should therefore attend to "our" stories, "their" stories, and the connections between them. The process of restructuring the past, in other words, requires a double vision that focuses at once on historians' modes of composition and their subjects' ways of conceiving the past.[29]

Given both the political ramifications of the possibilities of resistance to the dominant discourse in oral history as expressed by Thompson, Armitage, and Rosaldo and the understanding of oral history as an expression of lived experience as history, oral history combined with the feminist methodologies discussed earlier creates a productive method for writing a history of feminist theater. A characteristic common to all the interviews, identifying experience as the basis of feminist theater, emerged not only from the stories of the women cited at the beginning of this chapter, Malpede, Coss, and Sklar, but also in all the interviews I conducted. The women were adamant in their focus on this as the groups' primary interest.

One part of oral history is the story teller's relation to the experience she relates. This is demonstrated by the ways the women interviewed told their stories, the values and emphases they placed in their narratives, and the events they chose to relate. Another element is the historian who inserts herself into the community. This required me to understand myself, my feminism, and my theories of history discursively. I entered the communities as a self-proclaimed feminist but I was not part of these particular communities of feminists. I was differentiated by my generation, my status as an academic, and my post-1970s feminism. I was given entrée by members of the community who have since moved into academia. The possession of the initial set of names, addresses, and phone numbers gave me legitimacy in their eyes and I was thereby able to earn an element of trust.[30] The training I received in the university led me to question and investigate in very specific ways. My interests and focuses were readily apparent to the women I interviewed, and their stories were certainly tailored to suit their audience.

The picture of feminist theater groups I received was a tapestry marked by contradictions, loyalties, and disagreements that predated the interviews I conducted. The stories were obviously shaped by the women's relationships to the people in their narratives. In every interview each woman was adamant that she could only tell her own story and that her story was probably not the entire account. "You'll have to get other parts of the story from other people,"[31] was an attitude most women continually stressed. They felt my distance from their stories and recognized that there were limits to their personal conception of the past. Muriel Miguel, during the account of a particularly difficult moment in Spiderwoman Theater's history, paused to say "this is from *my* point of view, *personally*, Muriel Miguel talking about what happened then."[32] Terry Baum, narrating the events of her break with Lilith Theater, was firm that her account was not unconflicted. "Michele [Linfante] and I go back over what happened. I wouldn't say we recollect the same exact thing differently, but we recollect different pieces of the same thing."[33]

It would be impossible to write a seamless, traditional history of feminist theater because my interpretation of feminist theater is caught in the contradictions of a still vital community and it would radically alter the community I encountered to try to resolve those contradictions. This history follows Paul Thompson's definition of oral history in that it "brings history into, and out of, the community."[34] This focus continues the collective orientation of feminist theater into its history.

No one woman interviewed believed that her personal biography could encompass the entire story of what had been a collective movement. There was the distinct attitude that while it took several individual experiences to create the collaborative experience, neither the individual nor the collaboration was more important than the other. The history of the feminist theater movement was already collaborative before I arrived on the scene. My task was to unravel the collaborations by interpreting the interviews in the context of other accounts and other interviews I had conducted. Renato Rosaldo advocates this doubled interpretative move, proposing that the historian "must study historical consciousness because it is the medium through which oral testimonies present the shape of the past."[35] Thus, my conception of feminist theater had already begun to be shaped by the few available books, articles, and reviews before even I began to interview women in December of 1989. These published materials not only played a crucial role in my understanding of feminist theater groups but they continue to be the primary sources to which people turn in order to research the groups. This situation makes it crucial to understand the books and articles as well as the process of interviewing. The interviews, the ideas contained within them, and my interpretations of the interviews demonstrate how my feminism of the later 1980s and early 1990s reads the feminism of the 1970s and early 1980s. While the primary and emphasized source of information for this book was the interviews, the published and unpublished written materials were also vital. This book does not stand alone but emerges from and relies on previous works in the field. A review of the work on feminist theater will provide a perspective on the historicization of feminist theater, and a framework within which to read the articles.

PUBLISHED SOURCES AS HISTORY

Most of the available works on feminist theater have attempted to provide visibility to women in the field. There is an uneasy balance between the endeavor to create an aesthetic theory through which to critique feminist theater and the wish to validate and celebrate women's theatrical work. The authors discussed in this section celebrate unreservedly the achievements of feminists in theater, generally adopting a sociological approach which Jill Dolan characterizes as the consideration of "theater as an image of positive or negative social images."[36] The articles and books discussed here

21

were the first works on the subject of feminist theater, and for many readers were an introduction to feminist theater as a movement beyond their specific communities. They helped to move feminist theater from a community phenomenon to a national movement.

My critique concentrates on the texts that are central to any examination of the theater groups. There are currently five books available that are solely about the feminist theater movement in the U.S.A. They are: *Feminist Drama: Definition and Critical Analysis* by Janet Brown (1979), *Feminist Theater Groups* by Dinah Luise Leavitt (1980), *Feminist Theatre: An Introduction to Plays of Contemporary British and American Women* by Helene Keyssar (1984), and *Feminist Theater: A Study in Persuasion* by Elizabeth Natalle (1985). I will also examine four journal articles that influenced the reception and history of feminist theater: Patti Gillespie's (1978) *Quarterly Journal of Speech* "Feminist Theater: A Rhetorical Phenomenon," Charlotte Rea's (1972) "Women's Theater Groups" and (1974) "Women for Women" in *TDR*, and Rosemary Curb, Phyllis Mael, and Beverley Byers Pevitts' (1979) "Catalog of Feminist Theater" in *Chrysalis*.

The list represents divergent approaches to and understandings of feminist theater. For the most part they share very little except subject material, looking at a finite pool of common groups within a similar time period. The only analytical approach shared by more than two of the pieces is rhetorical theory and is used by Brown, Natalle, and Gillespie in their discussions of feminist theater. The rhetorical model was not a feminist model; it relied for the most part on definitions and theories developed long before the feminist movement. Rhetorical analysis emphasized thought as expressed in spoken language to influence others and could not account for feminist theater as representation or cultural production. Gillespie's definition of feminist theater is the best example of the rhetorical approach: "all feminist theaters are rhetorical enterprises: their primary aim is action, not art."[37] Each article or book that quotes Gillespie duplicates the absence in her definition of a clear understanding of what the differences are between art and action and why art and action should be considered as two separate entities. The definition also avoids the task of distinguishing aesthetic political production from political activism. The focus is instead on supporting the politic expressed by the groups discussed.

Janet Brown's *Feminist Drama* is a version of her 1978 dissertation for the University of Missouri at Columbia Department of

Theater. The book focuses on defining a feminist aesthetic; she uses traditional criteria and does not treat feminist production as a body of work requiring new criteria and/or paradigms. While Brown uses the work of many early feminists, including Kate Millett, Simone de Beauvoir, and Mary Daly, her primary model is Kenneth Burke's rhetorical theories. Brown's concentration is not on feminist theater groups but on playwrights, devoting a chapter each to Rosalyn Drexler's *The Bed Was Full*, David Rabe's *In the Boom Boom Room*, Tina Howe's *Birth and After Birth*, Alice Childress' *Wine in the Wilderness*, and Ntozake Shange's *For Colored Girls Who Have Considered Suicide/ When the Rainbow is Enuf.*

The critical model of *Feminist Drama* is based, for the most part, on the artistic production of a single individual, so when Brown turns to the groups she finds it difficult to theorize one of the hallmarks of feminist theater: collective production. Brown herself notes the problem: "Adaptations in the method employed here may be necessary if it is to continue to be relevant to the study of feminist drama."[38] Her concentration is not on the groups themselves but on the four devices she identifies as definitive in feminist theater texts: "(1) the sex-role reversal device; (2) the presentation of historical figures as role models; (3) satire of traditional sex roles; (4) the direct portrayal of women in oppressive situations."[39] She examines the various manifestations of each device in the works of five theater groups and then defines their relation to feminism according to their employment of each device.[40]

Janet Brown's dissertation was written in a theater department, unlike the majority of the other works which came out of speech departments, but an absence of feminist theory in theater brought her to rhetorical theory.[41] This theory provided a way to examine theater for its political aims and to differentiate feminist theater from other kinds of theater. While rhetorical theory analyzes form more than content, and avoids a specific political commitment on the part of the writer, it was not always necessarily intended to be apolitical; instead rhetorical theory provided a productive framework through which to theorize the new forms of theater feminism was creating. What rhetorical theory could not account for was how the theatrical forms being created were specifically feminist since it was not a theory shaped by the interests and demands of feminism.

In 1991 Brown published *Taking Center Stage: Feminism in Contemporary U.S. Drama*. This book is a substantially revised version of *Feminist Drama*. In the introduction she acknowledges

23

the difficulties she had using Burke's rhetorical analysis with its emphasis on the single agent. However, she also notes that it is through the inclusion of Burke that she was able to write the dissertation at all. "Burke is a respected male literary critic under whose aegis I was able to win approval of my dissertation topic for a thesis on the (then) questionable topic of feminist drama."[42] Brown retains her emphasis on individual playwrights but places them within the context of feminist theory in the U.S.A., acknowledging the emergence, since 1979, of feminist theory specifically concerned with theater.

Elizabeth Natalle dealt specifically with feminist theater and was interested, like Brown, in formal concerns. Her project focuses on documenting the new feminist perspectives on theater. In doing so, *Feminist Theater* relied heavily on interviews, manifestos, questionnaires, and first-hand experience, making the book an invaluable source of information.

She pursued her study from "the rhetorical point of view."[43] This point of view centered her methodology and definitions on "feminist theater as a communication process." According to Natalle: "The drama is a persuasive message designed to influence the beliefs and convictions of both the members of the audience and the members of the theater."[44] If theater was simply persuasive "communication" alone then it is difficult to see how it was different from public discussion, poetry, or public protest. Natalle's analysis dealt with theater not as representation but as a medium for communication, albeit a medium concerned with affecting the attitudes of both the spectators and performers. Theater as an aesthetic venture and cultural production are not strongly present in Natalle's analysis.

Patti Gillespie's "Feminist Theater: A Rhetorical Phenomenon" is the most rigorous of all the pieces utilizing rhetorical analysis. Gillespie managed to use rhetorical theory while also accounting for feminist theater in a political/historical context. It was an important article for feminist theater because it was thorough in its research, using both mainstream and alternative press sources, as well as interviews with the participants. She set two questions for herself as a way into feminist theater: "Why did these theaters form in such numbers and with such suddenness?" and "Why did the theaters assume such diverse, and often quite non-traditional, characteristics?"[45] The article is invaluable from the descriptive point of view but it does not provide a productive theoretical model for the analysis of feminist theater. As long as feminist theater was "action, not art" theater itself remained an inconsequential detail, as opposed to the shaping factor in the presentation of ideas, politics, and intentions. The article endeavored to legitimate feminist theater as both a theatrical and rhetorical enterprise, but did so from the outside, seeing the specifics of theater as extraneous. She did, however, make some interesting and important choices. She connected feminist theater to the feminist political grassroots movement as a whole, something neither Brown nor Natalle did, she resisted a racist comparison to Latino or African–American theaters by refusing to compare women's oppression to that experienced by people of color, and she distinguished among various feminisms and the different theaters those feminisms created. These three elements are important, as Gillespie introduced a more complex and less amorphous model for the identification of feminist theater. But she still operated within rhetorical models which kept her from examining theater as representation and cultural production. Her model was different from Brown's because Gillespie did not refer to male definitions of rhetoric, but instead used feminist rhetorical theory, specifically Karlyn Kors Campbell's definition of feminist rhetoric as distinct from other kinds of rhetoric.[46] Gillespie created a specifically feminist space for her critique but the critique did not emerge from theory specific to theater.

Rhetoric was not the only theoretical model women experimented with when trying to theorize feminist theater. Helene Keyssar did not propose any specific theoretical model but did oppose her understanding of feminist theater to an Aristotelian definition of theater. Feminist theater and drama was proposed as the opposite of Aristotelian theater and drama in that it was not based on "self-recognition and revelation of a true 'self'" but rather on "a recognition of others and a concomitant transformation of the self and the world."[47] Keyssar's book is no more than a general introductory survey, as the vast territory she proposed to cover prevented her from doing more than a cursory review of the material. She did place feminist theater in a specifically theatrical context, but unfortunately it was not a feminist or theoretical one.

Charlotte Rea used no explicit theoretical model, and her approach was a celebratory journalistic one that applauded and reported the efforts of women in theater, concentrating primarily on production. She could assume that her audience was knowledgeable about theater as she wrote for a theater journal, allowing her to discuss feminist theater from a production-oriented point of view. Her lack of explicit theory led her to over-generalize about feminist theater, however, and, as Patti Gillespie pointed out in her article, Rea designated all of the theaters under discussion "women's political theater groups."[48] Gillespie indicates that there was a wide range of relationships to politics, feminist politics specifically.[49] But Rea's two articles are significant because for many people they were the first on feminist theater. Both are indispensable to anyone interested in the topic, and Rea covers many important issues including the lesbian/straight split and relationships to audiences.

Dinah Luise Leavitt's 1980 work offered an interesting methodology. Her discussion of feminist theaters puts them squarely in the context of feminist activity. She traced the appearance of the work of Kate Millett, the creation of professional journals, and the foundation of women's studies as "[a] revolution in women's art and literature."[50] *Feminist Theater Groups* demonstrated that the basis for this radical change was in the grassroots feminist movement's fight for the rights of women and the elimination of sexism. According to Leavitt, these two related but distinct manifestations of feminism, the academic and the grassroots, came together to create the context and possibility for feminist theater.

Leavitt used feminist art theory to critique feminist theater. "Inasmuch as theories of art pertain to the performing art of theater, feminist artists' and critics' ideas are of value in identifying feminist theater."[51] Feminist art criticism was clearly foregrounded as of limited but important use. The choice was an interesting and appropriate one. Leavitt, unlike Brown, Natalle, Gillespie, Keyssar, or Rea, placed value not only on putting feminist theater into a strictly feminist context, but also on feminist theater as artistic representation and political action: "all art is political and the personal belongs within any definition of art"[52] is how she delineated the intersection of feminism and theater.

"Catalog of Feminist Theaters" is divided into four parts. The article is aptly named, for it provides listings of feminist plays, organizations, and theaters as an encyclopedic primer introducing the breadth of activities occurring under the heading feminist theater. The first section, "Feminism and Theater: A Drama of Our Own," is written by Phyllis Mael and served as an introduction to the entire piece. It surveyed the new field, noting that "hundreds of women are now turning to drama as a viable genre for expressing their newly awakened feminist consciousness."[53] Mael concen-

26

trated primarily on providing statistics and information that demonstrated the novelty of the activity.

The second section is written by all three authors, Rosemary Curb, Mael, and Beverley Byers Pevitts. "Feminism and Theater: A Sampler of Contemporary Drama by Women" is a highly detailed annotated bibliography that is broken down into anthologies, published plays, unpublished plays, and source information. They even provide brief plot summaries on all the plays they list.

The first and second sections comprise Part I of the article and the next sections, dealing primarily with the theater groups, constitute Part II. For the third section Curb wrote the survey article "The First Decade of Theater in America" to characterize the theater activity based on the information she received from surveys of the theaters. She then uses the information for the fourth section, also in Part II "Annotated List of Feminist Theaters." Curb, with occasional contributions from the other two authors, provided information about founding dates, addresses, phone numbers, brief histories, financial information, political and artistic orientations, audience composition, and repertory. The fifty-four theaters were organized chronologically in order of founding date. This article was a very important effort in compensatory documentation and it provided a contemporary sense of the excitement and urgency surrounding feminist theater activity.

The rhetorical model used by Gillespie, Brown, and Natalle was a useful one when determining the goals and effects of feminist theater. Seeing feminist theater as a type of political action is important when determining its place in and relation to the larger feminist movement. The rhetorical model also recognizes that theater is a political enterprise that can be used to resist and oppose or support and uphold the status quo. Where the model ceases to be effective is when it neglects theater as a diverse mode of representation. Rhetorical analysis still exists and has not been abandoned simply because there is now a substantial body of feminist theater theory and criticism. Judith Zivanovic, in a paper read at the Themes in Drama International Conference in Riverside, California in 1988 and subsequently published in the *Themes of Drama: Women in Drama*, used a rhetorical approach to critique the collaborative nature of feminist theater.[54] Her primary citations were Gillespie and Karlyn Kors Campbell's article. In a move similar to the Campbell piece, Zivanovic maintains a distance between herself and feminism, removing herself from the political implications of the material, despite her reference to personal experience in feminist theater. The article has interesting observations about feminist theater's creative processes, but has no critique or analysis because Zivanovic ignores ten years of feminist theater theory and scholarship. She is unable to account for the demise of most feminist theater groups and the survival of the few she discusses (Spiderwoman and At the Foot of the Mountain).

There are three obvious exceptions to this list. The first is Helen Krich Chinoy and Linda Walsh Jenkins' *Women in American Theater* (1981/1987). While it is a valuable resource volume on companies, bibliographies, and data, it is intended more as a source book and sampler on women in theater rather than an in-depth examination of feminist theater groups. Many of the women who wrote the books and articles listed above also wrote the pieces on feminist theater in Chinoy and Jenkins' book. The arguments and approaches in *Women in American Theater* are covered by the discussions on the other material. The second exception is Karen Malpede's *Women in Theater: Compassion and Hope* (1983). This book, too, contains valuable source material but is simply an anthology aiming to place women uncritically in theater history, where they might serve as models and foremothers, and includes excerpts from their writings. The last exception to the list is Sue-Ellen Case's *Feminism and Theater*. Case's book addresses some of the theater discussed later in this work, but its contribution is more to an understanding of the many possible intersections of feminism and theater rather than the single intersection known as the feminist theater groups.

All these articles and books, including Zivanovic's, have a distinct sense of excitement over the possibilities and the future of feminist theater. There is also a confidence that the movement would continue to flourish, despite changes in feminism, the economic picture, or the theater scene. The articles do lack a distinctly feminist theory of theater, but they are also efforts at creating that theory from the specifics of feminist performance. The work responds to the connections between theater and experience as it endeavors to shape an academic practice in keeping with the material.

Most of the historical works on feminist theaters, whether or not they concentrate specifically on groups, include a section developing a working definition of "feminist theater." Lizbeth Goodman, in her book on British feminist theaters, writes: "In fact, the most difficult thing about writing on feminist theatres is reaching a definition which both the theorists and practitioners might agree."[55] It is interesting that in both Goodman's work and others' work the goal of reaching some sort of working definition(s) is not questioned. The previous version of this book included a section entitled "Defining Feminist Theater." As I re-read it I became more and more disenchanted with the project of struggling toward a definition, however provisional, as ultimately artificial, exclusionary, and discriminatory. At the 1993 Women and Theater Program Conference in Philadelphia, "Making Feminism/Making Comedy," Peggy Phelan in a discussion on the foundations of comedy refused to offer a definition, demanding instead that we ask: "What are the uses of comedy?"[56] I was liberated by her question. Rather than being trapped in the detailed work of creating a definition either too vague to be useful or too restricted to include all the self-identified feminist groups, one could move to the uses of the form and the terms as a way to identify the practices that could be productively labelled "feminist theater"; in other words, to answering the question of how the label "feminist theater groups" is used by the groups, by the scholars and critics writing about the groups, and by the individual participants themselves. The theater of feminist groups resists categorization. Thus, the section that follows does not propose a definition of feminist theater groups but instead identifies practices, relationships, and methods that characterize the process of doing feminist theater.

THE USES OF FEMINIST THEATER

In *Feminist Theater* Helene Keyssar endeavors to propose a working definition but ends up by writing:

> [p]articularly in its early stages, some practitioners felt that to define the genre was to place inappropriate constraints on a form that aimed at diversification. To avoid the simple replacement of one elite and compound voice with another, it was argued that no individual voice should bear the authority of definition. It was not that this voice was necessarily wrong or corrupt, unimaginative or even unrepresentative of the group as a whole, but that it carried no power that no other individual or group as a whole could equal.[57]

The rejection of the individual as the definition of a movement directly confronts the tradition of theater history. One of the reasons why much of the experimental theater movement in the U.S.A. has been able to move into the standard theater history texts is that, despite whatever relation each group may have to collectivity, the groups are easily defined by the work of one individual, such as Joe Cino, Ellen Stewart, or R. G. Davis. The approach contradicts a collective notion and erases the labor of the other people involved. However, it is undeniable that the individual leaders of Caffe Cino, La Mama, and the San Francisco Mime Troupe defined much of what was produced at those organizations. The same is impossible to say about feminist groups. As Patti Gillespie points out, feminist theater is "an example of a grassroots movement seldom witnessed in the American theater."[58] Designating one or two groups or individuals as definitive contradicts the grassroots organization of feminist theater. Doing so would elide differences in performance, politics, process, and geography.

Sue-Ellen Case and Jill Dolan escape the problems of definition in their books by writing less about a self-identified theater movement and more about the relation of different types of performance to different kinds of feminism.[59] Patti Gillespie examines two types of feminism and their connections to feminist theater, but within that she finds too many diverse relations to politics and expressions of those politics to define all of feminist theater. An article in *Ms.* in 1972 did not try to define feminist theater *per se*, but instead described many different kinds of theater that evinced a feminist politic: "Sometimes called guerilla theater, street theater, loft theater (and potentially Broadway theater)."[60] In an article in *Feminist Art Journal*, Linda Killian's definition is so inclusive that the reader is left with no idea of what differentiates feminist theater from any other theater:

What is feminist theater? Perhaps the best way to describe it is a myriad of different styles and a divergence of ideologies. Feminist theater ranges from being satiric, to serious, to outré, to political. Some feminist groups are consciously unorganized, while others are more structured.[61]

Killian divided feminist theater into three manifestations: (1) "Consciousness-Raising oriented groups, such as It's All Right To Be Woman Theater (IARTBW)"; (2) "politically motivated groups," such as the Los Angeles Guerilla Theater; and (3) "structured producing groups," such as Women's Interart Center or the Women's Project.[62] This move is very helpful as it recognizes that

30

not all feminist theaters had similar goals, despite a generalized shared politic, but it does not separate feminist theaters from theaters that are not feminist. Susan Suntree, a member of the Women's Ensemble of the Berkeley Stage Company, sees the "significant commonality" as "they often derive their materials from the actual lives of women, including themselves."[63] Suntree makes a crucial point: the strong emphasis on the actual day to day experience of women is a distinguishing feature of feminist theater. Killian and Suntree make two helpful moves in identifying feminist theater, a distinction among aims of theaters and the category of women's experience.

Elizabeth Natalle and Janet Brown offer definitions based on product. For Brown, feminist theater is any theater producing drama based on the "feminist impulse." She says: "This feminist impulse is expressed dramatically in woman's struggle for autonomy against an oppressive, sexist society. When woman's struggle for autonomy is a play's central rhetorical motive, that play can be considered a feminist drama."[64] Natalle, on the other hand, defines feminist theater as a "communication process." She states:

> The drama is a persuasive message designed to influence the beliefs and convictions of both the members of the audience and the members of the theater. . . . By using the stage as a speaking platform, feminists argue against their own oppression, seeking a change in their identity as lesser human beings and their subordinate position in society.[65]

The definitions set forth by Natalle and Brown leave significant gaps. Brown sees feminist theater intra-textually, unconcerned with the production of text, and Natalle envisions feminist theater without accounting for representation and producing conditions. Both those absences are important because neither discusses the theater as a live event with important functions in the feminist communities.

While none of the previous views of theater is wrong or inaccurate, all of them beg certain questions. Patti Gillespie warns in a footnote that one of "the most frequent errors is the lumping of all theaters together,"[66] but many of the other writers ignore or downplay this important point. There is also little discussion of what it means to base a theater movement on lived experience, despite the general agreement among the writers that this element is one of utmost importance.

Killian's distinction among different theater organizations, Suntree's suggestion of women's experience as definitive, Brown's emphasis on struggle within a sexist society, Natalle's focus on an audience/performer interaction, Keyssar's notion of resistance to definition, Gillespie's stress on the grassroots, non-centralized emergence of feminist theater, as well as the explorations by Case and by Dolan of the political implications of reception, interpretation, and difference for feminist theater are productive parameters for understanding the uses of feminist theater. Taken together they suggest that what differentiates feminist theater from other theater movements are three separate, but inter-related, relationships of the theater experience. These relationships will be positioned throughout the book as vital to all the work on feminist theater and they come from an analysis of the issues identified as important and definitive by the women who actually created and ran the groups.

Thus, I believe that an understanding of feminist theater should concentrate on performance, in the dramatic texts and the audience/performer interaction; on structure, both in the creative process and the group itself, focusing on the relationship to collectivity and collaboration; and politics, in the extremely varied manifestations of feminisms and the way they shape theatrical expression. All three of these relationships are intertwined in a notion of feminist community. Despite the artificiality of these distinctions, they are useful in that they allow differences, biases, and commonalities to emerge.

One of the unique aspects of feminist theater is the relationship between performers and the audience. While all of the books and articles acknowledge the interaction to varying degrees, I think it is a highly significant feature of this theater movement. Performances of feminist theater have been credited with reactions as predictable as that of Suzanne Messing, when writing about her experience of reciting her matrilineage at a performance of *Daughters* by the Women's Experimental Theater (WET) in 1980:

> Of course I always knew it; however, when saying it aloud, I suddenly understand it. My mother, my daughter, and I are bound by more than kinship. We are survivors, the last of a clan, the last of who knows how many generations of related women.[67]

Performances have also elicited more extreme responses, as the New York Feminist Theater found during their tour of Canada in the summer of 1974. "Women in some of the towns the New York Feminist Theater performed for actually left their homes and joined the troupe."[68] All the women I interviewed or read interviews with felt that the relationship of both the performers and the performances to the audience was one of the defining characteristics of their experience. Great emphasis is placed by feminism on the relations of women to women, and feminist theater groups took this to heart. How each piece would affect and relate to the audience was always a significant part of the creation process. Susan Suntree wrote of her experience with the Women's Ensemble in 1975–76 that the performers always began every performance by mingling with the audience, emphasizing their collective commonalities. This grew out of the rehearsal process, as Suntree notes:

> Because we were audience to one another we grew accustomed to trying to speak with both honesty and tenderness. The atmosphere created the intimate tone of the piece we shaped and carried into performance. We never lost sight of our desire to communicate to an audience, the audience was always there.[69]

The majority of feminist theater artists working in groups consistently strived to create connections with the audience that emphasized commonalities and similarities. The artificiality of fourth wall voyeurism was seen as a male device that would divide women from one another. Emphasis was on responsibility to an audience composed not of passive spectators but of participants joined with the performers in a common movement.

Concomitant with the relationship to the audience is the way that the relationship was effected, or the various styles and approaches used to create the works and performances. When moving from male-defined experimental theaters or traditionally oriented academic training programs, women regarded their inherited tools and techniques with the greatest suspicion. Roberta Sklar told Cornelia Brunner that

> The Mutation Show [1974] was the end of my work with the Open Theater. I had to make a change that would articulate my being a woman. I was disillusioned enough . . . to think that the theater was not really "it" for me. I realized that the struggle for a woman in a sexist world is so vast that wherever I worked the struggle would be enormous. Until then I had

33

somehow thought that I was "equal" with the men in the company even though I knew the outside world did not think so. But when it came to struggles about women, the men could no longer see the issues as political; suddenly it was all very personal. I realized I would have to go through a very major struggle to do what I wanted ... I had to figure out if the theater – as I knew it – was the right arena for me.[70]

While she would later use the methods developed from her work with the Open Theater to create works with Womanrite and WET, Sklar did so in a highly conscious way. This kind of consciousness about the creation of theater was one form of theorizing and most groups created theories as they created theater.

Another source of inspiration for performance content and relationships came from the specifically feminist process of consciousness-raising. While this will be discussed at length in the next chapter it is important to note that the context for the relations of women to other women, and the process for their politicization, was an important influence on the style and content of feminist theater. The emphasis on relating the experiences of women necessitated a new way through which to tell the stories. Acting exercises such as At the Foot of the Mountain's (AFOM) feeling circle were "conceived as a means to train actors to identify their emotions."[71] Martha Boesing opposes AFOM's approach through the feeling circle, a direct outgrowth from consciousness-raising, to professional male-defined approaches, as she told Meredith Flynn in the early 1980s:

When we started Foot of the Mountain, one of the premises we used was that the actors were going to follow their feelings– train them as much as they did their bodies and their voices. We came with the premise that in the professional theater, people are told to leave their feelings at the door. . . . We try to start with the exact opposite – bring it in, use it so that the whole person, the whole actor can be there, not leaving part of yourself at the door.[72]

Thank-You Theater in Los Angeles, it was noted in 1973, toured a four-woman show that was intended to serve as a "consciousness-raising session, releasing the rage inside, and then in the after session allowing for the sharing of experience."[73] The play was organized as a trial of men for their oppression of women. Mythical women, such as Eve, are juxtaposed with literary characters, such as Gertrude and Ophelia, and with actual women such as Zelda Fitzgerald. The "denunciation of the patriarchy" was performed all over the Los Angeles area as an introduction to the women's movement.[74]

Some groups took their inspiration more directly from the political scene, performing on the street in confrontational ways, staging mock protests and fake events. Los Angeles Feminist Theater (LAFT, founded in 1969) staged "elevator plays" in corporate headquarters in downtown Los Angeles in the early 1970s. Sondra Lowell, who organized the events, described a couple of different scenarios. In one, women posing as secretaries get on the elevator carrying their personal effects, declaring loudly enough for everyone to hear that they are quitting. They then detail the reasons for their resignations:

> Her boss yelled at her for putting too much sugar in his coffee again; he told her not to question his authority again; he gets a bonus for her suggestions, etc. . . . At the ground floor, the women all rush out of the elevators shouting "I can't take this crap any longer!" – and burn their steno pads.[75]

Lowell admits that in performance the play was much less spectacular. They complained more and tried to spark conversations among other people in the elevators. Sometimes they overheard other women agreeing with them, but they never incited an actual walk-out nor did they burn any steno pads. But whether or not they followed their script to the letter, LAFT successfully blurred the lines between audience and performers and between theater and everyday life.[76]

The live elements of theater, performer, and audience would not have been shaped the way they were, with an emphasis on women's experience as the base of creation and interaction, if process and structure had not been shaped by this criterion as well. Not all feminist theater groups were collectively organized, but some women were so strongly committed to the collective ideal that they refused to be identified individually by name. When Karen Malpede interviewed IARTBW Theater in 1972 she noted that

> [w]hat follows is an interview with eight of the eleven members of the It's All Right to Be Woman Theater. At their request the remarks of the individuals have not been differentiated.

Therefore each answer is a combination of comments, sometimes conflicting, from most of the women present.[77]

As Patti Gillespie found in 1978, Womansong Theater, in a move similar to IARTBW's, omitted the names of the performers from programs in an effort to redirect the focus of the audience away from the individuality of the performers.[78]

While the two examples above are extremes of the desire for complete collectivity, they are indicative of the commitment to value group labor and ensemble work over personal ambition, as well as the rejection of a hierarchy founded on the glorification of one person's vision. There was a strong belief that the performance text created through collective process would be more illuminating than that produced by a single individual. Collectivity required active participation that moved the burden of creation from the individual to the group:

> If every member must rely on her own creative output instead of relying passively on the leader/director for inspiration and guidance, then the theatrical forms that the group produces must convey to the women in the audience that they, too, possess untapped potential for artistic creativity.[79]

Collectivity in theater was a microcosm of the larger women's movement and was a way to explore connections to the women participating as audience.

Collective collaboration was often claimed as the feminist approach but not all groups organized themselves collectively. The majority of feminist groups did feel a responsibility toward or, at least, accountability to the idea of collectivity. Groups not organized as collectives often felt the need to defend the choice. In 1972 Anselma Dell'Olio, the founder of the New Feminist Theater, believed "in the necessity of the director/leader because 'I care more than anyone else . . . the energy comes from me.'"[80] The majority of feminist theaters, however, placed value on work created through intense collaboration in which all input was welcome and ostensibly equal. Based on this, the roles of collectivity and collaboration are extremely significant to feminist theater, differentiating it from other theater movements, even when those movements valorized the collective structure. The collective was an important expression of the feminist belief that the personal was political and that a rejection of hierarchy was a step toward the demolition of the patriarchy.

"[C]ommunal organization ... expresses their rejection of the hierarchal organization of traditional theaters, which they identify with patriarchal values."[81] A theater's organization was connected to the kind of feminism the group espoused, but all the groups recognized that organization had political meaning. An examination of structure is integral to an exploration of feminist theater, since part of the legacy of that grassroots movement is the emphasis on new and alternative theater organizations and structures.

As has been emphasized previously, women's experience was definitive in many aspects of feminist theaters. This is nowhere more true than in the process of creating performance texts. Sometimes the work would be created from within the group using only the experiences of the members of the group, as in the first works of Lilith. Others, such as the Rhode Island Feminist Theater (RIFT) or WET, did research outside the group by reading feminist books and interviewing women. When RIFT developed a play on office workers in 1980 they interviewed many receptionists and secretaries who worked in the Providence area.[82] Spiderwoman began in 1975 as a workshop of Native American and non-Native American women exploring the concept of storyweaving using women's lives as the starting material.[83] Feminist theater was often process oriented; members considered the methods employed to create the work as important as the work itself. Labor was intended to be shared equally, no matter what the task, as the environment was part of the product. Feminist theaters tried to enact feminist ideals behind the scenes as well as on the stage.

Another important component of feminist theater is the political uses of feminism by the individual groups. Calling these forms of theater "feminist," as I have throughout my work, begs some questions. Many of the theaters called themselves women's theaters, rejecting the feminist label for a variety of reasons reflecting, in many cases, their conceptualization of feminism as an inherently narrow politic. Some, such as Nancy Rhodes, claimed that "isms" were limiting to an artist,[84] others, such as Margot Lewitin, as quoted by Jill Dolan, feel that many women decide not to call themselves feminists "so as not to limit their work."[85] Feminism, as each group understood it, determined the issues explored and the audiences interested in the work. When Anselma Dell'Olio said that she hoped to reach an audience of "housewives and businessmen"[86] she was working within a different politic than Women's Collage Theater who preferred all-women audiences for their show *Sirens* which toured from 1976 to the early 1980s.[87] If feminist theater is, as Elizabeth Natalle describes it, "not only a voice that reflects the ideas of the women's movement, but ... also a part of the movement as a contributor of ideas,"[88] then it is important to examine how it functioned as an expression of feminism and women-centered ideals. The analysis of feminist theater is centered on performance, in the performer and the audience dynamic, on structure, in the creation process and group organization, and on politics, in the different feminisms enacted and espoused. The acting/audience dynamic is an important axis along which to move in a definition of feminist theater because the relations of women was focused upon by feminism. Often feminist theater groups performed in non-theater contexts and few had money for elaborate production values. The focus was the people. This dynamic of the group's organization is important because many of the women had had experiences like Roberta Sklar's in finding their work devalued or thwarted. Women were determined that the strategies that had forced them out of male-defined groups would not be repeated. Their politics also varied, leading them to create diverse works on many subjects.

Despite my critique of the published works I still rely on them heavily as valuable resources. Although I realize the interviews I conducted are in no sense the singular or final truth about the feminist theaters discussed here, they are a provisional picture of those activities rooted in the times, places, and circumstances of their production. However, using those sources critically is another way of "using" feminist theater, meaning that all the sources discussed here contribute and contributed to how the term is and can be used, as well as what one can discuss as feminist theater. The groups, ideas, and performances that writers chose to include heavily influences what a historian, looking back, will see as feminist theater. Some of the names of potential interviewees were from the sources used here. Rather than see any of this as a "true" depiction of feminist theater groups, I see it as one possible interpretation rooted in a specific time and place. This does not make the subsequent work inaccurate but places it as part of a larger effort to put the work of the feminist theater groups into history with all their complexities and contradictions intact.

2

FEMINISM, THEATER, AND RADICAL POLITICS

Intersecting at experience

Feminist theater groups did not spring fully formed onto the stage, nor were they the next logical step in the linear development of experimental and consciously political theater. However, there were specific material circumstances that made feminist theater possible and this chapter will explore the contemporary political and theater scenes in order to document the interactions that produced the theater movement. A crucial focus that various political movements and theaters shared was a belief in the importance of everyday, material, lived experience. Suspicious of the focuses inherited from previous historical moments, the Left turned its attention to everyday lives and the theories and practices that could be derived from them. As an examination of the "Port Huron Statement" will demonstrate, erasing or ignoring what people experience in material existence was perceived as a dangerous, even hostile, mode of political analysis. Feminists believed that obscuring what women experienced was, in a large part, how women's oppression operated. Theater also participated in this investment producing texts and performances that were occasionally autobiographical, often based in improvisation, and usually based on events and information gathered from real women's lives.

RADICAL POLITICS AND FEMINISM

In June 1962, fifty-nine university students from across the United States gathered in Port Huron, Michigan, to draft a manifesto for their organization Students for a Democratic Society (SDS). Dismissing the "Old" Left as moribund and stagnant with staid and ineffective organizing tactics, the delegation, chaired by Tom Hayden, sought to offer a new agenda for political action on the Left.

39

Inspired by the civil rights movement, by the anti-HUAC (House Un-American Activities Committee which investigated alleged Communist activity) protests in 1960 by Berkeley students, and by theorists such as C. Wright Mills, John Dewey, and Herbert Marcuse, they proposed strategies that were to have a profound effect on the politics of the 1960s. Hayden borrowed the idea of "participatory democracy" from his teacher Arnold Kaufman and circulated an early draft of what would be later revised into the Port Huron Statement.[1] Beginning with their personal identifications as white middle-class students, the members of the SDS offered a new conception of the relation between the individual and the community, between the personal and the political:

We would replace power rooted in possession, privilege, or circumstances by power and uniqueness rooted in love, reflectiveness, reason, and creativity. As a *social system* we seek the establishment of a democracy of individual participation, governed by two central aims: that the individual share in those social decisions determining the quality and direction of his life; that society be organized to encourage independence in men and provide the media for their common participation.[2]

Believing that people were increasingly disaffected and alienated by the effects of mid- to late-twentieth century life, the students of SDS proposed an active political life to remedy the problem. "Politics," they wrote, "has the function of bringing people out of isolation and into community."[3] The SDS broke with the Old Left over traditional issues such as the U.S.S.R., communism, and Marxism. The standards of the U.S. Left were replaced with critiques of institutions and a concern with the processes through which decisions are made and agendas are formed.

It signaled an almost religious return to experience and a converse retreat from the abstractions of red politics of yesterday. One worked out personal and procedural issues in great and often exhausting detail as a way of fusing the personal with the political, of creating a community not primarily of interest (political rationalism) but of *feeling*.[4]

Establishing and sustaining community was one of the most important features of the New Left's approach to politics. While community was a group of people committed to similar goals and interests, it was intended that each person be considered individually, with unabridgable rights and privileges. It was not community in the sense of a Marxist collective where the interests of the group supersede the interests of the individual, but in the U.S. democratic tradition where the interests of the individual were seen to be the responsibility of the community. It was this kind of thinking that led members of different groups on the New Left to advocate the dismantling of the bureaucracy of the welfare state for "new institutions of popular participation."[5] They intended to take apart the existing structures of power and to replace them with ones run by people expressing similar political visions and intentions while retaining their individual voices and opinions.

By the mid-1960s the Youth International Party, or the Yippies, would fault the New Left for its unrelenting seriousness and its distrust of the more culturally oriented counter-culture movements. Influenced by the politics of the SDS, by the anarchy of the hippies, and by rock and roll music, the Yippies focused on symbolic politics under slogans such as "live as if the revolution had already happened." Formed in late 1967, the Yippies declined to engage in dialogue with the Old Left and unions, or to sponsor local actions to enfranchise the economically disadvantaged. Instead the Yippies concentrated on quick, decisive, and outrageous events designed to catch the eye of the mass media.

The two founders of the party had been developing a political aesthetic that would easily mesh when they met. Jerry Rubin first explored the relationship of pleasure and political action when he helped to organize the 1965 Berkeley Teach-In on the Vietnam War. He told Milton Viorst that the event was "fun, politics, and ideas together, an antidote to the main culture of the society around it."[6] In New York, Abbie Hoffman was developing a similar political approach with a group of hippies called the Diggers. The 1967 March on the Pentagon had originally been conceived of as a march on Washington but Rubin suggested focusing on the Pentagon as the center of military activity. While the New Left understood the march as a serious event Hoffman approached it as a huge joke, claiming he was going to levitate the Pentagon three hundred feet off the ground. Rubin, as one of the chief organizers of the march, had to remain on good terms with everyone involved but "as the weeks passed he moved further from the grim rebelliousness of the SDS to the saucy politics of Abbie Hoffman."[7] It was Hoffman who encouraged the hippies to put flowers in the barrels of the soldiers' guns, instantly creating an image that is one of the most reproduced and symbolic of the 1960s.[8]

The SDS and the New Left were responsible for the content and form of much of the politics of the 1960s. The student movements and anti-war protests came directly out of the New Left agenda. It was also the New Left that supported the notion that political strategies should find a balance between the community and the individual. The community was necessary as a forum through which the individual could find fulfillment and power, and the individual was the base of the community giving it shape and focus. The Yippies, on the other hand, spectacularized politics using the media to point up the representational nature of public action. Theater was almost inevitable because everyday life on the Left picked up on two of the important components of performance for most experimental theaters: the creation of work out of a collaborative community and the focus on representation and spectacle.

Feminism, too, found itself divided about the most productive path to take. Many of the women who organized the first political actions of the Women's Liberation Movement came from groups within the New Left. It was at a 1967 SDS convention that some of the basic premises of radical feminism were first articulated. Women argued for child-care, birth control and abortion information, and a policy of equal distribution of housework. Despite the theories of the New Left that valorized individual rights and egalitarian communities, the reception of the women's demands was not encouraging. The women were met with condescension and dismissed by the all-male leadership. This galvanized women and they eventually left the SDS to found their own movement. It was this contradiction between the theoretical liberation and the practical discrimination that led many women to move from the New Left to feminism.

Debates similar to the ones Stanley Aronowitz described over process, procedure, and about what strategies would be the most effective to end oppression and change material lives were duplicated in early feminist organizations. How discussions would proceed, who would represent the Women's Liberation Movement in the media, how to involve working-class women, and how to define their feminism were important and rancorous arguments within the different groups. Women identified themselves from the start as diverse types of feminists; politicos, radical feminists, or socialist feminists. Some groups mirrored the approaches of the

New Left in their emphasis on producing both theory and political action. Early protests such as the Counter-Inaugural March in 1969, the 1970 Ladies Home Journal sit-in, or the action to interrupt the 1969 New York State legislative hearings on abortion were familiar types of protests.[9] The Yippies also influenced feminist politics; WITCH, the Women's International Terrorist Conspiracy from Hell, was more interested in grabbing the public's attention than working with women to change their lives. WITCH, understanding the power of the mass-media and the importance of representation for politics, focused on zap actions rather than consciousness-raising. In 1968 the women dressed as witches and convened on Wall Street to "hex" the financial center.[10] Another New York based action was a 1969 protest at the Madison Square Garden Bridal Fair. WITCH members went to the fair wearing "black veils" and singing, "Here come the slaves/ off to their graves." The women also carried placards with slogans such as "Always a Bride, Never a Person" or "Ask Not For Whom the Wedding Bell Tolls." They ended the protest by releasing white mice into Madison Square Garden.[11]

A more infamous protest, planned by many of the women who would later form WITCH, was the September 1969 Miss America Protest. The event is significant for many reasons because, as Alice Echols points out, it "marked the end of the movement's obscurity because the protest . . . received extensive press coverage."[12] The protesters, almost a hundred in number, marched a live sheep on the boardwalk, crowned it Miss America, and performed guerilla theater sketches. As part of one sketch, for example, a demonstrator chained herself to a large cardboard woman with exaggerated features in a stars and stripes bikini. Women also "flung dishcloths, steno pads, girdles, and bras into a Freedom Trash Can."[13] Many feminists felt that this kind of protest was not appropriate because it attacked the women participating in the contest instead of simply attacking the power structure behind the contest. These women rejected the tactics of groups such as WITCH for marches, consciousness-raising, education of women, and legislative issues, including abortion, the Equal Rights Amendment, and women's civil rights.

As has already been discussed, one of the hallmarks of the New Left was an emphasis on experience. As the "Port Huron Statement" stressed: "It [the New Left] must form to the feelings of helplessness and indifference, so that people may see the political, social, and economic sources of their private troubles and organize to change society."[14] Feminists observed a great deal of hypocrisy in the realization of this goal – experience turned out to be shorthand for *men's* experience. Thus, when they broke with the New Left they took with them the investment in experience but not experience precisely as the New Left had defined it. The challenge facing feminists was how to identify women's experience. They needed to develop some process that would elicit the identifications of experience. The process that developed came to be called consciousness-raising.

The origins of consciousness-raising (C-R) are in a story that may or may not be apocryphal. During a meeting of the New York Radical Women (NYRW, 1967–69), an organization that included Shulamith Firestone, Robin Morgan, and Kathie Sarachild, one member, Ann Forer, commented that she wanted to understand the operations of oppression more clearly, especially the oppression she had experienced in her own life. "I think," she is supposed to have said, "we have a lot more to do just in the area of raising our consciousness."[15] The idea in the remark, that women's oppression was so much a part of their daily lives that they could not easily perceive it, led the NYRW to propose a series of exercises that feminists could use to analyze their own lives as a basis for feminist thought and action. The call for specifically feminist theory was to be answered by consciousness-raising discussion groups. Indeed, some of the earliest feminist works did come from women who had participated in consciousness-raising. Shulamith Firestone's *The Dialectic of Sex*, Anne Koedt's "The Myth of the Vaginal Orgasm," and Kate Millet's *Sexual Politics* are all founding texts in feminist theory and were all inspired, in part, by the revelations that came out of consciousness-raising.

The discussion group format of sharing lived events and reinterpreting them politically was based on many sources: the civil rights movement; the 1966 book *Fanshen* by William Hinton, popular with the New Left; and the distrust of all previous material on women. Starting with the assumption that all theory and thought had been based, until that time, on male-defined norms and values, feminists sought a way to resist and counteract the effects of this tradition. Experience was offered as testimony, then discussed and analyzed as political material. This practice was intended to counteract the divisive effect of patriarchy and to bond women by demonstrating that their experiences were not individual and unrelated occurrences, but part of a larger pattern in the material oppression of women. The new and politicized understanding of experience was then intended to be the basis of all political action.

According to bell hooks, consciousness-raising enables the participants to "talk about personal experience as part of a process of politicization," using one's own life as inspiration.[16] Understanding one's own life politically, through the comparison of one's experience with that of other women, revalued women's experience as a source of truth and political vision. Reading was no longer the basis for thought, because it was superseded by the actual materiality of lived events. Feminists ceased to believe that books could validate or invalidate what women thought and lived; instead women would validate or invalidate the books.[17] Only through experience could a concrete agenda for action be formed. Kathie Sarachild stated: "The purpose of consciousness-raising was to get to the most radical truths about the situation of women in order to take radical action."[18] Pam Allen asserted, even more forcefully than Sarachild, "We believe that theory and analysis not rooted in concrete experience (practice) are useless."[19] Experience was understood to possess specific and tangible truths not available from other sources. Anything undertaken in a systematic way by feminists would have to be based on experience, by this time considered an infallible guide.[20]

What was not understood, or at least left untheorized, was that experience was shaped by consciousness-raising, not the other way around. Consciousness-raising came about in a troubled time in feminist history, when the movement was beginning to fragment and issues of sexuality and race were making inroads in the primarily white, straight, and middle-class movement. Ann Snitow, a founding member of the New York Radical Feminists, told Alice Echols in an interview:

> The dream was that underneath our differences, our oppression unified us in a very fusing way. Women's experience had an interior coherence – both political and historical. There was a great desire to find in those C-R questions, different as we all were, we were not. The C-R questions structured the answers.[21]

Experience testimony was encouraged as unifying, rather than differentiating; difference was viewed as counterproductive. The questions referred to by Snitow certainly did construct and valorize certain experiences, as well as valorize a limited number of interpretations of those experiences.

In *Radical Feminism*, an anthology by the women affiliated with the radical New York groups, Anne Koedt suggested a fourteen-week series of questions as a guide for beginning consciousness-raising groups. The first four weeks were to be spent on family relationships, the next two on men and marriage, the seventh on motherhood, the eighth and ninth weeks on heterosexual relationships, and the tenth on relationships with other women (with a brief mention of being "attracted" to women). The eleventh through thirteenth weeks focused on understanding the self through questions about behavior, aging, and personal expectations. The last week used the information from the previous weeks to formulate an agenda for the movement.[22] The emphasis was on the experiences of those within the white, middle-class family. Women were seen primarily from the perspective of the heterosexual contract, and while that contract was to a certain extent problematized, it was not de-naturalized. There were no questions that allowed the complex experiences of race and class to emerge, nor were there any questions that allowed women to acknowledge and explore their complicity with systems of oppression. But the experience that was identified and constructed was collectively created through feminist collaboration in the discussion groups and through feminist paradigms. The experience of being a woman was not individual and private but public and cooperative. Consciousness-raising emphasized women working together to politicize and change their lives.

EXPERIMENTAL THEATERS AND FEMINISTS

On the one hand, many of the women who were involved in the feminist movement received their training in the experimental theaters of the 1960s or in more traditional academic settings. On the other hand, there were also significant numbers of women who participated in feminist theaters with little or no theater training and instead were motivated by their involvement with political movements. The two approaches are contiguous: the experimental theater movement shared political issues and concerns with the New Left. Indeed, Karen Malpede, who edited three Open Theater texts for publication, pointed out that "[i]t's impossible to imagine the Open Theater existing without the writings of Herbert Marcuse, Simone Weil, or R. D. Laing."[23] Women who came to feminist theater through the Women's Liberation Movement usually saw theater as an accessible medium through which political and personal issues could be merged and publicly explored. Whatever the beginnings of a woman's involvement with feminist theater might have been she was always, to some extent, politically motivated.

Margaret Croyden notes about the early 1960s experimental theater scene that the emphasis was on, and would remain on, "group work, creative communities, theater as politics."[24] It is not difficult to see how the agendas of most experimental theater groups were derived, at least in part, from the New Left. Intentionally political, these groups sought to bring people together through an agenda shared by both the performers and the audience. As the New Left had sponsored organizations and institutions that operated as alternatives to mainstream options, so people in experimental theater tested out forms of theater that brought politics to aesthetics and aesthetics to politics in original ways. Outside performance the actors were usually active in the protests and actions including draft counseling, civil rights protests, and sit-ins.

A strong emphasis was placed on a community of theater people working together over a long period of time to create theater pieces. Collaboration created new kinds of texts that relied upon improvisation, experience, and discussion, making the input of all members vital to the creation of works. Experimental theater produced theater in non-theatrical contexts such as churches, lofts, public parks, and cafes. These theater spaces were usually stripped down, without the apparatuses of lavish production values. Constraints of time and money placed the emphasis on the performers as the visual spectacle, de-emphasizing sets, props, and lights.

The audience was constituted as part of the larger political community. Generally the same group of people would attend performances by the radical theater groups and they shared a commitment to the same issues. The performance was dependent on the audience in a totally new way. Arthur Sainer noted about this new relationship that

> The spectator in the radical theater may be finding something that the play has been unable to find before his appearance on the scene. As the play breaks down many of the barriers between life and art, the spectator may find out something about his life through his physical entrance into art.[25]

This was beyond audience participation. According to this view a work was affected and completed by the presence of spectators. Spectators were not passive but active members of the communities of the performers.

On the east coast, New York was the hub of experimental activity. On the west coast theaters such as the San Francisco Mime Troupe proposed new and consciously political approaches to theater. In the mid-west, New York/San Francisco-influenced theater companies such as the Firehouse Theater in Minneapolis provided centers for experimentation. Many of the women who would go on to found or to participate in feminist theater companies came out of the theater experiments of the 1960s.

Margot Lewitin, a founder and current Artistic Director of the Women's Interart Center, commented on the relation of New York experimental theater to New York feminist theater:

> The entire world of off-Broadway and certainly the not-for-profit theater for anybody over the age of forty – it's not true for people younger than forty – but for people over the age of forty today, there's not one of us who didn't work in one of those theaters. That was how you got into the theater. . . . You can scratch the surface of any not-for-profit, off-Broadway, or experimental theater, we *all* worked there, every one of us. There were four places where you began. You began at either Judson Poets' Theater, at Caffe Cino, at Theater Genesis, [or] at La Mama.[26]

Most theater historians agree that off off-Broadway experimental theater was created in 1961 when the theater people who were patrons at Joe Cino's coffee house persuaded him that they could stage the poetry readings more effectively than the poets themselves could:

> [W]here there are poets there are readings. And where there are poets reading there are actors who know they could do it better. And where there are actors there are – other actors, at least a dozen of whom know in their hearts they're really playwrights.[27]

Caffe Cino was soon joined by Judson Poets' Theater founded in late 1961, Cafe La Mama begun by Ellen Stewart in 1961, and Theater Genesis in 1964. All these theaters were founded in response to the political and artistic needs that were not met by established theater.

The next chapter offers, in part, an analysis and narrative of four feminist theater groups. In order to provide a comparison the following sections examine four experimental theater groups: Caffe Cino, Cafe La Mama, Open Theater, and the San Francisco Mime Troupe. These groups and their leaders spawned much of the experimental theater of the 1960s as well as providing a start for many feminist theater practitioners. An in-depth and individual examination of the groups provides a clear picture of the practices and theories that feminists adopted and/or abandoned as they created their own work.

Caffe Cino

Shows at the Caffe Cino often ran less than sixty minutes, performed twice nightly and three times on Fridays and Saturdays.[28] The small coffee house had a raised platform that arranged the audience around it on three sides. While it was certainly a performance space it could scarcely be called a theater. Joe Cino, describing the Caffe, called it a "room," noting that it had severe physical limitations:

It's a very small room and there's no time ever to think about expanding or where you go from here – after eight years. The work has been endless. We try to change the feeling of the room as much as possible to go with the current production. When it works it's very rewarding.[29]

However, physical limitations were not considered artistic or creative stumbling blocks. The relative unimportance of a traditional theatrical setting was one of the hallmarks of experimental theater. Performances rarely occurred in the architectural context of a theater building. The lack of interest in mainstream theater was not an actual rejection or rebellion because no one involved in the Caffe was interested in or concerned with the requirements of traditional theater. According to Michael Feingold and Joe Cino, the interests and criteria of dominant theater practices were never a consideration. Michael Feingold wrote in the *Village Voice*, "They hadn't planned to overthrow an established theater because it never particularly occurred to them that one existed. An aesthetic to them was something to create, not challenge."[30] Joe Cino wrote about the experience of assessing established theater in the context of what occurred in his coffee house, "When I now go see something on a proscenium stage, it's like something else – with no comparisons with what is done here."[31] The theater at Caffe Cino was not theater to make money or theater to draw as large an audience as possible but theater responsible to and created by a community of people with shared concerns, interests, and approaches. By some standards it was not theater at all. But then ignoring or being unaware of those standards was, in a large part, what enabled people to do what they did.

One specific audience was the gay community. While Caffe Cino, founded in 1958, is often credited with beginning the experimental theater movement or at least providing a model for experimental theater, it is also important to credit it with being one of the primary forces behind the creation of an openly gay theater and aesthetics. William Hoffman wrote in his introduction to *Gay Plays: The First Collection* that, along with the willingness of the British "Angry Young Men" to place gay themes on the stage, the factor that liberated gay men to create their own theatrical sensibility was the Caffe Cino.[32]

Part of this lack of concern for mainstream theater stemmed from its irrelevance to gay concerns and representations. Homophobia had so long been institutionalized in society that men wanting to write gay theater had to look elsewhere for a venue. Hoffman observed: "Oddly enough, most of us who worked there were only barely aware that writing about gays was unusual. We lived in a fairly enclosed world . . . and thought little about the outside."[33] Roberta Sklar, one of the founders of the Women's Experimental Theater, worked in the Caffe Cino while she was in graduate school and found the context of Caffe Cino exhilarating because the openly gay sensibility required that the participants create new forms and ways of making theater:

> It was an environment that really allowed for experimenta-
> tion. It was the beginning of the male homosexual theater that
> was "out." It was really "anything goes." I was not ready for
> "anything goes," but it was a great place to learn in. It
> included a community of people who came night after night
> because they were interested. We'd watch each other's work,
> hang around and explore and chew the fat.[34]

The Caffe Cino presented works that were created especially for its own context. No one involved was worried about the interests and concerns of the theater community outside the community of the Caffe. It became a model for those who wished to foster a theater that was not hampered and defined by the concerns of a mainstream conservative audience. Instead, it provided a place for a new kind of theater to grow and develop.

Like Caffe Cino, Judson Poets' Theater, founded in 1961 by Al Carmines, rejected the mainstream straight theater scene for a theater shaped and bounded by gay criteria and conceptions. Creating the theater out of a $600 grant from the Judson's Memorial Church, Carmines believed that the most interesting and significant theater in New York at that time was in the off off-Broadway venues.[35] Caffe Cino paved the way for Judson Poets' Theater as it did for many other off off-Broadway theaters.

Cafe La Mama

Ellen Stewart's Cafe La Mama, founded in 1961, was supported and encouraged by Joe Cino and the possibilities his theater had created:

> "We didn't know anything about theater at La Mama," Ellen Stewart said at the ceremony opening the Lincoln Center exhibit [on the Caffe Cino]. "The Caffe Cino knew *everything*." As he did with so many others, Joe Cino took a paternal interest in the extravagantly dressed black woman who had opened a similar place on East 9th Street to put on her friends' plays. Sometimes after the Cino had closed, he would stroll across the Village to see how La Mama was getting on.[36]

Cafe La Mama was, like Caffe Cino, a coffee house that was dedicated to putting on the new works of local playwrights. Playwright development was Ellen Stewart's primary aim. "La Mama E.T.C. is an experimental theater club dedicated to the playwright and all aspects of theater. That tells everything."[37] For Stewart, the real crime of American theater, as it existed at that moment, was the lack of opportunities for untried, non-traditional playwrights to find a venue for their work. She herself did no theater work but created and maintained the context for experimentation.[38] "The plays that we're doing are the plays that I want to do. I don't interfere in how they get to be that way. I'm here to serve the playwright."[39] This approach allowed La Mama to produce hundreds of new plays of varied quality. The individual play was not important so much as the fact that the play could be performed and that the opportunity for experiment existed. It was this approach to theater that earned Caffe Cino and Cafe La Mama their special citation Obie for the 1964–65 season.[40] The award was given to the two companies for their unfailing support for the new and untried playwright and theater.

Margot Lewitin, who began her theater career as a stage manager at La Mama, said of Ellen Stewart's ability:

> Ellen Stewart had such an incredible intuitive ability to lock on to work that was worth doing. And I say intuitive because she never read scripts, she didn't do anything traditional. You could give Ellen a script but that was not how she determined whether she was going to produce your work or not.

I asked Lewitin how Stewart decided and she replied:

> She met you. She was unerring in her talent. She has the most extraordinary sense of what's good, what's worth pursuing, what to nurture of anyone in the business.[41]

The focal points of the communities such as those that formed around La Mama and Caffe Cino were individuals and the work they wanted to do rather than attracting large audiences or having lucrative hits. Ellen Stewart relied on her own sense of theater rather than on audience surveys or mainstream aesthetics and forms. She offered to serve a theater sensibility that had no home and did that by means that were as non-traditional as the theater she made possible.

Experimental theater provided a venue not merely for theater artists to create and perform their way out of the confines of realism and the "Method" but for people to create and perform away from the oppression they experienced in society at large. Alternative experimental theater was created by people who saw nothing for themselves in mainstream theater. Experimental theater was a theater in which they could represent themselves according to how they understood themselves.

Open Theater

In 1962 seventeen of Nola Chilton's acting students approached Joseph Chaiken, then with the Living Theater, about joining them to continue in a workshop environment the work begun with Chilton. Chaiken agreed and contributed his knowledge of the acting exercises of Viola Spolin.[42] The ensemble worked daily in a loft. The rent for the space represented their only expense and the group managed to pay this by passing the hat.[43] By 1965 they were conducting workshops and limited performances for outsiders and once a month in the 1964–65 theater season performed at the newly renamed La Mama Experimental Theater Club.[44]

The emphasis in the group was on work created collectively through improvisation. No one in the ensemble felt that the work they wanted and needed to perform existed in any form. In a 1974 interview with Arthur Sainer, Chaiken declared:

> What we've been doing at the Open Theater [is] the blank page. In other words saying, "The material doesn't exist," and we all put our heads together and our bodies together and see what we can bring into existence.[45]

The clean slate notion was one that pervaded alternative activities in the 1960s. Radicals on the Left were suspicious of historical practices and usually decided to begin with themselves and abandon established theater traditions for ones that they would invent.

The characterization of the Open as a collective must be informed by the lived experience of the members of the group. Collaborative creation was assumed by all to yield creations more powerful and more interesting than that of the individual. But, as Margaret Croyden describes,

> their collective effort was not only a way of making theater, but of sensitizing themselves in a mechanized and repressive society and of reinforcing the theory that collaboration can surpass individual creativity.[46]

The testimony of members describes a situation less collective than Chaiken would admit. One member of the ensemble told Chaiken, despite his protestations to the contrary, that "[t]he Open Theater is a dictatorship. Nothing gets done without you."[47] Theater collectives from this period were rarely genuine collectives. There was always a tension between the conventional theater hierarchy descending from the leadership of the artistic director and the idea of theater as a collaborative, community event with everyone having equal power. In most cases experimental theater was a hybrid of the two forms.

The Open Theater was essentially an improvisational theater based on Viola Spolin's contention that "improvisational theater requires very close group relationships because it is from group agreement and group playing that material evolves for scenes and plays."[48] Exercises such as "Transformations" created the basis for *Keep Tightly Closed in a Cool Dry Place* (performed in the 1964–65 season) scripted by Megan Terry and *The Mutation Show* (1971–72 season). The transformation exercise is intended to explore the possibilities of unstable and uncontextualized change. Rejecting the Stanislavski/Method reliance on motivation, obstacle, and object-ive, the ensemble used this exercise to explore relationships and creation. Spolin offers the possibility of "extraordinary break-throughs [that] occur as players sense that an endless succession of characters, ideas, and relationships exist within them for their use."[49] Peter Feldman, the director of *Keep Tightly Closed* for the Open Theater, described a transformation as

> an improvisation in which the established realities or "given circumstances" (the method phrase) of the scene change several times during the course of action. What may change are character and/or situation and/or time and/or objectives, etc. Whatever realities are established at the beginning are destroyed after a few minutes and replaced by others. These changes are in turn destroyed and replaced. These changes occur swiftly and *almost without transition* until the audi-ence's dependence on any fixed reality is called into ques-tion.[50]

Realities and identities shift constantly during a transformation emphasizing not the actor's skill of sustaining an internally and externally coherent character, but the ability to change, adapt, and respond to external circumstances without any transitional moment whatsoever. Sidney S. Walter, a member of the Open Theater who became the Artistic Director of the Firehouse Theater in Minne-apolis, directed *Keep Tightly Closed* at the Firehouse and sees the work as sub-text made text.[51] The manifestation of the implied is a method in keeping with Chaiken's goal of giving "testimony" through the body to varied "experiences and conditions."[52] Chaiken believed that if the familiar parameters of acting were abandoned then previously unknown theatrical exploration could emerge. Rather than emphasize performance based on an emotional state experienced by the actor and translated into the character's emotional state, Chaiken and the Open Theater explored the body's ability to generate emotion through sound and movement. "Using kinetic impulses to locate inner states, actors were able to discover emotions that had not been in their experience before."[53] This process created texts through interaction in which the writer was decentered and displaced as the primary visionary for an emphasis on the bodies of the actors and the texts they could create physically.

The Open Theater, like many experimental theater groups in the 1960s, had a strong political awareness. However, unlike theaters with a specific political orientation, such as Caffe Cino or the feminist theaters, the politics of the Open were more vague. The political commitment of the Open Theater is indicative of the split between the rhetoric and action of many theater groups. Chaiken's articulation of the ensemble's relationship to the political changed over time. In early 1966 Eileen Blumenthal quotes Chaiken as committed to encouraging "'a certain kind of political honesty' doing frankly propagandist work."[54] By 1969 he had moved away from this confrontational mode of political theater to a murkier understanding of the relation of politics to theater. "He felt that whatever separation existed between the political, the personal, and the artistic should be unified, but he wanted to steer clear of agit-prop or guerilla theater."[55] One of the most obvious political expressions of the Open Theater was the dedication of performances to political groups, figures, and causes "such as the Indians occupying Wounded Knee, the United Farm workers, or Angela Davis."[56] Chaiken later said that he thought overt political theater made more sense when it came out of personal experience of oppression, othewise there was the danger of the theater positioning itself as superior and the educators of the "unenlightened."[57] Without the lived material dimension, the work could also become an end in itself without political goals or strategy other than performances.

By 1974 Chaiken had moved in the direction of the personal as political. In an interview with Arthur Sainer, Chaiken stated that it seemed to him (Chaiken)

> absolutely essential that people not only ask themselves "how can I work from myself in a true way?" but also "And in what way does this connect to my community or to my whatever – you know, whatever group that I would also perform for?" You can't do it alone any more.[58]

In the same year, in his commentary "Notes on Acting Time and Repetition" for *Three Works by the Open Theater*, Chaiken wrote "[t]he significant political choices are involved in the artist's relationships to his or her collaborators, to the audience, and to commerce."[59] This emphasis on the relation of the personal and political was expressed in the last scene of *The Mutation Show* when all the actors onstage held poster-sized pictures of themselves in pre-Open Theater days. The audience was told the height, eye color, hair color, body type, and birth place of each actor. To this was added personal details such as "Tom Lillard's cousin is a Ku Klux Klansman," or "In the sixth grade Paul Zimet won the American Legion Citizenship Award."[60] The details named the actors and foregrounded their roles onstage as characters constructed specifically for the performance. By doing this the ensemble rejected the mimetic impersonation of character for the open recognition that the actor is consciously pretending to be someone or something else.

San Francisco Mime Troupe

East coast experimental theaters were neither the only theaters women worked in before moving onto their own endeavors, nor the only theaters affecting the ways feminists thought of theater. On the west coast the San Francisco Mime Troupe (SFMT) had a significant impact on the theater throughout the country.

By 1959 Ronnie Davis was completely disenchanted with the established theater world, including experimental theater. He had trained with Etienne Decroux and Marcel Marceau and was one of the directors at the prestigious Actors' Workshop. It was there that he first presented an early version of what would later be the San Francisco Mime Troupe, the R. G. Davis Mime Troupe, infrequently doing small shows. The first show was done under the auspices of the Actors' Workshop, performing at eleven o'clock in the evening after the regular show. Called the "11th Hour Mime Show," Davis remarks that it "didn't have much competition, who else was doing free mime shows at 11:00 pm?"[61] Soon after this Davis broke from the Workshop and established the Mime Troupe on its own. In the first few years the Troupe was unconcerned with establishing itself as a legitimate theater, it did not present a season, nor did it hire a business staff. Instead, it spent time developing its style, experimenting with the *commedia dell'arte* tradition, and building a repertory. In 1962, despite opposition from the city of

San Francisco, the Troupe began to perform outdoors in the parks. In 1963 Davis changed the name from the R. G. Davis Mime Troupe to the San Francisco Mime Troupe.

The first play to emerge with the recognizable Mime Troupe style was *A Minstrel Show or Civil Rights in a Cracker Barrel* in 1965. Based on actual minstrel show scripts and staging, the show was performed by six actors in blackface (three white men and three African–American men). The play intended to confront racism in society and the audience as well as "deal with the personal liberation of each actor."[62] Davis comments that the show was considered quite dangerous by some, but that it was in keeping with the Mime Troupe's mission: "In 1965 the objective of our group was to teach, direct toward change and to be an example of change. We were to exemplify the message that we asked others to accept."[63] This kind of internal and external political congruence was an important feature of the radical Left: in order to bring about change one had to live the change. In 1967 Davis trimmed the company from its unwieldy fifty members to ten or fifteen. The company could not support all the members and the Mime Troupe's sense of purpose was being diluted by the size of the group. The remaining practitioners were dedicated to the Troupe, and were "politically and aesthetically trained."[64] The new company began work on *L'Amante Militaire*. This was an anti-Vietnam War play, and was the first show adapted for the company by Joan Holden who would become playwright for the collective. Two years later the company was running into organizational trouble again.

From the beginning the audience was primarily drawn from the Radical Left counter-culture community in San Francisco. However, the Mime Troupe, in keeping with its politics, was committed to interesting a more diverse audience, including the working class and people of color. The move into the parks started that process, but many in the Troupe felt that they were still not seeing much diversity in the audience. While they had from the beginning rejected psychological, realistic acting, it was over time that they learned to avoid "those forms which tend[ed] to be more contemplative than energetic."[65] Two specific issues caused the split in the Troupe. The first was the organization of the group; should it form itself as a collective, or should Davis be the sole artistic director? The second area of contention was over the targeted audience: middle-class intellectuals, or the working class? After much debate Davis chose to leave the group, as did the Marxists, and in 1970 the SFMT recreated itself as a collective doing theater for working-class audiences.[66]

The SFMT's formation as a collective represented

> a shift from intellectuals commenting on political issues to political activists; from artists who had a proprietary attitude about their individual contributions to art workers with a common objective of bringing about social change.[67]

These shifts also represented a commitment to their community, both artistically and organizationally. They began to do plays about women, Latinos, Asian–Americans, and city politics. The SFMT's home base was the Mission District of San Francisco, a working-class, predominantly Latino neighborhood. They radically changed the racial composition of the group from all-white to seven white, five Latino, and three African–American. This came from Joan Holden's belief that theater can and should operate as an event that creates as well as reinforces the bonds of community especially to people who are experiencing the erosion of those ties:

> There is a sense of community from gathering together to share a common experience, and that sense of community is important because people know they cannot change the world by themselves. The potential for change is felt when they are part of an energy, a movement, that is bigger than they are.[68]

The Mime Troupe and Holden believed that when an audience experiences a common purpose and a positive potential for achieving that purpose, the people in it no longer believe that they cannot affect their world. A community needs to see its bonds represented and the representation reinforces them.

The histories of these four theaters demonstrate that political commitment, the connections among communities and theaters, and personal experiences were crucial to experimental groups in the 1960s. Women played signal roles in the explorations conducted by these groups and others like them. However, not all their experiences were positive, nor were they ultimately fulfilling enough for some women.

By the mid- to late 1960s large numbers of women were leaving the experimental theaters to found ones for themselves. Not all of them left their theaters in the same way, and not all of them left permanently. Martha Kearns was extremely bitter about her involvement in the Bread and Puppet Theater, as she told Elizabeth Natalle in a 1982 interview:

> By the time I left Bread and Puppet Theater, I was disenchanted by their one, single-minded view of women: which meant women should be barefoot and pregnant, and not be artistic leaders in the theater. Nor were the roles for women particularly interesting, and I didn't like that.[69]

Joan Mankin, a member of Lilith (1974) in San Francisco, worked with the SFMT before joining Lilith, but had no particularly bad feelings toward the Mime Troupe:

> I . . . left the Mime Troupe after five years because I felt like my politics weren't coming from any experience that I knew about, because the Mime Troupe at that time was very ideological, we were always having these discussions about Marx and Mao.[70]

Most women were conflicted about their experiences with other theaters. What they had learned was useful and important, but they often worked in less than ideal conditions. Many women experienced a sharp contradiction between the spoken intentions of a given theater and its sometimes unexamined actions. Terry Baum left a theater company she had co-founded because she was the only woman member, and "I wanted to work with women."[71] Kay Codish left La Mama where she had stage managed, abandoning it to form a feminist theater outside New York City with some friends in New Haven. Codish believed the New York scene was too competitive and judgmental.[72] Margot Lewitin also stage managed for La Mama, leaving first to work for Mobilization For Youth, and then later to be one of the founders of Women's Interart. She credits founding the organization with giving her the support she needed to move from stage management to directing. "Whether I would have moved from stage managing without Women's Interart, I don't know. But being here gave me the courage to direct plays."[73] In an atmosphere politically dedicated to producing women's work, Lewitin grew beyond the capacity defined for her by less feminist oriented theater. For all women who founded feminist theaters, whether out of experimental theater, political activism, or from a consciousness-raising group, there was something compelling about creating theater for women and by women out of women's experience.

Working with the Open Theater, although not one of the theaters mentioned by Margot Lewitin, was a significant experience for many of the women who later founded feminist theaters on the East Coast. Writers, such as Susan Yankowitz and Megan Terry; performers, including Jo Ann Schmidman, Muriel Miguel, and Tina Shepard; and directors, especially Roberta Sklar, drew inspiration from their experiences there. Patti Gillespie notes: "Of the fifteen women identified by Joseph Chaikin [in 1976] as particularly significant members of his group, ten are now, or have been at some time, involved in feminist theater."[74] The experience of working at the Open Theater was inspiring in two contradictory senses. The women involved learned acting, rehearsal, and process techniques that rejected the standard "Method" approach. The focus was on more experimentation with an emphasis on improvisation and the performer, as opposed to the text and the writer.

At the same time, however, the women of the Open Theater were forced to acknowledge that the labor of women was devalued because the political commitment of the ensemble did not extend to a critique of the discriminatory actions of the ensemble itself:

> For years . . . many of the men had been doing draft counseling whenever we did performances on college campuses. But when Tina Shepard and I started doing abortion outreach (not counseling, just short speeches announcing demonstrations and such), there was a lot of tension about it: Would it interfere with rehearsal time? Would it alienate the audience?, etc. Unbelievable![75]

These political good intentions stopped short of an actual critique of the practices of the theater as Roberta Sklar points out over the issue of sexism, "The company seemed outraged at first . . . at the sexism of the outside world, but internal struggles soon made it clear that there was a lot of it inside as well."[76] Sklar experienced continually operating contradictions despite the political statements made by the group.

Roberta Sklar believes that it was during *The Mutation Show*, which she directed for the Open Theater, that the latent sexism of the group was most apparent and that her own feminism was sharply focused, driving her to leave the company. In section five of the play, titled "Ropes," Kamala, a girl raised by wolves killed by missionaries in order to capture her, is forced to stand straight and learn to walk like a human.

We will name her.
We will straighten her bones.
We will give her words.
We will caress her.
We will name her.[77]

Roberta Sklar and the other women in the company were profoundly affected by this moment. To them it was representative of the repeated separation of mother and daughter, the dictates of a misogynist fashion industry, and behaviors that shaped the female body in ways unfamiliar to the body's natural construction. Sklar proposes that the Kamala narrative of *The Mutation Show* plays out the domination of women by the patriarchy. The men, however, did not make a similar connection:

> A man from the company was pulling her [Tina Shepard/ Kamala] up by the rope. One of the actors said at the time, "Maybe a woman should be doing this because this way it looks as if it is saying something about men and women, rather than about power relationships." The women understood that this was *not* a contradiction.[78]

It is important to realize that while the actual work pioneered by the Open made possible many non-traditional, non-realistic, and non-method techniques that could be and were used productively by feminist theater artists, the Open was also a painful experience for the women involved. Working within the Open Theater gave them a new theatrical expression while systematically devaluing their part in creating the new expressions.

Of the groups discussed in this book the following were either founded by or made up of women who had previously participated in experimental theater groups: Women's Experimental Theater, Spiderwoman Theater, New Cycle Theater, At the Foot of the Mountain, Lilith, Omaha Magic Theater, Westbeth Playwrights Feminist Collective, Theater of Light and Shadow, Interart, the Wilma Theater, Womanspace, and the Woman's Unit. Dissatisfaction with conventional political expression, discussions, marches, and protests, and frustration with hostile or apolitical theater were part of what encouraged women to produce theater out of their own experiences, beliefs, and visions. Their antecedents gave them an emphasis on community, one that they probably would have developed anyway, but as Sally Banes pointed out about experimental art: "The rhetoric of community – the desire for community – is everywhere evident in the artworks and institutions of the Sixties avant-garde.[79] This was just as true for theater as in any other art form. Experience, as interested and political, struggles over the relationship of personal experience to production, and the connections between the community and the individual were everywhere at issue during this time and feminist theaters were no strangers to these questions.

3

COLLECTIVITY AND COLLABORATION

"The personal is political" is a phrase that has enormous resonance for any feminist; indeed for many it summarizes feminism. It had and has come to have a number of different, even contradictory, meanings. One of the interpretations feminists have of the phrase is that what is done to accomplish something profoundly shapes the accomplishment itself. Thus, contradictions between public declarations and private actions can undermine the public declaration. It was a tenet of oppositional politics of the 1960s and 1970s that one had to live one's beliefs to their fullest extent. Rejecting hierarchies and committing to egalitarian principles while systematically excluding people from decision-making, as seen in many of the radical political groups and experimental theaters discussed earlier, were practices that contradicted the stated commitments of alternative politics. The situation was perceived by many women as a demonstration that those who denied a voice to women did not really believe in their visions and goals for a new society but instead wanted to maintain traditional power relations at least as far as gender was concerned. As has been described, many women in alternative organizations perceived the contradiction and their experiences led them to reject those organizations for ones of their own creation.

A theater could not present a production that was supposed to emerge from alternative politics and not be conscious of it as a product of a specific way of thinking and acting. Theaters were cast as microcosms of society that did and could play out the individual's relation to society both actual, as in mainstream and conventional theaters, and potential, as in alternative and political theaters. Feminist theaters saw their tasks very clearly; in order to work toward an end of the oppression of women they had to create organizations that would empower women both in the process of creation and in the product of performance. Exploration of ideas through the collective was the most significant manifestation of the attempt to reconcile politics with structure. Feminist theaters were not the only groups struggling with the idea of the collective; the San Francisco Mime Troupe had wrestled with the desire to reorganize as a collective, and the issue split the group. Those kinds of struggles and commitments were hallmarks of alternative theaters in the 1960s. The collective model's potential resonated for all feminist theaters, and each woman believed herself accountable to notions of collectivity and these notions were often a part of every facet of the theaters' operations. There were vestiges of collective organization everywhere, even in groups that rejected the model outright; each theater articulated some kind of relationship to collectivity. Collective organization within the theater groups tried closely to imitate the egalitarian community ideals of the feminist movement. Every area of the groups' functioning was subjected to a collective standard and scrutiny: the creation of texts, the selection of members, the interactions with the audience and with other theater groups, and the day to day operations of the theater. This chapter will interrogate notions of collectivity as they were shaped by the participants' understanding of their activities, as they brought theater groups together to collaborate and interact, and as the notions functioned when the theaters grappled with the differences of race, class, and sexuality. Finally there is an in-depth examination of the stories of four specific feminist theaters: the Women's Experimental Theater, Spiderwoman Theater, Lilith Theater, and Front Room Theater Guild. These narratives are not intended to be read as perfect representatives of all feminist theaters; certain elements are repeated in the histories of many theater groups, but they also offer narratives not easily available elsewhere as a reference and basis for comparison. By discussing ideas of collectivity, interactions among theaters, and the issue of difference as it is played out in class, race, and sexuality as the most important and explicit issues in feminist theater, it is possible to examine the congruence not simply of theory and practice but of the theory proposed for practice and the theory that can be extrapolated from practice.

COLLABORATING ON COLLECTIVES

It is probably impossible to talk about feminist theater, or indeed any alternative theater of the 1960s and after, without discussing the collective. As Alice Echols pointed out about all the radical movements of the time, there was an "enormous interest in creating political processes that would maximize individual participation and equalize power" by developing "alternatives to hierarchy and centralized decision-making."[1] Experiences with male-run collectives, such as the ones discussed in chapter two, demonstrated to many feminists that the commitment to this idea was often either mere lip service or existed exclusive of women. As the feminist movement grew larger, and more and more organizations came into existence, the commitment to the idea of the collective, to the group without leader or hierarchy, grew as well.[2] Feminist theater, as a part of the larger feminist movement, was committed to the idea of the collective for many reasons, some having to do with participation in the feminist movement and some growing out of the history and traditions of theater.

The process of creating collectively was not limited to feminist theater groups. As mentioned earlier the majority of alternative theaters organized themselves in relation to the idea of collectivity. Ted Shank characterized the movement toward the collective as a movement away from the perceived "fragmentation of the established society."[3] Collectives were seized upon as an antidote to specialization, a prescription for what was seen as the malaise of contemporary life and theater. Each person in traditional theater structures was believed to be so concerned with his or her individual responsibilities – the actor with creating the role, the playwright with producing the written text, and the director with imposing coherence on the different contributions – that there was no responsibility taken for the creative process from start to finish, and for its implications in the larger world of society and politics.

Shank opposes the above system of traditional theater with what he terms "the two-process method" to that of the collective group, "the one-process method."[4] Traditional theater isolates writing from production, the two processes of theatrical creation; the playwright writes the play apart from the theater group and then the director takes the play and produces it, usually with little or no input from the playwright.[5] The one-process method of the collective ensures that the same people are responsible for a production from its moment of inception to its final performance and responsibilities are not usually as delineated as they are in conventional theater. Michelene Wandor points out that collective organization,

Shank's "one-process method," empowers the performer. The implications of the system were such that a collective works as "a challenge to the conventional powerlessness of the performer . . . they could control the context and content of their work."[6] Collectives challenged not only the specialization and fragmentation of conventional theaters, but also the results of the diversification, especially passivity and disempowerment. The belief was that collectives would give everyone an equal chance to create the future.

It is important to distinguish between collective in the Marxist sense and collective in the sense that it was commonly used by feminist and most other types of alternative theaters in the United States. Rather than concentrate on the needs of each individual and the validation of personal identity, Marxist collectives stress the greater good of the group, believing that it is only through the subordination of individual needs and desires that the collective good can emerge. According to Sue-Ellen Case, feminist collectives represented more "a break with patriarchal organizations of power than . . . a break from individualism."[7] Case also points out that the feminist ideas of collective were based on the American democratic tradition of one person, one vote, stressing, as the "Port Huron Statement" did, that the greater good can emerge only when individual rights and needs are honored.

Collectives were an investment in process. No longer ruled by the primacy of the finished product, feminist theaters sought to emphasize the continuous act of creation itself, or the means rather than the end. In fact, as Dinah Leavitt has pointed out, it could be said that there were no ends, simply means.[8] Productions were usually changed during the run of a show to reflect changing consciousness on the part of the theater about the issues and approaches or in response to audience feedback. Rosemary Curb documents that at least half of feminist theaters in existence in 1979 were organized as collectives and over two-thirds used a collective/collaborative process to create works for performance.[9] Despite these statistics it is important not to create an impression that collective meant the same thing in every theater group. Probably due in part to the absence of a single definitive theorist or party line, the definitions of what exactly constitutes a collective feminist theater group are as varied in number as the theater groups themselves. As Dinah Leavitt points out about the four Minneapolis feminist theaters in her book *Feminist Theater Groups,* while collective organization is the hallmark of feminist theater, all groups do not employ it in the same way. The Alive and Trucking group set up *ad hoc* committees for various duties; the Circle of the Witch assigned tasks to individuals and rotated duties; the Lavender Cellar had no standing committees or tasks but worked from production to production encouraging flexibility in work assignments; and At the Foot of the Mountain tried to recognize abilities within the group without designating leaders.[10]

While these four groups shared many attributes – a commitment to feminism, geographical location, and a collective orientation – they understood and implemented collectivity in different ways. Indeed, the "collective" worked as a label to cover disparate and idiosyncratic methods of structural organization and creation.

Emma Missouri of Chrysalis Theater Eclectic (founded 1978) in Northampton, Massachusetts, says that this theater group was "rooted in feminist principles" which meant that they were collaborative without a consolidated hierarchy. "We got more astute in the process of collaboration and collectivism," she said, "and we realized that everybody didn't have to do everything, in fact, not everybody wanted to do everything or liked it."[11] Chrysalis was small enough (five members), that it could succeed with a loosely structured organization. But no matter how any group worked out the actual mechanics of their particular collective, their definition in relation to their ideas about collective was part of their definition as a feminist theater, there could not be one without the other.

Anita Mattos, a Latina feminist who has been involved in political and alternative theater since the mid-1960s, remains committed to collectives although she is not currently involved in one. She worked with El Teatro Latino but resigned in 1982 because they would not become a collective. She defines collectivity as a "horizontal" mode of working.

> The means are the ends. In this goal-oriented society everyone's so busy getting to the goal first. If you're so busy getting to the goal you don't see so many things along the path. I am into focussing on the process as it happens.[12]

The most important and productive theater work is, in Mattos' view, ensemble work where everyone is involved in every area of the theater from performing to business decisions.

Some theaters confined collectivity to the process of play creation. In Spiderwoman Theater, Muriel Miguel is the Artistic Director and spokeswoman for the group. After her first feminist theater group, Womanspace, broke up she told one interviewer that she wanted to found a feminist theater group "in which the women worked together more as an ensemble. . . . where the actresses were as much in tune with each other as possible."[13] In their creative process called storyweaving everyone offers themes, ideas, experiences, and dreams, which are reduced to their essential core and then worked into the fabric of the production. While there is an Artistic Director, "everyone in the group has a voice and doesn't hesitate to use it to express herself."[14] When the show is close to its final shape Miguel works as a conventional director, to give the show its polished and final form.

At the Women's Experimental Theater (WET, 1977, New York) the three Artistic Directors, Clare Coss, Sondra Segal, and Roberta Sklar, made all the decisions. The research process, where topics and content were determined through improvisation and interview, was conducted with the participation of all the performers who worked with WET, as well as the hundreds of women invited through a network of audiences, feminist community groups, and workshops to explore specific themes. These workshops, while planned by all three women, were usually conducted by Segal and Sklar with Coss recording and participating. Throughout the process of improvisation all the Artistic Directors also contributed to the writing. When the workshop process was completed an "inventory period" was declared. During this stage Segal took the lead in structuring the play and "thematic and material choices are made by all three of us."[15] When the play reached draft form the three members took more traditional roles: Segal acted, Sklar directed, and Coss wrote. There was still, however, a significant amount of interaction across the boundaries of roles.

Lilith Theater was a collective for much of its existence. Within the group they developed what came to be known as the "Lilith process;" four working methods that framed every gathering of the group. Harriet Schiffer describes it:

> The first thing you do is you check in. The reason is to leave behind at the door whatever concerns you have – to acknowledge to yourself that you've got this concern that you are putting aside so that you can come to the work. Then there's

a physical component and a vocal component. We must sing, we must move our bodies. Even in business meetings we would sing a song.[16]

Schiffer laughs at her insistence at bringing the process into the business meetings but is emphatic that it was just as productive there as it was in rehearsals. The physical warm-up was particularly important: "Your body is going to tune in and tune up with everybody's. That creates ensemble too."[17] After the warm-ups were complete the rehearsal would begin and at the end there would be a feedback session. The point of the feedback session was to assess the process and to build a transition from rehearsal back to one's life. Schiffer described it as saying to the director: "I am giving up to you my well-being but it's just for this time, it's not for my life."[18] She added: "There's accountability for not what you've said to me but the ways in which it has come down."[19] After the feedback session the women gathered in a circle, made eye contact with one another, and said: "I dare not say I have finished." Later it was changed to: "A woman's work is never done." Ultimately: "It empowers everybody to come back to themselves at the end and say what they feel."[20] Thus the group ran by consensus and everyone contributed to its progress.

Joan Mankin recalls the way plays were written:

We would do an improvisation and then we'd tape it. Then Terry [Baum] and Carolyn [Meyers] would go home and listen to it and come in with a scene the next day. We'd play the scene and we'd say "this doesn't make it" or "that doesn't make it," or "that conflict has to be sharper." We'd work on it some more and then they'd go back and write it again and then they'd come back and we'd do it.[21]

While Mankin remembers this as a satisfactory and productive process, Terry Baum is less enthusiastic in her estimation of it as a way to create theater. She never directly rejects the work that Lilith did but she is no longer committed to the collective as a method of theater and would never work that way again. She remembers that when Lilith was deciding what two shows to take on their first European tour they considered *Sacrifices*.[22] In order to tour it, everyone agreed that it would need massive rewrites and the argument that occurred during the process was typical, in Baum's opinion, of the flaws in the collective system:

LILITH
A WOMEN'S THEATRE COLLECTIVE
SACRIFICES
A FABLE ABOUT THE WOMEN'S MOVEMENT

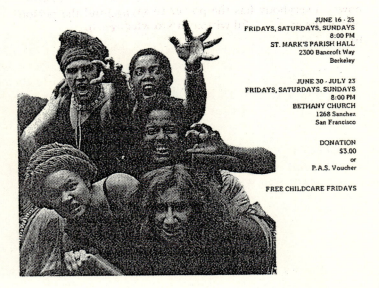

JUNE 16 - 25
FRIDAYS, SATURDAYS, SUNDAYS
8:00 PM
ST. MARK'S PARISH HALL
2300 Bancroft Way
Berkeley

JUNE 30 - JULY 23
FRIDAYS, SATURDAYS, SUNDAYS
8:00 PM
BETHANY CHURCH
1268 Sanchez
San Francisco

DONATION
$3.00
or
P.A.S. Voucher

FREE CHILDCARE FRIDAYS

Figure 1 Poster for Lilith's *Sacrifices* (1977). Photo courtesy of Ruby Rochetto

Some of us wanted to make it that Lilith, who was the main character, was thrown out of the village for being a lesbian. Now I don't remember how much lesbianism was in the play. There was at least the implication that Lilith – it was not really an issue – but some of the women just put their foot down and said no. I remember that all the women who said "no, we won't do it" were straight. Carolyn [Meyers] was straight and she was on the side of making Lilith a lesbian. But I thought, I'm not interested in this. Straight women are afraid. It was real clear; one of them was in line to play Lilith and she didn't want to play a dyke.[23]

The play was abandoned and never rewritten, partly because of the disagreements over the lesbian issue. As far as Baum is concerned the incident was indicative of the problems with collective organization. If everyone has an equal say then risks will rarely get taken because those who are hesitant will veto the new idea or image:

> In a collective, I feel, the most cowardly person has the most power. Everybody has the power to say no, and the person who is the most fearful will say no to whatever they are afraid to do. So you're just tied up and bound by the fears of the most timid person. . . . I would never put myself in that position creatively again, not in a million years.[24]

Baum does circumscribe her rejection of collectives with the memory that she did find support in the group. It was an important thing to have tried but on the whole it was not, for Baum, successful.

Adele Prandini, when asked if San Francisco's It's Just a Stage (IJAS, founded 1974) was a collective, answered, "In a way, sort of, kind of, not really." She went on to define further the relationship between IJAS and collectivity:

> The collective process is a very difficult process because although everyone wants equal power, most of the time people do not want to share equal responsibility. That is the breakdown in the collective process.[25]

It was obvious that Prandini felt accountable to a collective approach; decisions were always discussed, although Prandini made the final choices. She could not completely dismiss that form of organization, but it is clear that it is an extremely difficult one to implement.

Barbara Tholfsen, the founder of Women's Collage Theater, shares Baum's skepticism about collectives:

> There was a lot of belief in non-hierarchal organization which was a cover for a hierarchy that really existed. In my theater

71

I was the mother and towards the end a lot of people were furious with me, just furious.[26]

Tholfsen used the same term, the mother, to describe her position in Women's Collage as Linfante and Baum used to describe their position in Lilith.[27] All three women feel that they were often treated like the traditional definition of a mother: expected to support everyone, while not taking control or imposing her own decisions on the company.

Patricia Van Kirk shares with Tholfsen, Baum, and Prandini a wariness about collectives. She acknowledges that her theater owed a debt to earlier feminist collectives, "I felt like we were able to succeed in part because so much had gone before us, was collective, and had the heartache of the collective."[28] Despite the recognition, or perhaps because of it, Van Kirk was firm that the Front Room Theater Guild (FRTG, founded 1980) was not to be a collective and that she had never envisioned the theater that way:

I wasn't into collectives. I was enough of a feminist; I'd been around long enough that I'd seen most things go down the tubes before they barely got started. I felt strongly that I was artistic director and that I picked the plays. I certainly had a lot of people who worked with me on that but ultimately I felt like it was my responsibility.[29]

Van Kirk envisioned making FRTG a professional theater at some point and was convinced that a collective structure would be too unwieldy and cumbersome for that end. She was emphatic that she was never a dictator, nor did she ignore the input of other members of the group, but she did want a structure that included a position that could make final decisions and provide a vision for the theater.

Van Kirk's position toward collectives is similar to the one finally adopted by the members of the Theater of Light and Shadow in New Haven (TLS, founded 1977). Early in the history of the group all decisions were made by consensus and anyone who wanted to join could do so. In fact, over fifty women showed up for the first auditions and all were accepted into the company. In 1979 the choice was made to trim the company from its large number to just fifteen members. "That step was seen as necessary for both continuity and discipline, best reflected in their commitment to working on the physical foundation of acting."[30] After this step the theater stayed collaborative by sharing decision-making and allowing people to change positions but it was not a collective, "authority [wa]s clearly defined."[31] The group came to the conclusion that a horizontal structure that spreads responsibility and decision-making powers among all the members equally is ineffective for the theater. "'A collective is a great idea,' Codish adds, 'But you can't do it when aesthetics are involved.'"[32] TLS tried both the alternative structuring of theater with the collective and the more traditional form, albeit with adaptations, and decided that the traditional structuring was easier to handle and more productive for a theater that wanted to be considered professional and competitive.

Collectivity often ended up as a way publicly to declare a group leaderless while putting the labor of the leader on to one person and later forcing her to take all the blame for any mishaps. Collectivity could relieve individuals of personal culpability by allowing an avenue of blame; the person who "took" power was, by definition then, working "against" feminist principles, ignoring that in many instances it was an unspoken agreement that the person serve as *ad hoc* leader as it happened with Lilith and the Women's Collage Theater. But collectives could also be enormously exciting ways to work. They forced individuals to examine their assumptions about creation and their approaches to relating with other people. An enormous body of plays and performances came out of collective theaters; plays that dealt with issues never before placed onstage. The influence of collectivity was felt beyond the confines of individual groups. The importance of reaching from one's group to others' was also a highly prized ideal and part of the notion of working together as a larger community of women.

CONNECTIONS AND INTERACTIONS

We *always* intended to stay in touch with other women's theaters. . . .
We always tried to maintain those connections. This is where we lived, this is what we were after.

(Michele Linfante)[33]

Many articles, most notably Patti Gillespie's, make the point that one of the most interesting features of the feminist theater movement is its amazing grassroots and independent nature.[34] Without a single defining figure, it is argued, feminist theater groups appeared almost spontaneously throughout the United States. While this is not completely untrue, it is misleading. Many of the women who founded the theaters had previous experience in theater and saw feminist theater as a way to combine their professional skills with their commitment to feminism. Nor were they entirely isolated from one another, for there were discussions during conferences and festivals, as well as collaborations. Much of this interchange occurred after the groups came into existence, so that most groups were independently founded but sought ties with other groups as survival mechanisms. As the previous chapters have indicated, there were many factors that brought individual women to feminist theater and there was a variety of ways these women interacted with one another.

The most obvious example of theater groups coming together to share performances, information, and skills is the number of festivals that occurred around the United States in the early 1980s. While not an exhaustive list, the following examples provide a sense of the various activities. In 1980 and 1981 in Boston the Feminist Amerikan Theater produced the Boston Womyn's Theater Festival. In 1985 the festival was taken over by the Boston Women in Theater. On the West Coast the National Festival of Women in Theater sponsored festivals annually from 1981 to 1985. In 1980 and 1981 the Women's One World Festival brought feminist theater from Europe to perform in New York.[35] The Theater of Light and Shadow in New Haven sponsored a five-week series of performances and panels in February and March of 1982 at Albertus Magnus College titled "Women in Theater." Participants included Helen Krich Chinoy and the Women's Experimental Theater.[36] At every one of these festivals feminist performers and theater groups gathered from all over the country to perform, conduct workshops, network, and present panels. The 1983 Santa Cruz festival offered Lilith's *Daughters of Erin*, Beah Richards' *A Black Woman Speaks*, and pieces from At the Foot Of the Mountain, Rhode Island Feminist Theater, as well as companies from Ithaca, New York; Eugene, Oregon; New Haven, Connecticut; Brooklyn, New York; and Seattle, Washington.[37] However, by 1985 the festival organizers in Santa Cruz were closing their doors because they were "unable to continue to generate sufficient funding to maintain the broad scope which we achieved in the first two festivals."[38] But all the festivals were important inspirations for women in theater, as well as serving as avenues of support and contact among women dedicated to similar approaches to theater.

The Women's One World Festivals (WOW) emerged from Lois Weaver and Peggy Shaw's experiences touring in Europe. After participating in many festivals there they felt there should be a similar venue in the United States for women to see European groups. When they were finally ready to invite groups and hold the festival in 1980 they were able to extend little more than a chance to perform in New York City:

> Groups came from Europe paying their own way and sleeping on floors of friends of the festival. "We couldn't offer much," Weaver explains, "but just having a spot to perform in New York was a great deal for them. And they got some press. That actually generated enough interest that they could come back on their own later." "We couldn't pay them," Shaw adds, "but they got a lot of attention and made a lot of contacts."[39]

After the second festival in 1981 the organizing group did not want to lose the momentum generated by the festivals and decided to continue the festival as a local community gathering place and performance venue. Through community dances and benefits they funded theater, poetry, movies, and art. The space was named the WOW Cafe 330 and opened in March 1982.

Academic organizations also provided opportunities for theater groups to perform and interact with scholars, as well as with each other. The Women's Collage Theater performed at the first conference of the National Women's Studies Association where they were able also to see a performance by WET.[40] The Women and Theater Program of the American Theater Association (later reorganized as the Association for Theater in Higher Education) has been holding conferences every year since 1980. At those conferences it has been a firm tradition to commit a significant amount of time to discussing and critiquing performances presented at the conference by various feminist performers and theater groups.[41]

National organizations were not the only means for women to see one another's work or for exchanges and inspirations to occur. At the Foot of the Mountain was an important focus for collaboration because of its size, stability, longevity, and resources. In 1977 AFOM joined with Caravan Theater of Boston (founded 1965) to spend a summer collaborating on a piece about mothers and daughters. During their time there they realized that far more interesting and to the point was the topic of their own collaboration. "'From the start, there was a question about whether the priority should be theater work or the emotional work of building a community,' says Bobbi Ausubel of Caravan."[42] The compromise was to create theater out of the struggles of working together to create performance collectively, the importance of reaching across "divisions," and the responsibilities of caring for children.

Another significant AFOM collaboration occurred in 1985 with Spiderwoman Theater. Spiderwoman joined AFOM to recruit an ensemble of eight women: three Native Americans, two Chicanas, one African–American, one Jewish, and one Chinese–American.[43] The ensemble was gathered without a clear topic for performance in mind. After almost a month of working improvisationally and using the storyweaving technique the focus of performance began to emerge:

> During different parts of that month we started to work on a piece and the main thrust of people talking was talking about how exotic they were, that how people always see them as exotic. So we did a piece called *Neurotic Erotic Exotics*.[44]

The piece was enormously successful but the ensemble was not able to stay together after Spiderwoman left.

AFOM also included in their own seasons many works performed and/or originated at other feminist theaters. *Pizza*, written by Michele Linfante for Lilith Theater, was done in a "Broadcloth" series of staged readings in 1980, *Internal Injury* created by the Rhode Island Feminist Theater was produced at AFOM in 1982, and *The Clue in the Old Birdbath: An Affectionate Satire of Nancy Drew* by Kate Kasten and Sandra DeHelen with music by Paul Boesing, included in the 1978 season, was also done by the Theater of Light and Shadow in 1979 and by the Front Room Theater Guild in 1986. Women also moved from one theater group to another facilitating the communication of ideas and methods of working. Judith Katz worked as an apprentice to Megan Terry and was later a founding member of Chrysalis Theater Eclectic for whom she wrote *Tribes*. Later she joined AFOM after *Tribes* was presented there in 1982. Bernadette Cha was another person who worked for more than one feminist theater group; until she joined AFOM in 1986 she was a member of Lilith Theater.

Some of the women who worked in feminist theater cited other theater groups as inspiration and influence. Iris Landsberg of It's Just A Stage in San Francisco made occasional trips to New York City where she saw and was impressed by the work of Split Britches, Karen Malpede, and Eleanor Johnson.[45] Anita Mattos is convinced that her work with Cherrie Moraga and seeing performances by

Split Britches and Julie Aber have had a profound impact on her work.[46] Deborah Margolin, a member of Split Britches, describing her reactions to *Electra Speaks* to Julie Malnig and Judy Rosenthal, echoes the reactions of Sklar and Coss to It's All Right To Be Woman Theater: "I never saw theater like this. I never saw women that weren't perfect little blondes singing arpeggios. These were skinny women, large women, of different ethnic backgrounds. They affirmed that women's lives have theatrically viable images."[47] Michele Linfante credits a residency in Iowa for which Martha Boesing recommended her as being extremely beneficial to her playwrighting.[48] Patricia Van Kirk is convinced that her theater could never have existed if it were not for the precedent set by the feminist theaters before her.[49] Dinah Leavitt has demonstrated in her work on four Minneapolis feminist theaters that their histories and experiences have been intertwined and related.[50]

While the list here is not especially long it implies that there were many instances of collaboration, inspiration, and mutual dependence. Some groups sprang up without any knowledge of other groups, but many did not. Feminism stressed the interaction of women and the connections among them. To claim that connections did not exist in feminist theater would be misleading. It would also deny that the values and methods learned from working collectively had an impact outside a given group when in fact they made women determined to reach out to other groups, to see, and to produce each other's work. But these interactions both within and without the groups were not always untroubled and unmarked by disagreements. The more groups broadened their horizons, the more they found themselves challenged by and challenging the very structures they had created.

DEALING WITH DIFFERENCE

You don't go into a coalition because you just *like* it. The only reason you would consider trying to team up with somebody who could possibly kill you, is because that's the only way you can figure you can stay alive. . . . Today wherever women gather together it is not necessarily nurturing. It is coalition building. And if you feel the strain, you may be doing some good work.

(Berenice Johnson Reagon)[51]

One of the strongest and most divisive conflicts within feminism has been the issue of differences among women, especially those of race, sexual orientation, and class. Feminists in the 1960s and 1970s alternated between routine denunciations of all feminist groups as extremely racist and/or classist and claiming that issues of differences were either falsely manufactured by outsiders to split the movement or were intended to dilute feminism by turning its attention away from the oppression of women. There were also many women who wanted to foster discussion and change but were unsure as to how to go about it. There were no models for the kind of work they wanted to do and this made the task very difficult. The initial struggle over differences was made far more explosive and divisive than it might otherwise have been by the unwillingness to admit to difference and the confusion over how to make it a positive resource, not a negative barrier.

Just as the issue was always present in the larger women's movement, feminist theaters understood it to be a central and important concern. Audiences were one source of challenge for the theaters. They were outspoken in their approval and disapproval, feeling a significant investment in and responsibility for what appeared on the stage. Audiences were not hesitant to critique harshly when a theater was perceived as failing to address an important issue, concern, or idea. The frustration Terry Baum experienced over the homophobic women in Lilith who limited the creative and political possibilities of *Sacrifices* has already been discussed. Baum's struggle within her theater group was similar to the struggles initiated by audiences with the theaters that were consistently ignoring lesbians. Roberta Sklar, who performed with students from Bard College in a group called The Women's Unit, noted that when lesbians and lesbian issues appeared in performance lesbians could be counted upon to be very vocal and forthcoming with their support. However, when lesbian issues and characters were believed to be lacking or absent, "you get confronted. 'Why aren't you raising these issues?' 'Are there any gay women in your group?' 'If not, have you considered why?' 'Why aren't you talking about your own homosexuality?'"[52] Exclusion from mainstream representation was no surprise, it was a painful and destructive part of homophobia, but exclusion from feminism, while frequent, was met with strong protest and rigorous critique. Early feminist theaters, such as New York Feminist Theater, offered the solution of having all company members, regardless of sexual orientation, play a lesbian character at some point in the show. At the end of each performance, as a show of solidarity, "the entire cast declare[d] their lesbianism."[53] The declaration was a clumsy attempt at making lesbians more present in representation and at fighting homophobia, but the simple appropriation of the lesbian position was not an especially productive solution to a complicated problem. The declaration originated more from a liberal attempt to prove commonality than an in-depth investigation of lesbian experiences.

Lesbian audiences challenged theaters to acknowledge omitting lesbian characters and to change their practices. The Women's Collage Theater received a lot of negative reactions from lesbians about their show *Sirens*. In the piece the central character, Anna, has an affair with a woman while involved with a man. One woman in Detroit wrote:

> [a] large part of the women's movement – a large segment of the women who insist on liberation – are lesbians, good old dykes, and we were totally ignored in your presentation – a bisexual affair is not lesbianism. Lesbians make the women's liberation movement and we need to be here.[54]

Another woman made a similar critique and reminded the theater of the feminist commitment to women. "You have an opportunity in this context to stop perpetuating fear of and lack of support for women loving women."[55] In the face of this invisibility and lack of commitment to lesbian issues, many lesbians began to form theaters of their own that could put onstage what many heterosexual-dominated theaters could or would not do.[56]

While conflicts and splits between lesbians and heterosexuals were being played out, white women and women of color were also struggling in the 1970s to discover a way to work together. Many white women were aware that to claim to be united with all women against sexist oppression and to present work created by an all-white ensemble with an all-white cast was a sharp contradiction. Clare Coss published a journal excerpt in 1977 written while Womanrite worked on *Daughters*. After hearing one group member express relief that "third world women" would not be a part of the theater group because "just working on my own stuff is/ hard enough/ without having to handle/ all those other issues,"[57] Coss describes her reaction:

> I clenched my teeth/ felt my chest flush with anger/ and thought/ this is a project to explore my womanline/. . . . / what

79

kind of issues would/ third world women/ world women/
bring to this group/ that would not be part/ not be part/ of our
stuff which is hard enough[58]

The "them and us" rhetoric would mark the attempts of many
groups to abandon an all-white composition and approach to
theater and in many ways be part of the failure of the work. The
problem became how to achieve actual integration that brings
together women from different classes, races, and sexualities to
produce theater while still acknowledging and representing all their
differences.

Throughout its existence Lilith (1974, San Francisco) endeavored
to present a multi-cultural vision. This project was plagued by
conflicts, disagreements, and burn-outs. There were two productions where the theater made an enormous effort to do significant integration work, the first on *Sacrifices* in 1977 and the second
on *Exit the Maids* in 1981. On the first occasion that they tried to
bring in performers from outside the company there were no
significant events that doomed the attempt but on the whole it was
not a success. Terry Baum remembers that two African–American
women and one Filipina entered the company with the understanding that

they were sick of talking about racial problems and racism.
They just wanted to work as actresses. That was it, that was
their rule coming in. It doesn't work. You can't not talk about
that stuff. If you don't talk about it, it just festers and gets
worse.[59]

Michele Linfante believes that part of the problem with the collaboration was that the three women were brought in after the show
was complete and they were not members of the collective. It was
also unclear as to whether they were going to become members.
Thrusting people into an ensemble and in the middle of a process
is, Linfante believes, "an unbalancing thing, and predisposed the
project to failure."[60] All three women left Lilith once *Sacrifices*
closed.

After the European tour and Baum's departure in 1979, the
company decided to try again. *Exit the Maids* was the first large
play since the tour where they committed themselves to collective
playwrighting. It will be discussed later how Linfante could not
stand behind the play created by the collective; that ultimately she

felt it was not a Lilith play and did not match her artistic vision. It is not surprising, then, that she feels that due to the difficulty of collective work it is not easy to separate racism from professional difficulties:

> It's hard to know was it strictly racism or was it other stuff? Was it new company members versus old company members? Was it being on a lower rung? Those are the kinds of thing I don't remember enough of the details. That in and of itself would have been worthy at the time of a seminar but we brought them in to put up a show.[61]

Linfante also notes that there were conflicts about discipline and commitment because some of the new women lacked experience in the theater.[62] Joan Mankin has similar memories in that there was a lot of acrimonious and "intense" conflicts during the rehearsal period over the logistics of rehearsals and performances.[63]

While Michele Linfante does not want to credit the entire conflict to racist tensions within the company she is quick to agree that racism certainly played a part in the difficulties. "The racist stuff *did* happen. You can't combat it overnight from both sides just for the sake of putting up a show."[64] It is important to keep the problems surrounding the creation of *Exit the Maids* in the context of the company's history. The founder had just resigned after a battle, the company was losing members to exhaustion, and rehearsals were floundering in a company unsure for the first time of its mission.

One Chinese–American woman wrote an article about her dissatisfying collaboration with Lilith. Kitty Tsui had limited experience in the theater but was very interested in working in a theater company that was dedicated to "defin[ing] the responsibilities of the liberated woman and affirm[ing] the power of every woman to make our world a better place."[65] She auditioned and was cast. There was no script as it was to be created in rehearsals:

> One of the actors was to write the script from the improvisation work. When it was clear she was unable to produce one, the director took on the role of writer. To her credit she turned out a script in four days. However, it was an ordeal for me to read through it. My character, Jenny, the "quiet one," had minimal lines. When she did speak it was to tell fortunes from the wrinkles of a sheet. Speaking in versee likee dis.[66]

COLLECTIVITY AND COLLABORATION

The stereotype Tsui understood to be at work angered her because she had expected more from a feminist group. The play did not, as she had hoped, provide insight into "why women and women of color, foreign-born and American, are often forced into work as maids." Instead it was, in her opinion, "a figment of fantasy that distorts, trivializes and makes a mockery of a woman's work."[67] Despite her problems with the script she decided to continue to work with the group, hoping that perhaps through dialogue she could change the script's assumptions and characters.

Her initial reactions to her character's fortune-telling were ignored but after Tsui poured a considerable amount of time and energy into explaining why she objected to the activity and why she felt it was inappropriate, the director reassigned the "exotic activity" to a Cuban maid:

> Anxieties and emotions were high. There was rewriting, reshaping, cutting, and shaping to be done . . . . From the first when I spoke out against the racist characterization, I had been alienated from the rest of the cast. . . . Though they felt my politics were "right on" they resented having to take the time and energy to make the needed changes.[68]

Tsui believed strongly that the changes were imperative to avoid the more blatant stereotypes she saw in the script.

After the show opened and before it went on tour Tsui was told by the management of the theater company that she would not be able to go on tour with them because of her "personal problems."[69] Her anger at Lilith stems from her belief that she was never informed that the company had personal problems with her and her belief that all personal problems, especially in situations like this one, are political. She writes that the decision was never discussed with her, so she felt like the "hired help" exploited in the play. "The group conveniently dismissed me to avoid confrontation and debate."[70] Tsui's article and the interviews with Baum, Linfante, and Mankin all testify to the difficulty of coalition work and to Linfante's belief that it cannot be accomplished in one production, that it is work that must be developed slowly over a long period of time. Without taking the time to develop trust and a working relationship there cannot be any movement towards productive multi-cultural creation.[71]

At the same time as Lilith was painfully trying to integrate itself, Spiderwoman Theater found itself unravelling because of the multiple burdens of trying to work through the racism, homophobia, and classism in the company. The situation was aggravated by the incredible strain of touring for six months out of the year and by the fact that the conflicts were taking form as a power struggle over control of the company. The clash of artistic visions eventually led to the formation of two separate theater companies, Spiderwoman Theater and Split Britches. One aspect of the struggle that was especially difficult for Muriel Miguel was that Lois Weaver wanted to direct and Miguel did not want to relinquish that role. Discussions, the very basis of the kind of work Spiderwoman did, became heated and confusing. They also became less and less productive. What was surprising to everyone was that there seemed to be a real lack of communication. As Miguel said: "The scary thing was we talked about everything because our work depended on it."[72] Meetings disintegrated into taking sides and hiding true opinions:

> Now this is from *my* point of view, *personally*, Muriel Miguel talking about what happened then. Elizabeth would start talking about her feelings and Lois would cry. So we can't talk about that; Lois is crying. We'd start talking about other stuff, other times and Peggy would get mad, so we can't talk about that. So that kind of stuff happened. Or we would talk and we would talk and people would not tell their feelings and then there would be regrouping outside of the meeting. This is how women work unless they really trust you.[73]

Outside the meetings campaigning occurred and feelings and opinions not brought out in meetings would be laid bare. Miguel believes that everyone's lack of trust in the process was causing her to let go of the company she had founded and run. "I was letting it go because I was feeling liberal, I was not letting people grow is what they were telling me. I would have to free up and get loose and I was holding too tight to my ideas."[74] But Miguel was urged by others, especially her sisters Lisa Mayo and Gloria Miguel, to retain her artistic vision, one that they shared, and to fight for it. Muriel Miguel is also sure that class differences played a large role in the crisis. "It was all those wonderful things; 'you're not being fair,' 'we have to look at this in a logical way.' These were the middle-class values that came into the group with the middle-class fair women."[75] The temporary solution was to produce two separate productions under the auspices of Spiderwoman Theater. Miguel and her sisters did *Sun, Moon, and Feather* about their own childhoods and their encounters with racism and Lois Weaver, Peggy Shaw, and Pam Verge did *Split Britches* about women in Weaver's family in West Virginia. After the 1981 premiere of *Split Britches* and a subsequent reworking of the play, Weaver and Shaw were confident that their collaboration could form the basis for a separate company.[76]

In 1985 the company reunited to remount *Cabaret* after not speaking for several years. At that point they told Alisa Solomon that they were no longer completely clear as to what all the causes of the fight had been but "sexual politics probably had plenty to do with it. Tensions among gay and straight women in the company increased as lesbians wanted to express and explore their experiences in the group's theatrical work."[77] The reconciliation came at a party where the members of Spiderwoman and Split Britches talked for hours and decided to pick up their friendships where they had left off.

Some years after Spiderwoman was split into two groups and Lilith was unable successfully to integrate their company, At the Foot of the Mountain (AFOM) made a commitment to anti-racist work that eventually brought about monumental changes in their acting company, administrative structure, and artistic vision. Beginning in 1986 the theater contracted to do two intensive anti-racism workshops. They brought in specialists from the outside, two white women who worked from the notion that the initial anti-racism work should be taken in groups composed exclusively of white people, so that the burden for teaching did not fall on the shoulders of people of color. The first workshop was focused generally; they watched movies, tackled assigned readings, and held discussions about the material. The second workshop concentrated on the specifics of the theater company.[78] What was learned in the workshops formed a significant part of the decision to create a new multi-cultural acting ensemble early in 1987:

> We were not, as we imagined, *all* women. . . . We were overwhelmingly white and middle-class, and with the arrogance of race and class privilege – dismayingly like the gender privilege we deplored in men – we generalized from our own experiences, took ourselves as the unmarked norms.[79]

Working from the principle that the theater was more than what was presented onstage they resolved to extend the multi-cultural commitment into the management of the theater as well, and began a search for a new Managing Director with the intention of hiring a woman of color. In addition to a new Managing Director, AFOM also auditioned and cast a new company: Carmen Maria Rosario, a Puerto Rican–American; Rebecca Rice, an African–American; Antoinette Maher, a Polish–Irish–American; Sherry Blakey Banai, a Native American; and Bernadette Hak Eun Cha, Korean born. The Managing Director's job was filled by Nayo-Barbara Watkins, an African–American woman who had been working at the University of Mississippi. Phyllis Jane Rose, who had been serving as both the Managing Director and the Artistic Director, remained to serve as Artistic Director.

For a few months in 1978 things seemed to be going quite smoothly; all the positions were filled, the company and the theater were working together and committed to the experiment. AFOM seemed to have a new and exciting purpose. Then things began to fall apart disastrously. The announced season was changed several times and then abandoned, Phyllis Jane Rose resigned as Artistic Director, and the theater stopped production to rethink the process of multi-culturalism. Carol Itawa, president of the board of directors, explained:

> There aren't a lot of examples to follow.... Setting up in advance how you expect things to work out and what you plan to do is part of the problem. You obviously have to find a balance between something that is so experimental that you can't make predictions and something that is so fixed that you can't achieve what you want.[80]

The original idea for the new company was to remount the two productions that had established AFOM as an important feminist theater and that had been the hallmark of their style: *The Story of A Mother* and *Raped: A Woman's Look at Bertolt Brecht's "The Exception and the Rule"*. Martha Boesing was to return after a two-year absence to rework both plays with the new acting ensemble.[81] Rather than create a new company with its own history and its own successes, sharing only the name with the original company, the theater wanted to start by acknowledging the white past and revising white history as the beginning of the creation of a new multi-cultural present. Not surprisingly, they found that *Mother* needed to be completely rewritten, almost from scratch, and the work needed to complete that collaboration left no time for *Raped*.[82]

In the fall of 1987, before she resigned, Phyllis Jane Rose found herself at odds with the board over how the new mission would influence the interaction between the board and the artistic management and what the balance would be between traditional board activities and activities created in response to the multi-cultural experiment. Rose was told by the board that all major artistic decisions would have to be approved by the board before they could be implemented. Rose felt that this was a threat to the traditional independence of the artistic area of the theater. Carol Itawa, president of the board, disagreed with Rose's interpretation of the decision. It was not their intention, according to Itawa, that the board take over all the artistic functions of the Artistic Director nor was it a second-guessing vote of no confidence:

> It was the board's way of ensuring that we use our lines of communications and open up new lines. Being truly multi-cultural in a society such as ours is difficult. It requires that we be different from the way we were socialized to be.[83]

Itawa was also adamant that the increased interaction between board and Artistic Director would not dilute the artistic quality of the theater's productions, feeling that the argument over art versus politics has long been used to diminish the work of feminist theater collectives.

Rose's subsequent resignation forced the theater to do some more thinking and revising of their plan for multi-culturalism. The theater devised two solutions. One was to continue work on *Mother* and the other was to appoint three members of the artistic ensemble as co-Artistic Directors. In December 1987, AFOM announced that Rebecca Rice, Bernadette Cha, and Jan Magrane (an original member of the theater) would serve as co-Artistic Directors.[84] To continue the work of the ensemble the theater sought and received a $225,000 grant from the Ford Foundation.[85]

The problem that AFOM was facing was that no one was quite sure what multi-cultural art should look like. The model created from the re-collaboration on *Mother* was one that stressed similarities and shared interpretations of experience. But the company was not sure that was the model with which they were most comfortable. Nayo-Barbara Watkins tried to work out in a newsletter article in 1988 just what it was that the theater was doing.

We are aware that it is not the simple presence of people of different colors and cultures on a stage at the same time. We are aware that different peoples perceive and conceive theater differently. . . . We are mindful of the rigidness of the guardians of the tradition of American and Western Theater in perpetuating concepts and practices which do not serve the interests of all Americans. And finally, the one thing we know is that there is much we simply don't know: we don't know the image that is created when peoples with very different motives, drives, and concepts of fulfillment intersect *democratically* in a space that honors no dominant cultural view.[86]

While Watkins' statement is honest in its admission that the theater is experimenting without precedent and looking for a solution for what has never been envisioned, it is difficult to produce theater without a positive vision. Therefore, it is not surprising that the new ensemble stayed together for only five months, proving correct perhaps one critic who told AFOM that the idea behind the ensemble was "an excellent example of what pleases white audiences but does not serve audiences of color."[87] The company turned to other ways of realizing a multi-cultural theater. In September and October of 1988 they produced a festival of one-woman shows by multi-cultural performers and offered workshops by many of the performers.

The theater's biggest step was to abandon production altogether. In 1991 they concentrated on skill sharing and training because "an immediate concern was the fact that few artists are trained in cross cultural work or collaboration and a body of works to draw upon was yet to be created."[88] AFOM moved its focus to producing and supporting a diversity of performers, providing them with performance space and financial resources.

AFOM cannot do justice to the works of many women, to many audiences, or to its own survival if it relies on what it is able to create, produce and show on its stage. The Education and Outreach components, as ongoing service areas, provide additional ways to support artists, serve audiences, and generate income.[89]

Process became the focus of the theater company, recalling the early 1970s when the politics of feminism forced theater artists to concentrate not only on what they put onstage but also on how it got there. However, this solution did not solve the problems of the company and by the end of 1991 AFOM no longer existed.

The experiences of Lilith, Spiderwoman, and AFOM all raise important and interesting questions about the future of feminism and theater's ability to tackle the questions of multi-culturalism and racism, representation and sexuality, and integration and difference. Michele Linfante believes that moving away from an all-white focus to a multi-cultural one is "a delicate thing that must be done over years."[90] The stories of the three theater companies demonstrate that it is extremely difficult to work productively through the intersections of oppression, especially when they are complicated by artistic questions and goals. But these problems emerged from almost a decade of work within variously defined communities and it is not surprising that feminist theater groups were having these crises at the same moment as the larger feminist movement. It was a crisis of community and a crisis of communication. The argument has been made that no one group can stand in for the whole of feminist theater, just as no one woman can be said to represent all feminists or all feminist perspectives. However, that is not to argue the exact converse, in other words, that no groups shared any characteristics or that nothing can be learned from an in-depth examination of a small number of theaters. In fact, one thing that scrutinizing a limited number of groups will demonstrate is that the struggles over issues such as diversity, organization, or their relation to feminism demonstrate the dynamism and heterogeneity of the groups.

The four groups in question are the Women's Experimental Theater, Spiderwoman Theater, Lilith, and Front Room Theater Guild. Their histories span 1972 to the present (of the four, only Spiderwoman Theater continues to produce); regionally they span the country and all (except Front Room Theater Guild) toured extensively. Their experiences and emphases are both similar and in great contrast to one another. Each history is primarily drawn from the memories of the participants which were usually partial and sometimes contradictory. Hopefully what will be communicated is the strong sense of importance and value that each woman invested in the struggles and achievements of her group, serving as a demonstration of the vitality of the feminist theater group movement.

THE WOMEN'S EXPERIMENTAL THEATER

The Women's Experimental Theater (WET) was founded in New York City in 1977 by Clare Coss, Sondra Segal, and Roberta Sklar out of an earlier company, Womanrite. In 1972 Womanrite had begun as a consciousness-raising group that focused on what Segal called "theater techniques" as a method for becoming more "self-aware."[91] Sondra Segal, a founder of the group, had an emotional, intellectual, and political commitment to explore women's experiences through theater that emerged from her own feminist consciousness and, realizing performance's potential to affect and address women, urged that the group reform as a theater. The group began to train in earnest and, despite the emphasis on theater as process over product, in 1973 created and performed a piece that explored the traditional roles of women in the family and society, *The Cinderella Project*. After the production the group split into two factions: one that wanted to continue to emphasize consciousness-raising and self-examination and another that wanted to concentrate actively on becoming a more professional performance group. Segal was the driving force behind the second faction. Performing in *Cinderella* resolved for her that her commitment was to theater, performance, and the audiences of women rather than to individualized consciousness-raising alone. At some point in 1972–73 Segal and other members of Womanrite attended performances of the Open Theater. What they saw there excited them and they decided to hire someone to teach them the techniques of the Open Theater. They contacted Roberta Sklar to obtain the name of someone qualified to teach them. Sklar remembers that

> they asked me to recommend someone and I recommended myself. While the disparity in our theater experience was very great, as a feminist, a woman trying to understand my own condition, I was at the starting point. It was here that we were peers and where we could join forces and work productively. I knew it would be extremely challenging to bring my experience as a director and teacher of theater to work with women who were seeking to change their lives.[92]

By 1971–72 Roberta Sklar was both directing at the Open Theater and teaching acting at Bard College in New York. There, out of a theater course for women, grew a feminist theater group, the Woman's Unit. While this was Sklar's first attempt at feminist theater, the work shared a similar line of inquiry with the work she would later do at WET.

What we were most interested in [in the Woman's Unit] were questions about the distinct acting problems women have. We had no idea what would apply of the traditional techniques. I was starting from scratch because I was going on the assumption that everything I knew was generated by male traditions, so I had to start from what I did *not* know. . . . The traditional approach to acting – stripping away layers, breaking down defenses, and building up from nothing – didn't seem to apply to women. . . . She has learned to survive by developing defenses in a world that doesn't perceive her as part of the human race. . . . So, instead of tearing down, we located, supported, and built up strengths. . . . We worked with feelings. . . . We had to learn to shape, control, and consciously project our feelings. [93]

The performance material emerged from personal experiences shaped as songs, sketches, and monologues and was part of Sklar's interest in investigating feminist methods of acting and evolving a feminist theory for women actors. The group did *Obscenities and Other Questions* in women's prisons, for community groups on Long Island, and for all-women audiences in the New York area.[94]

Clare Coss and Sklar met in 1974 when they were both on the faculty at Hunter College. Coss was an established playwright. She had undergraduate and graduate degrees in theater and in the 1960s worked with Maryat Lee at the Soul and Latin Theater doing improvisation and sociodrama in East Harlem. Coss' work had been performed at the American Place Theater in 1969 (*Madame U.S.A.*) and at the Berkshire Theater Festival in 1971 (*The Star Strangled Banner* directed by Maxine Klein). When, in 1976, Womanrite decided to open the group to new people Coss was invited to join. Coss, Segal, and Sklar felt that they worked well together and "a very exciting collaboration occurred."[95]

The first work they created together was *Daughters* in 1976. The original idea for the production was Segal's: she suggested that the group examine the psychological and social consequences of the idea that every woman is a daughter. This concept resonated strongly for all three women and served as the foundation for all future work by WET.[96] While *Daughters* was in progress the conflict over the purpose and focus of the group resurfaced. Coss, Segal, and Sklar were determined that the work continue and that production and performance obligations be respected. Others felt equally strongly that the groups should remain primarily committed to consciousness-raising, with performance of secondary importance. Segal commented on the situation:

> We had performances scheduled and some people wanted to cancel them and do "group dynamics." There were others of us who felt we would rather kill than do that. It was critical to honor our commitments to our feminist producers, to the audience of women looking forward to this work, to women who had been assigned to write about it, and to ourselves.[97]

The disagreements over process and product led to the formation of the Women's Experimental Theater. Sklar recalls that the break was actually quite liberating as the arguments had created a great deal of tension, making it difficult to work. After the break, for the most part, the three women felt "wonderful. [We were] unfettered from conflict."[98] *Daughters* was then finished and two more plays on the theme of women's roles in the family were created: *The Daughters Cycle Trilogy*.[99]

For most of its nine years of active existence, WET was fortunate enough to have a home base at the Women's Interart. While many feminist theater groups expended considerable time and energy booking both rehearsal and performance space, WET's residency gave them a continuity of location, access to an administrative structure, and the non-interfering support of an organization sympathetic to their project. It was that last point that WET stressed strongly for Helen Chinoy: "They don't just leave us alone," Roberta Sklar told Chinoy, "they leave us alone with love and support."[100] Interart provided a free rehearsal and performance space, used solely by WET. Their agreement was not overly formal, though occasionally the group would discuss their work with Margot Lewitin and verbally agree to continue their association.

The responsibility for fund raising and administrating was on the shoulders of the three Artistic Directors. WET received grants from the National Endowment for the Arts, New York State Council on the Arts, CETA Title VI Funds, the Women's Fund of the Joint Foundation Support, and sponsored benefits and fundraisers.[101] The burden of writing grant applications, of planning and executing benefits, and of all the other business demands (publicity, scheduling, and bookkeeping) fell on Coss, Segal, and Sklar. While the theater charged admission, the ticket price was minimal and, according to Coss, no one was ever turned away for being unable to pay the admission price.[102] The runs at the Interart tended to be about eight weeks, at which point they would go on tour, primarily on the East Coast. They performed in a variety of venues including theaters, festivals, and conferences. For example, they presented their work at the National Women's Studies Association, at the Feminist and the Scholar Conference at Barnard College, and at the first Women's One World Festival.[103]

In 1980, upon completion of *The Daughters Cycle Trilogy*, Clare Coss left WET to return to her work as an independent playwright.[104] Coss was missed but the transition from three to two was less difficult than it might have been, coming as it did at the end of one phase, the interest in women and the family, and the beginning of another, the investigation of women's relationships to food and the body. Focusing on food and the body Segal and Sklar created three more plays; *Food* in 1980, *Foodtalk* in 1981, and finally *Feast or Famine* in 1985. Collectively the three plays were titled *Woman's Body and Other Natural Resources*. Both Segal and Sklar consider the work on these three plays, especially *Feast or Famine*, to be the most advanced work that WET produced – technically, visually, and theoretically. The last play enabled them to further "develop technique, and hone and question feminist principles."[105] It was also the first WET production that involved sophisticated and complicated production values. "Until that point nearly everything rested on the performer alone," said Segal.[106] That was the production that Segal and Sklar believe began to use the full range of the new feminist acting and producing theories they had been developing.

The acting approaches developed within WET concentrated heavily on the relationship between the audience and the performer. Sondra Segal stressed this dynamic: "I was not at all looking to pretend that the audience was not there. I was looking to communicate with that audience, and to be very direct and forthright about it. . . . I understood that the audience could see very well and that camouflage was not to the point."[107] In her view, the connection with the audience, based as it was on communicating with them directly and relying on the recognition of shared lived experiences, precluded the traditional definitions of character.

> Every woman plays many roles all the time and knows what she's doing and why she's doing it. . . . The audience wanted to see that, wanted to see someone who knows what she's

doing, understands why she's doing it, is thinking all the time, a mile a minute. And I let that be seen.[108]

The Women's Experimental Theater realized this in two ways. The first was to develop exercises that concentrated on the ways women express themselves physically and vocally. For example, as much of *Electra Speaks* focused on women's access to language, WET workshopped with hundreds of women "who were not in the performance group, on issues of speaking and silence and tried to explore ways of speaking that articulated inner realities that weren't necessarily expressed verbally."[109] Another method was to choose material that seemed relevant to the members of the group and to their audiences. Sklar describes the questions and research process that began the development of each play.

> What makes this particular moment, thing, activity, feeling particular to women and particular to these women with whom we are working together? So that was really a guideline. Ask the question from the position of being female. What's the result? What do you get?[110]

From initial idea through workshop, writing, and rehearsal to performance there was a an emphasis on women's lived experience and the connections among women. This was achieved not by educating the audience/workshop participants but by "acknowledging [together] what we know" and learning from it.[111]

Feast or Famine was the last production of the Women's Experimental Theater. In 1986 they stopped performing. Sondra Segal and Roberta Sklar wrote of their decision to close their theater:

> Although thinking seriously about women's lives is as important as it was a decade ago, it no longer seems to be a conscious, pressing part of a mass movement. The Women's Experimental Theater is not currently active. The decline of economic and audience support tells us this is not the time. We have decided, however, not to formally close up shop. We want to remain open to the rumblings of a distant thunder – that of an old, or new, feminist need.[112]

SPIDERWOMAN THEATER

Spiderwoman Theater was founded at roughly the same time as WET. While the group has been as large as seven members, Muriel

Miguel, Lisa Mayo, and Gloria Miguel, three Cuna–Rappahan-nock Native American sisters, form the core of the group. The name of the theater company comes from the Hopi goddess of creation who gave her people the art of design and weaving. All of the goddess' work contained her spirit so a flaw had to be woven into every piece ensuring that the goddess could escape. Consequently, all of the group's creations are flawed or explore flaws, whether it be in the characters, subject matter, or performers. The group explained their use of the concept of the flaw in their publicity material. "Finding, loving and transcending our own flaws, as in the flaw in the goddess' tapestry, provides the means for our spirits to find their way out, and be free."[113] The process is called storyweaving; performance pieces are created from personal stories and experiences, cultural icons and texts, and political issues and concerns.

Muriel Miguel was a member of the Open Theater. From there she founded, with two women who were untrained and inexperienced in theater, a feminist theater, Womanspace, in 1972. Miguel, Laura Foner, and Carol Grosberg had spent eight months together in discussion and improvisation when they hit upon the idea of creating a theater piece out of the experiences of their collaboration.[114] The piece, entitled *Cycles*, was intended to "find common ground as political women of different class and racial origin, and to work out their problems in dramatic terms."[115] *Cycles* concentrated on a part of each woman's identity that set her apart from mainstream life, Miguel's as a Native American, Foner's as a former weatherwoman, and Grosberg's as a lesbian. It was, like Womanrite, consciousness-raising as theater and, also like Womanrite, it split apart because the group and group process eventually became more important than performing and creating new works. Because Foner and Grosberg lacked theater experience Miguel ultimately found it frustrating to work with them.

> It was really disappointing. I expected them to know things. I learned on my feet, I expected other people to. I expected them to know that if you say onstage that you love somebody and offstage you hate their guts, at that moment that moment is really true. They were calling me a bullshitter, a hypocrite. They couldn't maintain that kind of professionalism, that kind of craft.[116]

While Miguel was invested in the issues explored by Womanspace she was primarily interested in pursuing the investment through theater. She broke with Grosberg and Foner because "they weren't committed as theater people."[117] Miguel was committed to theater, as a feminist and as a Native American, and to doing political theater with a professional attitude. Despite her disappointment she decided to form another theater group.

Miguel invited her two sisters to create a theater piece with her but neither was interested in doing so at that point. Instead, with Lois Weaver, who would later be a member of Spiderwoman and then a founder of Split Britches, and a childhood friend, a Hopi woman, Miguel created a show about spirituality and performed it at Washington Square Methodist Church. Her friend's piece was about fingerweaving and the goddess Spiderwoman, Lois Weaver spoke on Jesus Christ, and Miguel performed a monologue based on her experiences at the Sun Dance. Later, when her friend died before reaching the age of forty, Miguel was devastated by the loss and saw her friend's death as emblematic of the fate of too many Native Americans. Miguel made two resolutions: to reach forty herself and to start a feminist theater group with her sisters.[118]

Soon after the show closed the group folded. However, Miguel received a grant she had applied for when working with Womanspace. Teaching at Bard College at the time, she used the money to create Spiderwoman Theater's first production, *Women in Violence*, in 1976.[119] Lisa Mayo and Gloria Miguel finally committed to Miguel and the theater company. In addition to her sisters, Miguel asked Lois Weaver and two other women to be a part of the company.[120]

This time Miguel found herself collaborating with people trained and experienced in theater and committed to performance. Lisa Mayo, her elder sister, is a classically trained mezzo-soprano. During her opera training she decided that acting lessons would be useful, and she entered the HB Studios with the intention of taking classes for the summer and ended up training there for ten years.[121] She had also worked extensively with Uta Hagen, so when Mayo began her work with Spiderwoman she had a clear idea of the discipline it took to work in the theater. Gloria Miguel too had professional experience. She studied theater at Oberlin College where she earned her B.A. Gloria Miguel maintains an acting career outside of Spiderwoman and has toured with other theater companies.[122]

While performing *Women in Violence* at the Baltimore Theater Festival in 1977, Luis Valdez saw Spiderwoman and recommended them to the organizers of the World Festival of Theater, an international event held in Nancy, France. On the strength of that recommendation Spiderwoman was invited to perform: "We were the first feminist theater group to go to an international theater festival."[123] The company raised the money through a series of benefits, including one at the Public Theater, and arrived in France totally unprepared for the interest and acclaim they received, or for the controversy they would cause.

The audiences in Nancy were larger than any audiences they had ever had. This experience was both exciting and nerve-wracking. Muriel Miguel remembers that after their show people would "scream and yell down the street 'Spiderwoman.'"[124] They also found themselves at the center of feminist organizing. During the run of *Women and Violence* a woman was beaten up in the street by a drunken man. Unable to force the police into action, she went to her boss and asked him to demand action on her complaint. He convinced the police to arrest her assailant. The police complied, but required her to identify the man while in the same room with him, offering her no protection or anonymity. He was released with only a warning and the woman was afraid he might attack her again. "She came to us because she was so frustrated and terrified," Spiderwoman told interviewer Renfreu Neff.[125] The story touched at the heart of their play and they agreed to try to help her. They sponsored nightly discussions about the incident and offered to organize a protest.

> After each show we would tell the story and say "if you want to do something about it, we're going to do something this Saturday, what do you suggest?" A lot of women came, and men too, and we did a piece in Stanislaus Square in Nancy and these women showed up. . . . It was wonderful because all the networking happened. In the next town over there was a feminist group who did not know there was anything happening in Nancy. So the whole networking thing came out of that.[126]

Miguel believes that the protest organized that weekend helped to bring French feminist activists into closer participation with one another and it brought Spiderwoman a number of booking offers. While they planned to stay abroad for the length of the festival, three weeks, they ended up booking several European appearances and toured for seven months.[127]

In 1977 they chose a classical text, something many feminist theater groups were doing at the time. However, rather than work from the House of Atreus stories or the Oedipus myths, they chose Aristophanes' *Lysistrata*. Renamed *Lysistrata Numbah*, the title coming from the idea that they were doing a "number" on the play, the company used the well-known plot to explore, among other things, violence against women, sexuality, and popular culture.[128] The tone and style of the pieces they produced in the following year differed from that of their previous works; for example, *Trilogy* was three serious monologues: *Friday Night, Jealousy*, and *My Sister Ate Dirt*. The three separate performance pieces concerned loneliness and isolation, male/female relationships, and personal experiences and family history.[129]

While touring in Amsterdam in 1979 members of the performing group Hot Peaches, a gay performance group inspired by the Theater of the Ridiculous style, went to see Spiderwoman perform.[130] Later in the year when Muriel Miguel wanted to expand her one-woman show *Cabaret* into a full-scale production the company "opened up the group" to new members, including Peggy Shaw of Hot Peaches.[131] The show, re-titled *Cabaret: An Evening of Disgusting Songs and Pukey Images*, was first performed in 1979 and later revived in 1985. Critiquing and satirizing "how women are forced to swallow male platitudes about love,"[132] the show explored romance through songs, monologues, and sketches. It followed the Spiderwoman style of weaving personal experiences and narratives with cultural icons and "challenge[d] classical, commercial, homogenizing images of women."[133] The play also presented a critique of heterosexuality in which Shaw and Weaver, in Jill Dolan's words, "conduct[ed] a subtextual seduction that clearly represent[ed] lesbian sexuality."[134] It was during this show that Shaw and Weaver became interested in working with one another on what would eventually become the play *Split Britches*, about women in Weaver's family from the Blue Ridge Mountains in Virginia.

Before *Split Britches* was created, Spiderwoman produced one more play as a company that included Shaw and Weaver, *The Fittin' Room*. The play critiqued the way categories create expectations that women feel forced to meet. Both heterosexuality and lesbianism were scrutinized: "Butch Meets Butch – Encounters in New

York City Bathrooms" was a soap opera throughline, juxtaposed with sketches about mothers and grandmothers, a young woman who wants to grow up to be the perfect wife, and a "how-to-be-attractive-to-men lesson."[135] It was during this play that the tensions that would force Spiderwoman Theater to split into two companies, Spiderwoman Theater and Split Britches, erupted.

Because working as a single group was becoming increasingly difficult, for the next project Spiderwoman produced two shows, *Split Britches* directed by Weaver, and *Sun, Moon, and Feather* directed by Miguel. Both plays were about family. Miguel's concentrated on the experiences of the three Miguel sisters as they grew up in Brooklyn and on the racism they encountered. Included were sketches about the influences of movie "Indians" on their self-perceptions, about witnessing their Father's violent and self-destructive behavior, and about their own sibling rivalry. *Split Britches* was performed in one version during the 1980 Women's One World (WOW) Festival and then in 1981 as part of a series of performances about women in families. It was the 1981 run that convinced Weaver and Shaw that they had created an independent theater piece. They broke with Spiderwoman and went on to form their own theater, Split Britches.[136]

Since 1981 Spiderwoman Theater has produced *The Three Sisters from Here to There* (1982), reworking Chekhov's *Three Sisters* through cast members' autobiographies, *I'll Be Right Back* (1984) about the nuclear threat, and *3 Up, 3 Down* (1986), combining personal narratives and Native American politics through a spoof of *Jane Eyre* and *Wuthering Heights*. In the late 1980s and early 1990s they toured *Winnetou's Snake Oil Show from Wigwam City*. The piece alternates among three narrative strands: a comedic but critical parody of Karl May's book *Winnetou*, a snake oil show that sells "ripped-off" imitation Indian spirituality to white people, and more serious and tragic stories of the toll of racism on the performers' families. Spiderwoman Theater continues to perform work with a rigorous feminist content but Miguel feels that since the early 1980s their work has begun to concentrate more heavily on Native American issues.[137] This is certainly borne out by their show *Power Pipes* performed with the Colorado Sisters, Vira and Hortensia, who were inspired to perform together by Spiderwoman. Developed in 1991 and performed at the 1992 Next Wave Festival at the Brooklyn Academy of Music, the play explores the performers' spiritual heritage through dance, music, and dialogue. Though concerned less with popular and European–American culture than their previous works, it continues their tradition of bringing together Native American and feminist concerns.

LILITH

On the West Coast, in San Francisco, Lilith Theater emerged at about the same time as WET and Spiderwoman. Terry Baum left Bear Republic Theater, a predominantly male theater group in Santa Barbara she had co-founded with friends from college, when they voted against admitting a woman she had recommended. She resigned because "having been with all men, I wanted to be with all women."[138] She moved back to the Bay Area and with some friends of friends, Charlotte Colavin and Shelley Fields, created *Lilith Theater* in 1974, a collection of improvisations and sketches concerning women's lives: getting older, housing, shopping for a bra, and falling in love with another woman. The audiences were very enthusiastic; Joan Mankin, who saw the show and would later, in 1976, join the company, remembered enjoying *Lilith Theater* a great deal and described it as focusing on "being a woman in a changing era of consciousness."[139] The following year Carolyn Meyers joined the group, now named Lilith after the first show, and they created the second production, *Good Food* (1975), about five waitresses in a restaurant with four tables. Each waitress has a dream and the other four act it out, "it was about us trying to figure out how to work together," Baum remembers.[140] Neither play had any production values to speak of, both were intended to be performed anywhere the theater could get a booking and both shows connected strongly with their audiences who were enthusiastic about Lilith's work.

For the next play, *Moonlighting*, in 1976, Lilith decided to be more ambitious and put out a call for more women to join to create a play about women and work. Joan Mankin, a former member of the San Francisco Mime Troupe, and Michele Linfante both joined at this time. Linfante remembers that they did improvisations in the style of Viola Spolin and the Firehouse Theater, and Mankin recalls that the bulk of the writing was done by Meyers and Baum.[141] The show opened with a recitation of group statistics, who and how many went to college and what jobs they had had, in order to make the group composition clear.[142] The play consisted primarily of short vignettes that resonated powerfully with the audience:

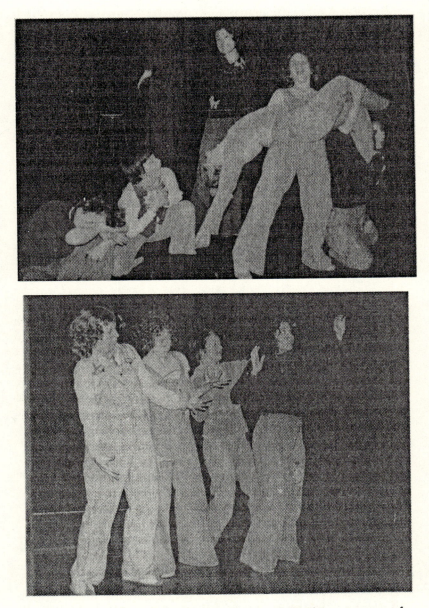

Figure 2 Lilith in rehearsal in the mid- to late 1970s. Photos courtesy of Tohu Bohu Lesbian Arts Conspiracy

We knew we wanted to do a scene about women and the idea of their abilities. We had this very small scene about fixing a toilet. It got to be very small but it was about being able to do something. You know, they say we can't do something mechanical, typical of women. We had people mimetically playing a toilet, snarling and growling. It was one of those things you could conquer and those scenes were very successful.[143]

Baum recalls there was also a revolutionary housework ballet done in "heroic Chinese style."[144]

Figure 3 The "toilet" scene from Lilith's *Moonlighting* (1976). The three women kneeling are the parts of the toilet that the woman standing is trying to fix

Between 1977 and 1978 Lilith produced two more plays, the first, *Sacrifices*, being written by Baum, Meyers, Linfante, and Resnais Winter.[145] The second, *Manifesto*, adapted and performed after *Sacrifices*, was by Dacia Maraini, one of the founders of the Italian feminist theater, Teatro La Maddalena.[146] Harriet Schiffer who saw *Sacrifices* remembers it as an incredibly powerful experience. "I was inspired, it was very profound."[147] She later joined the group when they did *Manifesto*. The 1978–79 season was a crucial turning point for the Lilith members. Linfante, through friends and friends of friends, was able to secure several European bookings for the company, including a large international theater festival in Munich.[148] Baum, exhausted and burned out, decided to remain in San Francisco and join the tour later. She deputized her lover, Alice Thompson, a talented director, to take on the director's responsibilities. While the company generally agrees that Thompson was talented and had the ability to do the job, they remember her as someone with whom it was difficult to work. This turned the tour into an emotionally charged experience for those involved. Performances were exciting, audiences were receptive and enthusiastic and Linfante describes the whole experience as "mind-blowing, people just opened their arms to us."[149] Terry Baum also remembers the tour primarily as an extremely positive experience. "People were just so – it was like spreading the good word. People were just so thrilled. There was a wonderful feeling that we were doing something new that people really needed to hear."[150] However, difficulties with Thompson and other disagreements made the women feel confined and cramped. Consequently, the company fired Thompson before returning to the United States. The group found that Baum was very angry at the company's treatment of Thompson and she resigned from the company.

Members give various reasons for Baum's resignation and Baum echoes many of them. Her position was that the group which she had founded, and of which she was the Artistic Director, albeit unofficially, had thrown her out when they fired Thompson. "I was the mama."[151] Initially, her resignation was a one-year leave of absence with the understanding that she might return. Michele Linfante recalls that Carolyn Meyers had Baum write down that the name Lilith belonged to the company, not Baum. Terry Baum tried, a year later, to use the name of Lilith to produce her own work but the Board of Directors denied her request. Baum felt "crushed" because she had founded the company, she had named it, and she had written Lilith's first grant. She felt keenly that her subsequent shows were often ignored while Lilith flourished because they were an established and known quantity. She could not help but think that Lilith was receiving money and attention that should have, in part, been hers.[152] Of the entire incident Linfante said, "in a lot of ways it wasn't a fair thing to have happened. But that's the way it happened."[153]

Terry Baum's departure was hard on the company because, no

matter how much collaborative work they had done and how much they proclaimed themselves a collective, Baum's absence left the company without a guiding artistic leader. Once again, unofficially, Linfante found herself in the position of leader, describing herself as the "mom."[154] The first play done after Baum's resignation was also the first play to be written by an individual playwright. Michelle Linfante wrote *Pizza* in 1980 as a one-act about her relationship with her mother.[155] Performed with this was another one-act, *Trespaso* by Martha Boesing. At this point Carolyn Meyers left the company to move to Ashland, Oregon, with her new baby. Joan Mankin believes that part of Meyers' decision came from her closeness to Baum and her reluctance to take sides in the debate over Lilith's leadership and name.[156]

Exit the Maids (1981) was a crisis production for Michele Linfante and another problematic period for the theater. A political piece about a recent hotel maids' strike, the play was, in Linfante's estimation, more a Mime Troupe play than a Lilith play. The company brought in a lot of new people, including several women of color, who had not previously been part of the company, to perform the piece. The new women had little say in the creation of the piece. As mentioned earlier in this chapter, Linfante did not support the play as she did not feel it reflected her personal artistic vision. However, the power dynamics of the company were hazy enough that she was not sure if she had the power to stop the play or if, even if she had the power, she would want to stop it. The instability of her position and the situation itself were painful to Linfante and she felt that the issue was an old one resurfacing, namely who controlled the company and how that control worked:

> *Exit the Maids* was the play that cracked me and sent me out of the company. It was, in fact, that I was having a nervous breakdown. . . . It wasn't creatively happening for me, I was losing the control I was supposed to be having . . . so I actually left.[157]

Joan Mankin succeeded Linfante as Artistic Director and was the third of the "big mothers who came along and mothered the company for a while."[158] But Linfante believes that after *Sacrifices* in 1977 and the European tour of 1979 "the company lost some essential vision."[159] According to Mankin the company was in a crisis after *Pizza* and *Trespaso*: "we entered a phase of really having a hard time figuring out what to do next."[160] People were leaving the company; Marga Gomez wanted to pursue a career in stand-up comedy, Vicky Lewis moved to Los Angeles to do professional acting, and Meyers and Linfante had also left. It was at this time that Lilith committed resources to hiring a business manager but the "artistic vision was splintering."[161] The "splintering" was occurring for many reasons, but one of the strongest was that no one could make a living wage off her work in the theater group. This increased burden made dedication to the theater often difficult, hastened burn-out, and shortened tempers.

In 1983 Carolyn Meyers became the Artistic Director, now an established and official role, and Lilith committed themselves to doing *Daughters of Erin*, a period drama about the Irish countess and revolutionary Constance de Markieviez and actress/rebel Maud Gonne, written by Meyers in collaboration with Elizabeth Rodin.[162] The idea had been discussed as a basis for a play in 1976 but was abandoned and now the company returned to the idea, deciding to pay company members full wages and re-orienting toward a more professional organization. They hired an outside director and seven San Francisco Equity actresses, and invested a significant amount of time and energy into fund-raising. As happened during *Exit the Maids*, when many outside people had been brought in to work with Lilith, the influx of new people destabilized the company. The production was too inflexible to tour, it had complicated production values, and was never popular with the press because the writing was rough and unpolished. The experiment in professionalism was an attempt at legitimacy that did not pay off. "It was a phase we went through and we paid for it."[163] At the same time the play was important because it dealt with a signal moment in women's history and, despite its flaws, audiences responded very positively, especially those at the second women's theater festival in Santa Cruz in 1983. It was after this production that Mankin left the theater to work with the Dell'Arte players. But she took with her what she had developed and learned in Lilith. She summed it up as a "very trusting atmosphere that was set up where you were encouraged to open up and just reveal and be vulnerable – I felt very supported by the whole process."[164]

After *Daughters of Erin* there was the strong sense that something was missing, that something crucial had gone out of the group. Harriet Schiffer, now Artistic Director, had a mandate from the other members and the board to restore the "Lilith process," described earlier in the chapter, to all areas of operations.[165]

Everyone agreed with Schiffer's suggestion that the next piece Lilith produced should be about reproductive rights and that it should be a play which they did not just produce but in which the "ensemble had to evolve."[166]

Four areas of activity were defined and 80–100 women became involved in Lilith at its weakest financial moment. Each area would be headed by one woman who would build a committee to assist her and who would be accountable to the core ensemble. That way the theater group was defined by a structure that did not depend on the work of any one individual woman and established a stronger, more centralized leadership. The first area was a series of full-moon rituals for which they charged no admission. The rituals were story telling sessions specific to the kind of full-moon (for example, the Harvest or Hunter's moon would elicit stories related to harvesting or hunting as themes) and were led by a member of Lilith. The second area was a play-reading series that drew on plays solicited from across the country. The third area concentrated on outreach through workshops and classes. The fourth area was the production based on reproduction rights. Two different performance pieces emerged from this emphasis: *Fetal Positions* (1983–84), a series of monologues which emerged through workshops, and *Breeding Grounds* (1984–86) which was quite different.

Five of the women in *Breeding Grounds* came out of the classes and outreach conducted by the women of Lilith, and Schiffer feels it was here that the rededication to process began to pay off. She integrated community service organizations interested in the issues into the piece as well. "I wanted to have them interested in the piece." But since she knew they did not have the money to give her: "I wanted to get their time."[167] Doing the piece in the open air of public parks, allowing much of the show to be dictated by the choices made by the spectators, and bringing the other organizations into the mix met Schiffer's goal that *Breeding Grounds* be "[n]ot just a performance piece but an event."[168] Schiffer felt that the piece was thus an incredibly positive note on which to end Lilith. Despite that, however, it did not make the end any easier.

In 1986 many of the core members gathered and had a closing ceremony to mark the formal end of Lilith. Schiffer remembers little of the ceremony itself mainly, she believes, because it was such a painful event for her. "I learned a tremendous amount from Lilith and the women in it. To me what we did was spectacular, I really had a great time doing it."[169]

FRONT ROOM THEATER GUILD

"It was really out of frustration that it started," said Patricia Van Kirk.[170] During a visit to Seattle from Alaska Van Kirk was inspired by the work she had seen at the Womyn's Theater, a Seattle producing group. She subsequently moved to Seattle hoping to become involved with the theater as a volunteer or as a performer, but she and the theater were never able to collaborate successfully. Instead, Van Kirk began to audition for the mainstream Seattle theaters. She did not succeed in being cast but her desire to do theater remained strong. It was then that she called several friends and asked them, hesitantly and only half-seriously, if they would like to put on a play with her. To her great surprise they agreed quickly and enthusiastically.

The house she was renting inspired her to produce a play. The living room was the largest one Van Kirk had ever seen in her life:

> it housed two overstuffed couches, two overstuffed chairs, a dining room table and chairs, and had room to spare. It was just a mammoth square room with a fireplace and bookcases and a trap door that went to the cellar. . . . I think it was built to house a theater in.[171]

The theater was named appropriately enough after the space in which it was born, Van Kirk's "front room."

Inspired by the romantic, gothic quality of the room and its furnishings, Van Kirk chose Sarah Dreher's *This Brooding Sky* and opened in March of 1980. Dreher's play is a lesbian spoof on gothic romances and FRTG played it to the hilt. The audience was brought into the theater through the backyard which was overgrown and wild, and Van Kirk used the trapdoor, the house setting, and the look of the place to great effect. Advertising to attract audiences other than the twelve women friends and relatives who attended the first performance was entirely based on word-of-mouth and the community grapevine. The experiment proved popular beyond Van Kirk and her friends' wildest imaginations. "By the second performance, the seventy seats and pillows were filled and women were turned away at the door."[172] But it was not simply the audience who sensed that something special was happening in that living room, the performers were aware as well. "It was fabulous, the energy, something happened. I knew that something had been born, there was no denying it."[173] While Van Kirk had both directed and performed in *This Brooding Sky*, she suddenly found herself the artistic director responsible for a new theater company.

FRTG was very popular, and people used to line up early outside the theater (Van Kirk's home) to get in to the see the shows. Initially the group funded the theater themselves, helped by the occasional small unsolicited donation, but later they started to charge fixed admission and to fund-raise with *In Search of the Hammer* in 1983.[174] They got a grant from the Seattle Art Commission and held popular fund-raising dances at a local women's bar. The group was never able to raise large amounts of money, which meant they had to keep expenses to a minimum. Two Halloween fund-raising dances in 1984 netted the theater $1,700 and in the same year they received a $600 grant from the Gay Community Social Services who also allowed FRTG to use the GCSS bulk mailing permit.[175] These grants and financial resources were typical of the size of grants FRTG had available to them throughout their existence. But the growth from the first show in 1981 to the four show season, a board of directors, and a paid artistic director was a gradual one. They kept adding to their responsibilities

> so that by the end when we tried to pass on the baton, you would have to be out of your mind to take the job with no pay. I got paid the last year and a half $400 a month. Nobody else got paid, we couldn't afford to pay anyone else.[176]

In 1986 when the theater ended, Van Kirk points out that part of the problem was that no one with any sense would take what was essentially a full-time job for a meager part-time salary.

Van Kirk was responsible for choosing the seasons and finding plays. She did not find this easy, for though certain playwrights such as Jane Chambers were well known and indeed published there were not many lesbian or even feminist texts from which Van Kirk could choose:

> I wrote around a lot, but it's hard. They're not published. You have to know someone who knows someone who used to live in Atlanta or St. Louis who remembers that their best friend's ex-lover's sister wrote plays. Minneapolis had At the Foot of the Mountain as a kind of model and RIFT had published some plays – I don't think we did any of theirs.[177]

Last Summer at Bluefish Cove, performed in 1985, one year before the theater closed, was very popular, as were all the Jane

Chambers' plays the company did. One reviewer wrote: "As strongly positive and beneficial to the gay image, it must not be missed by the community. . . . This production of *Bluefish Cove* is one of the best plays I've seen in Seattle."[178] Another reviewer had similarly strong feelings about the production. She recommended it because "[n]ot only does it show a group of strong women, supportive of each other and willing to work together, it should also effectively shoot down the myth that Lesbians have no sense of humor."[179] This kind of reception was typical; it was important not only that the theater fulfill the usual expectations of a theater company, but also that it would in some way add to the empowering representation of lesbians in and for the lesbian community.

The most popular production the FRTG ever did was the original musical *In Search of the Hammer: The First Adventure of the Three Mustbequeers* in 1983. The book was by Cappy Kotz, music and lyrics by Phrin Pickett, and Van Kirk directed. The show, the biggest the theater had attempted to date, broke all attendance records.[180] In the musical archaeologists uncover the ancient symbol of women's power, the hammer, "an item that looks much like a labyris, [and] was ritualistically important to matriarchal culture."[181] Ronald Reagan and his cohorts steal the hammer for their own use and the women must reclaim it. There is disagreement about the appropriate way to recover the hammer; should it be done through collective committee action and protest or by the individual efforts of the three Mustbequeers? The three women get exasperated by the committee's slow processes, and leave for the capitol on their own. On the way to Washington D.C. the three women meet a young lesbian about to come out to her parents, the members of a collective household, and fall in love. When they arrive in Washington they team up with the committees they had earlier abandoned and together they seize the hammer. A time warp returns them to the bar of the opening scene and everyone sings the finale "Sweet Success."

The company rented the Seattle Mime Theater for this large production, and for the first time charged a set admission as opposed to passing the hat after a performance. The enormous cast included over forty-five women and six musicians. The show had full production values; lighting, set, sound, and costume designers are listed in the program.[182] The primary set piece was a large fourteen-foot by twenty-foot comic book with a page for each scene's location. As the three Mustbequeers travelled pages turned,

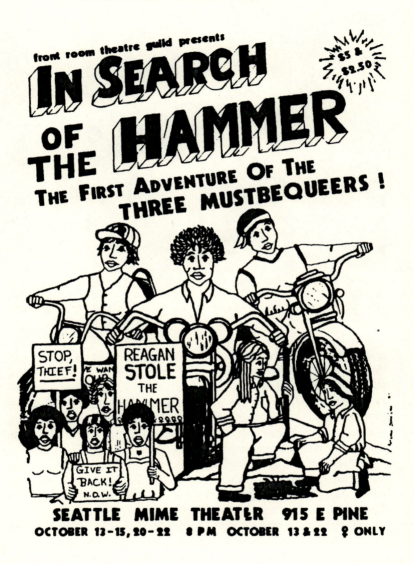

Figure 4 Cover from the program for the Front Room Theater Guild's *In Search of the Hammer: The First Adventure of the Three Mustbequeers* (1983)

109

Figure 5 Women in the Sleazy Gal bar sing "Give Us Our Hammer Back" at the start of Front Room Theater Guild's *In Search of the Hammer: The First Adventure of the Three Mustbequeers* (1983). The 14' x 20' comic book that served as scenery is in the background

revealing new locations. "We had no idea if it would fly or not [but] they came in droves. We added extra performances, we didn't know what we had . . . [it] could have run forever," Van Kirk said.[183] However, the play ran for only two weeks because, in Van Kirk's estimation, the non-professional orientation of the theater made it difficult, if not impossible, to sustain a long run. There were also two performances, opening and closing nights, for women only.

Besides the overwhelming support and enthusiasm of audiences, local critics were also enthusiastic about the show. One reviewer stated that she was "beguiled beyond my wildest expectations."[184] The play and the company were praised because the "depiction of generic lesbians achieves a marvelous balance between tender satire and modern anthropology. It elevates typecasting to an honor."[185] Two years later Pickett and Kotz wrote a sequel to the play, *The Return of the Hammer*, described by the director, Patty Contaxis, as similar to the first in that, "this production . . . is gay theater serving the gay community. *The Return of the Hammer* is an all-out gay event, with dyke charisma, in jokes, celebration and gay pride."[186] It was important that the humor of the play, spoofing various lesbian stereotypes and lifestyles, was never derogatory or deprecating. The comedy focused on community strengths rather than individual weaknesses for its humor.

Front Room Theater Guild was officially closed in 1987. It was difficult to hold together the non-professional company without money and difficult to move into the professional area without the non-professional people who had supported the theater for years. The theater was revived in 1990 for one production and a few play readings but it has not attempted the full scale theater company of its earlier incarnation.

For each theater company the collective was an important idea. For Lilith it meant writing plays collaboratively through improvisation and running the theater by consensus; the WET considered the collective to be a useful, if limited, way to organize the creation and rehearsal process; to Spiderwoman Theater it was also useful primarily in the initial stages of creation; and to Front Room Theater, coming later than the other three groups, collectivity was failed idealism on the part of the earlier years of the 1970s women's movement. The exploration of organizational structures in this chapter is intended to provide the framework to understand production and reception because, as will be discussed later, it is crucial to situate feminist theater both within feminist communities and within more local conditions. Performances were meant to be received in the context of their specific communities, but they were also produced in the context of debates over how what was seen onstage would reach the stage.

4

REPRESENTING COMMUNITY AND EXPERIENCE

Plays about mothers and daughters

Interest in alternatives to institutions seen as male-dominated or patriarchal was an important constituent of feminism in the late 1960s and 1970s because the alternatives were to function as resistances and challenges. The introduction to *Feminism, Culture, and Politics* notes that a "major form of feminist cultural politics is the construction of alternatives. This involves not only changes in the cultural 'product,' like books, films, and theater, but more importantly in the establishment of different ways of working."[1] This activity was not unique to cultural production. Indeed, Alice Echols observed that the establishment of alternatives was a hallmark of the women's movement as a whole. "Women's liberationists created an amazing panoply of counter-institutions, including health clinics, abortion referral services, rape crisis centers and credit unions."[2] The valorization of counter-institutions, indeed, of a counter-culture, opened new opportunities for feminists because both dramatic texts and theatrical event had to be transformed.

Even the non-feminist experimental and alternative theaters of the period continued to reflect mainstream sexist attitudes and many of the women who had helped to create them left because their voices were stifled and their ideas ignored. This experience taught feminists that good intentions and politically appropriate material were insufficient because they did not guarantee the intended understanding. The politically effective reception required a feminist audience and feminist event to provide the context necessary for the intended interpretation. While a dramatic work could be strategically envisioned as a feminist text, the circumstances surrounding the theatrical production of the dramatic text

112

could work to undermine or diffuse those feminist meanings. Michèle Barrett documented an incident at her University when a feminist theater group performed a play that involved a rape scene: "it was clear that the meaning of the scene was very different for the feminists at the front and the men from the rugby club who rushed in from the bar (laughing) when they heard what was going on."[3] Experiences like Barrett's and the experiences of women in male-dominated theaters taught feminists that they needed to create theater that was not only feminist in content and form, but feminist in context and event as well.

Since operating in previously established paradigms or simply changing the material presented was inadequate, the question became, what would constitute a "feminist event?" The concentration on both reception and production as categories carrying political weight was the obvious answer to the question; it was not enough simply to insist that performance texts be related to or represent, in some way, the material experience of women's oppression. Instead, feminist theater practitioners oriented their energies toward the project Michèle Barrett would later identify as "the creation of a cultural milieu in which feminist vision is creatively consumed as well as imaginatively produced."[4] A feminist event, then, hinged on both the creation and the consumption, on the performer and the audience. Chapters four, five, and six will investigate two constituents of the cultural "milieu"; production and reception. This chapter focuses on production through an examination of one subject widely dramatized by theaters: mothers and daughters. The following chapter will present another popular topic, violence against women, and chapter six will examine how the audiences responded to the productions they saw.

FEMINIST COMMUNITY AND THEATER

During the 1970s and early 1980s feminism was broadly defined as a politic emerging from a common experience of oppression. Indeed, it was "not possible to conceive of a feminist art that could be detached from a shared experience of oppression."[5] Feminist theater worked within the feminist community with the understanding that the construction of feminist art was a politically effective enterprise. This role should not be simplistically reduced to "preaching to the converted." This would imply that feminist theater shirked its more appropriate use as a tool for conversion or medium for advertisement. While it could act in those two roles, and a small number of theaters saw their function as bringing feminism to non-feminist audiences, the majority of theaters situated themselves within the community as a mode of support, strength, and renewal.[6] Theater worked as a model through which the larger movement could see women's aims and aspirations, as well as women's oppression and erasure, dramatized in narratives of celebration and triumph.

Within communities of women, the aligned theater movement worked to communicate values held in common and to induce actions based on those values. One value, self-worth as a mode of resistance, was easily represented by feminist theater as it portrayed women actively affecting the courses of their lives in stories that were intended to recall the experiences of the audience. Women were urged to support women as a way to provide the agency denied them in mainstream culture. The most important connection between the theaters and their communities was the positive portrayal of those aspects of women's experience erased and excluded by the male-dominated and defined culture and society. In this way, feminist theaters could serve as catalysts for their communities, returning women to everyday existence with renewed energy and commitment. Lucy Winer saw the role of the New York Feminist Theater (NYFT, founded 1973), in just this way. For her, the NYFT worked as "consciousness-raising crammed into a few hours. Finally, it means going back to their [the audience's] lives with a kind of anger and energy – saying they will try to change their lives."[7] The point of performance was a shared political cause: changing women's lives. The theaters did not intend to defend the cause, as they might have had to do as agents of conversion, but rather to support and to reaffirm feminism by joining audiences and performers in the mutual task of resisting oppression.

The relationship of theater to community/audience was also built on the notion of accountability. Because the theater was responsible to and for the political agenda and because performers and audience were understood as belonging equally to the same community, the theater was expected to answer to the community for the representations onstage. Adele Prandini, founder of San Francisco's It's Just A Stage (IJAS, founded 1974), said in an interview, "We felt very much accountable to the community we were trying to serve.... We were 100 percent accountable."[8] As they were situated within larger communities, the theaters were part of the struggle over the definition of feminism and the fight against oppression. The stakes were believed to be too high for feminist theaters to hold themselves aloof from the community. Indeed, their agenda was derived from that community. In this way, the theater/community relationship was reciprocal, the communities saw their concerns represented in the theaters and the theaters could look to the communities for support and encouragement. This does not mean to imply that there was never any conflict in these relations or that the relations were duplicated in all theater/community configurations but, rather, to affirm the relation as a significant one for every feminist theater.

For everyone, feminist theater was impossible without some notion of community. Community was defined in a multiplicity of ways by the various theaters but each group had some kind of working definition. Community was both the motivating force and the intended target for theatrical expression. Roberta Sklar understood all feminist theater as community theater because it was "current and topical," as well as small, local, and "for themselves."[9] The perceptions of community that the theaters held were affirmed and sustained by a commitment to social change. The theaters reinforced a sense of commonality that grew from dedication to a political agenda by both the audience and the theater practitioners.

However, there seemed to be as many definitions of community as there were feminist theater groups, and configurations of community were affected by class, race, ethnicity, sexuality, relations to feminism, and theater style. Lilith Theater and Chrysalis Eclectic had very general notions of what community meant to the theaters. Michele Linfante placed Lilith Theater (1974) of San Francisco in the community of the entire counter-culture scene; community was a loosely knit set of affiliations. "The women's movement brought our audiences . . . and the fact that we were part of a larger counter-culture."[10] For Linfante, community was defined oppositionally by what it was not, the mainstream, rather than by what it was, feminist and experimental. Linfante's relatively open notion of the community Lilith served allowed community to be largely a matter of self-identification.

For Emma Missouri of Chrysalis Theater Eclectic (1978) in Northampton, Massachusetts, community was a relatively simple notion. Missouri understood Chrysalis as community theater because "we knew there was a group of people who would always come to see the show."[11] This view of community is rather similar

115

to Linfante's, for community is constituted by people who hold similar ideas and beliefs and are concerned about specific issues. The members of the community as defined by Missouri, and to a certain extent Linfante, are bound together through a shared political point of view.

Community also helped to determine the focus of performance. It was not simply that communities assigned material to the theaters, although individual members often tried, it was more that specific issues seemed relevant and crucial at certain moments. Emma Missouri saw the relationship in a straightforward way: the topics around which Chrysalis developed theater were "ideas circulating in the community."[12] Adele Prandini saw the relationship as being more complex and random. Her theater used

> a very feminist approach, and what I mean by that is that it was sort of a holistic approach to the search for material. You looked everywhere in your life: your personal life, what was going on in the world at the time, your family, the newspapers, what was particularly impacting on your community, and tried to pull things from all those different areas of experience.[13]

Whether the connection was viewed casually or formally, it is difficult to deny that there was a link between what a community was focused on and what the theater linked to that community performed.

Lesbian community and lesbian theater

> The Front Room Theater Guild is . . . dedicated to the proposition that . . . all dykes need and deserve to see their lives represented on stage; that we best know what our lives are like and that we deserve an opportunity to portray the lives we live.
>
> (Front Room Theater)[14]

By 1981 Patricia Van Kirk came to the realization that if she wanted to attend or participate in theater that openly acknowledged and celebrated lesbians she was going to have to create it herself. She knew that few lesbians went to the theater in Seattle. "Why would you? You don't see yourself there. There's no reflection."[15] Adele Prandini had reached the same decision six years earlier, that if she wanted to perform in theater that dealt with lesbian issues, concerns, and experiences she would have to start one. Tired of concealing her lesbian sexuality for heterosexual theater, Prandini formed her own company primarily because

> there were no plays with lesbian characters and so if you wanted to act you had to pass and you had to do this very straight, very alienating material. Starting the company was a way to do what I wanted to do about material I wanted to do.[16]

The spirit and tradition of feminist theater demanded that where material did not exist it be created by and for those who needed it. If there were no lesbian plays, lesbian roles or lesbian theater then lesbians would have to make them for themselves. Working within their own particular community and orienting their productions primarily toward that community, lesbians began to see theater entirely shaped by their own culture, sexuality, and experience.

The mission statement of Front Room Theater Guild (FRTG, 1980, Seattle) demonstrates the importance and strength of the ties between theater and community, as well as the value placed on the representation of experience. In its Statement of Purpose, the theater declared that:

> We believe that lesbians are under-represented in American art and culture; that the opportunity to experience the dramatic portrayal of the unique issues of our lives, as audience and performers, enriches the artistic and personal growth of ourselves and our community.[17]

The dearth of lesbian images in the mainstream, and elsewhere, led members of the lesbian community to establish a medium through which the community, understanding community as including the members of the theater group, would be able to see itself. The opportunity to see itself strengthened the community and enabled growth and action in the process. The "unique issues" were best explicated within the community because that was the context within which they had meaning and relevance.

Despite this common ground there was no common agreement on how to go about this task. A theater's relations with a community were not always harmonious, nor was every theater/community relation the same. One contested area was the relation, if any, the theater would have to the heterosexual world outside the lesbian community. Red Dyke Theater in Atlanta (founded 1974) firmly stated that their "main purpose is to entertain lesbians and celebrate their sexuality, *not* to educate straight people about lesbians and gay issues."[18] On the other hand, and far rarer, was the Lesbian–Feminist Theater Collective of Pittsburgh (1977). They performed mostly in educational outreach situations, for colleges or chapters of NOW, but they endeavored to "dispel myths about lesbians for straight audiences."[19] The majority of lesbian theaters began because there was an abundance of cultural institutions founded and maintained on heterosexuality and a dearth of institutions founded on lesbian aesthetics and politics. For lesbians that absence was strongly negative, so it was therefore significant, and politically charged, when the members of the Lavender Cellar in Minneapolis told *Ms.* that they use "various themes to entertain while providing a positive perspective of lesbian lifestyles" because the heterosexual institutions denied even the existence of lesbians.[20] This form of education, positive reinforcement, was important but it was not the most radical.

Patricia Van Kirk thinks that FRTG provided for lesbians what was provided for heterosexuals by mainstream representation, the chance to see their sexuality enacted, enabling them to grow out of adolescent discomfort and into an adult understanding and pleasure with sexuality. The first time FRTG presented a kiss onstage, Van Kirk recalled that there were adolescent giggles and embarrassed laughter. Everyone had been socialized to accept the representation of heterosexual kissing, but for many of the women this was the first time they had ever seen a lesbian kiss in the frame of representation:

> You don't get to see yourself at age ten learning what it's like to be an adult by kissing every day of your life. That's what heterosexuals get, they don't have to titter by the time they're sixteen. But here are all these lesbians who've only ever done it in the closet, almost literally, seeing somebody standing in public. It's revolutionary. That was part of the beauty of what happened – we matured as an audience.[21]

By the time the theater closed in 1986 Van Kirk said that the kisses had become longer and more passionate and that the audience no longer responded so uncomfortably.

What FRTG provided was a resistance that made lesbian sexuality seem matter of fact and commonplace. Rather than occupying a marginalized and devalued place in representation it was placed at the center. Sequoia, the Artistic Director of the Cambridge

Lesbian Theater in Massachusetts (no founding date), believed that the audience shared the understanding that just to "get onstage and cry, sing and laugh out loud that you are a lesbian, that you believe in lesbians, that you are happy to be a lesbian" is a liberating experience and that it was equally as liberating to witness it from the audience as it was to perform it.[22] It was this kind of education that made the bonds of community more solid.

> We made lesbians more public in a theatrical sense and they came and supported us incredibly. I still have people who come up to me and thank me on the street and it has been years. It really was an educational tool and I think it was incredibly valuable in that respect.[23]

Not only were theaters places to meet and come together in a large group but they were also places to see the common culture enacted and celebrated. This opportunity was so rare that the theater was valued far more than in mainstream communities, or even straight feminist communities.

Theater often became one of the main focuses of the community because it was a relaxed social occasion. The FRTG's fund-raisers at a local lesbian bar, The Wild Rose, were often the events of the season; the company became known for its great dances, as well as its theater.[24] But this is not to say that there was no conflict and that the relationship with the community could not have its problematic side. Both Van Kirk and Iris Landsberg of It's Just A Stage felt that while there was audience support in the form of ticket sales, there was rarely support over and above the cost of tickets. Both women suspected that lesbians would give to a gay organization before giving to a lesbian one but neither is sure why that was. Van Kirk felt that even the wealthier women were "skeptical about donating to a lesbian organization" and Landsberg was not even sure that her group got the full audience support they should have.[25] "Lesbians would go to a lesbian play at the Julian [a San Francisco gay theater] but they wouldn't come to a lesbian play by a lesbian theater group."[26] While this conflict is not insignificant it is also not the dominant experience of working in lesbian–feminist theater. For the most part people involved in the groups as practitioners and spectators experienced the theater that was produced as an important and exciting part of their culture. The opportunity to see themselves onstage, not with disgust as so often happened in mainstream representation, but with love, approval, and celebration, was vital to the survival and growth of the lesbian community. The theater was a community project, the audience and the performers were connected across the boundaries of performer and audience, changing the dynamic of performance.

Race, ethnicity, and feminist community

There is, in this work, an obvious absence of theater groups composed primarily or entirely of Chicanas, Latinas, African–Americans, Asian–Americans, or Jewish women. This reflects much of the history of feminism as well as of theater.

Consciousness-raising was entirely inadequate when it came to the experiences of women who were not white or middle-class. Audre Lorde writes that in the discussion groups, there was

> usually little attempt to articulate the genuine differences between women, such as those of race, color, age, class, and sexual identity. There was no apparent need at that time to examine the contradictions of self, woman as oppressor.[27]

The methodology of consciousness-raising rested on the belief that all oppression experienced by women "had a common root."[28] White women in their eagerness to abandon patriarchal practice were not self-critical enough to see that they repeated that practice by forcing women to conform to the dominant feminist narrative of experience, that of the heterosexual, middle-class white woman. These women abandoned a white male universal and set about constructing a white female universal. bell hooks notes that adding the categories of race and class to consciousness-raising, where they had been absent, would have "radically call[ed] into question the notion of a fundamentally common female experience."[29] Given these biases it is not surprising that women of color did not flock to work within the feminist movement, preferring instead to organize women from their own communities of color. For example, *This Bridge Called My Back: Writings by Radical Women of Color*, a signal anthology for women of color and white women, was first conceived in early 1979 when Cherrie Moraga was the only participant of color at a conference and the "management and some of the staff made her feel an outsider, the poor relative, the token woman of color."[30] The anthology that sprang from this experience was intended to address divisions of race, class, sexuality from the perspectives of women of color. "What began as a reaction to the racism of white feminism became a positive affirmation of the commitment of women of color to our own feminism."[31] These experiences were repeated in feminist theaters. While there were many women of color doing theater in alternative groups, solo performances, or more mainstream theaters, they usually did not choose to become involved with the feminist groups. When they did, their experiences were often highly negative, as the accounts from the previous chapter document.

Within their own communities, women of color did work to confront the sexism they encountered. Yvonne Yarbro-Bejarano documents the existence of two Chicana feminist theaters. Teatro Raices, she noted in 1985, did theater in the "Chicano agit-prop tradition."[32] Valentina Productions was founded in 1981 by members of WIT (Women in Teatro), a sub-group of TENAZ (Teatros Nacionales de Aztlan). The group managed only one production, *Voz de la Mujer* (*The Woman's Voice*), a

> collage of poetry, prose, dance and song by and about Latinas and Chicanas, which had been adapted for performance. The script covered a range of sources from Sor Juana Ines de la Cruz and Gabriela Mistal to contemporary Chicana writers Angela de Hoyos and Phyllis Lopez.[33]

Voz de la Mujer was performed by Irene Burgos, Rosie Campos-Pantoja, Cara Hill de Castañón, Anita Mattos, Liz Robinson, and Juanita Vargas to "overwhelmingly positive response."[34] Anita Mattos, a member of the troupe, recalls that the play was primarily about the devaluation of women's work.[35] Mattos also remembers that the group could not stay together because of the responsibilities of child-care and jobs. They were committed to supporting the rest of the community, and the work declared a solidarity with men.

In San Francisco, Las Cucurachas (1974) was one of the projects of the Concilo de Mujeres that organized Raza women's activities about the material existence of women in the community. Rosemary Curb notes that it grew out of a task force at San Francisco State University. The group was committed to the search for "more economically rewarding individual cultural history from the Maya to the present."[36]

Other than the African–American women working in the groups discussed here, there are only two self-identified African–American women's theaters in the written sources of groups. Onyx Women's Theater in New York City was founded in 1973 and originated their own works as well as performing that of other playwrights. They also conducted "skills workshops and perform[ed] for black organizations and women's groups." Onyx's work focused primarily on "being black and female."[37] In Cambridge, Massachusetts, Black Star (founded 1978) presented a wide range of plays from Beckett to Myrna Lamb, Aristophanes to Joanna Russ. About ten of their thirty to forty members were male.[38] Many African–American women, such as Charlayne Woodard, Ellen Sebastian, and Anna Deavere Smith, followed in Beah Richard's footsteps and produced one-woman shows.[39] But for most women of color, the separation of oppression through race and the separation of oppression through gender were not distinct, and they often preferred to work from their ethnic communities in gender mixed groups.

Spiderwoman Theater negotiated between two communities, one identified by ethnicity, the other by gender. Their strong identification as Native Americans and as feminists placed Spiderwoman as both members of and outsiders to those communities. Their work has always been confrontational, even when feminist theater was more commonly celebratory and inclusive. When asked how the Native American community had received their first work, *Women in Violence* (1976), Muriel Miguel said, "They get up and walk out, with very heavy boots, big cowboy boots. One very famous Indian man said, "Bullshit.'"[40] The reaction to Spiderwoman in the feminist community was no less dramatic. Miguel remembers that when touring *Women and Violence* in 1977–78 discussions would become very heated. "In Boston we separated the [women's] community. Then we went to Baltimore with it, same thing happened there in the theater community."[41] Muriel Miguel understands very keenly that it is Spiderwoman's marginalized and contradictory status that makes them so controversial. When presenting to the Native American community, their feminism is problematic; when presenting to the feminist community, their commitment to exposing and confronting racism is often unwelcome; and when presenting to the theater community, their nontraditional style as a deliberate choice and commentary on theater is confusing. As Miguel has pointed out:

> You have to remember that this was fifteen years ago. Feminism at that time, and certainly feminist theater, was all holding hands and going off into the sunset, and not making fun of each other and not doing the gesture because that was male-

oriented. We did everything like that, we just put our big feet in the middle of feminism and went plop, plop, plop. So either you loved us or you absolutely hated us. Some of the radical feminists (none of us was gay) called us. We put make-up on, we had husbands, children. Theater people – was this art or was this feminism? Are you a housewife that's an actress or an actress that's a housewife? Theater was suspicious of us because we looked amateur and we'd get them.[42]

Fifteen years later people are still walking out of Spiderwoman shows offended by what they see onstage.

Rather than stress commonalities, as was prevalent at that time, Spiderwoman explored differences. The theater they wanted to create and the experiences they wanted to express did not exist in other theaters. For much of their history they have been a coalition theater, committed to working across the differences of race, sexual preference, and class. This was not, as has previously been discussed, an easy task. It also made Spiderwoman more of an anomaly in every community they connected with by always serving as a confrontation.

It should be apparent that feminist theater is best understood within the context of feminist community. As Loren Kruger observed, feminist theater is "work conceived and performed in response to the needs and tastes of a specific, even localized audience."[43] The events represented in performance found their meaning in reference to the material conditions of existence, or experience, as constructed by the community. Within the general category of feminist community there were often more specific communities, sometimes marginalized and sometimes positioned oppositionally but still identifying with the political focus on women, challenging the larger feminist community's biases on issues such as homophobia and racism.

ESTABLISHING COMMUNAL FORMS

Now listen carefully and you will guess the secret to who I am, who you are, and how we are the same.
What changes with the moon and yet remains the same?
What bleeds and yet is not wounded?
What nourishes with its body and is not devoured?
What carries a room that we all can leave but none can enter?
(*Sacrifices: A Fable of the Women's Movement*)[44]

123

In order to express the experience and vision of community onstage, feminist theater groups had to find forms that would enable them to translate material existence to the stage. To do this, they turned to forms associated with community representation: those of ritual. Rituals have traditionally been the type of performance that demonstrated the bonds and fabric of a community through its history, conventions, and myths. Concomitant with the use of ritual forms was the creation of a mythic heritage. Whether this took the form of the reclamation of traditional myths, such as the Greek pantheon, or the creation of new myths, as in At the Foot of the Mountain's *The Story of a Mother* or Naomi Newman's *Snake Talk*, both discussed later in the chapter, there was an active attempt to sponsor a mythic heritage and legitimacy for women out of a feminist sensibility.

In 1981 Batya Podos published an article theorizing feminist ritual theater using her work as the basis for discussion. Podos had dramatized Monique Wittig's novel *Les Guérilles* in 1977 at San Francisco State and Charlene Spretnak's *The Myth of the Triad of the Moon* in 1978. By 1981 she had also created two original productions, *Ariadne* and *The Story of Athena and Other Tales Our Mothers Never Told Us*.[45] Podos believed that the origins of theater were in "spiritual and ritual magic"[46] that predated by centuries the commonly accepted roots of theater in Greek festivals and drama. This early connection was, for Podos, the most important element of theater. "Pageants, festivals, ceremonies, and seasonal celebrations were all parts of early theater and were linked to the daily spiritual life of the people who participated in them."[47] The events had been fully integrated into the material day to day lives of the participants, demonstrating the links between the material and the spiritual, the theater and daily life. These connections became the key to feminist ritual theater. It linked the basis of feminist thought and belief, the primacy of women's experience, with the spiritual realm. According to Podos, feminist ritual theater provided alternative interpretations and understandings to those offered by patriarchal myth and ritual. Ritual theater resisted the separation imposed by the patriarchy of public and private, mind and body, spiritual and quotidian by substituting integrated points of view that emphasized the place of the spirit in the world and the everyday. Podos stated firmly that

not only must ritual theater seek to provide a transformative spiritual experience, it must educate an audience whose spiritual experiences, self-definitions, and world perceptions have been taught and nurtured by a misogynist society – an audience that has been denied knowledge of its own history and power.[48]

She posits ritual theater as the medium through which women can recapture the connections with their power that have been destroyed by the patriarchy. Podos also placed herself in a slightly different position than many other theater practitioners. While embracing the communal connection between audience and performers, she understood the theater's purpose as educational.

Ritual as a route to history was another crucial function of feminist ritual theater. While ritual provided the means for self-transformation through emotional and spiritual catharsis, it simultaneously provided the precedent for transformation by demonstrating that women's history contradicts the history of the patriarchy.[49] "By unlocking the past, we open ourselves to a deeper understanding of who we are in the present and, therefore, who we might become in the future. Ritual theater is a vehicle for this understanding."[50] The historical aspect of the project encouraged women to take control of their lives, stressing that the possibilities for such actions exist and have always existed.

Part of the benefit of producing and presenting a shared past was that it served as a reinforcement of the links between audience and performers, obliquely recalling the larger group of community. What the individual was to realize through the experience of the ritual is that her experience could be analogized directly to those of the other women present giving them a connection through shared experience. "The personal realization extends itself to the larger community of womanhood . . . . In order for a ritual to succeed, both the players and the audience must experience it."[51] Rituals healed women by bringing them together to discover and encourage communal, as well as individual, strengths. Rituals served to "dramatize the unique powers and experiences of women among women."[52] The destructive effect of the patriarchy was resisted and healed through rituals whether they were created for theater, spiritual/religious practices, or individual satisfaction.

Interest in ritual is not unique to feminist theater, nor did it originate with feminist theater. An emphasis on ritual is an important part of the feminist spirituality movement. This manifestation of feminism is widespread and popular, and by 1982 *Heresies: A Feminist Publication on Arts and Politics* had done a special issue on women's spirituality entitled "The Great Goddess," as had *Chrysalis: A Magazine of Women's Culture* and *Quest: A Feminist Quarterly.*[53] In 1986 Anne Carson published an annotated bibliography about women's spirituality that listed over 730 works on the subject.[54] Carole P. Christ notes that by 1976 there were two journals available that dealt solely with women's spirituality, *Womanspirit* and *Lady-Unique-Inclination-of-the-Night.*[55] It becomes obvious that the theater's interest in and utilization of ritual as one of its most productive forms was participating in a larger focus of the feminist movement as a whole. The work on the creation and exploration of feminist spirituality has occurred in two intertwined modes. The first, a scholarly and archaeological approach, endeavors to prove the existence of a pre-patriarchal matriarchal society. Merlin Stone, Marija Gimbutas, and Sophie Drinker have all worked to establish the historical precedent for a goddess-based worship and matriarchy.[56] The other focus is the creation of religious-like practices aimed at expressing "the need for revitalization and as an impetus for political action."[57] While feminist theater drew on both kinds of feminist spirituality, the second expression was more productive and closer to the aims of feminist theater itself.

Rituals could be used for many purposes; hexing a rapist, protecting loved ones, requesting money, or giving thanks. They are primarily undertaken as a community project. While women could perform rituals alone, and many women had developed personal rituals around, for instance, menstruation, the emphasis was on events strengthening communal bonds. The woman leading or creating the rituals is often referred to as the "ritualist" and her work within the community intended to "make available, clarify, and intensify powers that are the essence of the community."[58] The invisibility of the communal bonds emphasized the commonalities and connections among women. Kay Turner stressed that ritual "marks the ultimate idea of relationship between self and community, the fusion of two distinct realities rather than separation."[59] Rituals welcomed women and gave them a sense of connection to one another and involvement in their world denied them by patriarchal religion. The exploration and development of rituals was interpreted by spiritual feminists as the spiritual equivalent to the material struggle for legal, political, economic, and societal gains for women. It was the feminist desire to recreate the symbolic, as the other was the feminist desire to recreate the material.

Rituals specifically, and women's spirituality generally, focused on woman's body as the source of inspiration and origin for spiritual beliefs and practices. "The body is our first and last outward reality; it defines and conditions our life experience and gives us personal identity and continuity."[60] Concomitantly, a woman's body was also believed to be the site upon which the oppression of the patriarchy is made visible. Practices such as rape or enforced sterilization were tangible manifestations of patriarchal power. As a corollary, women's power emanated from the physical body and the most politically efficacious act, according to women's spirituality, was to take control of one's own body.[61] Ritual was a popular way to heal the wounds on the body and protect it from further harm. For Martha Boesing, founder of At the Foot of the Mountain Theater, ritualistic art is "a very healing force."[62] Feminist theater practitioners turned to ritual as a way to create feminist theater because ritual emphasized the bonds of community, sought to deny differences and barriers between audience and performer, and served the feminist community by encouraging the celebration of women and their potential and actual power.

Used as a way to recognize the trivialized domestic, ritually created myths offered new paradigms through which to revalue women's experience. This was Roberta Sklar's particular reading of the use of myth and ritual. "We tackled the trivialization of our lives, resurrecting domains made small by sexism – the domestic sphere, the kitchen, childbirth, women's relationships, the female psyche, our sustenance, our place in the world."[63] By harking back nostalgically to a pre-Athenian moment in civilization, to a gyno-centric matriarchy, feminists sought to counter the andro-centric biases of Greek based myths.[64] The new and/or reclaimed stories, it was hoped, would become the new paradigms through which women's experience was interpreted and understood. This was important because, as Joanna Russ understands myth, it was the embodiment of a culture's accepted beliefs. She notes that "we interpret our own experiences in terms of them [myths]. Worse still, we actually perceive what happens to us in the mythic terms our culture provides."[65] But, believing that the previous male-centered myths "no longer tell the truth about any of us," she encourages the creation of new myths for alternative interpretations of culture and society.[66] Judith Antonelli, like Russ, sees myth as an important foundation to culture and society. "There is a wealth of information in mythology ... which tells us about the transition from matriarchy to patriarchy. Myth is hystory [sic], but in allegorical, not literal form."[67] Myth was an important factor in the feminist historical project to envision women of the past because it offered alternative ways to interpret events and ideas. Old, seemingly patriarchal, myths could also be utilized in this way because they could demonstrate the power of interpretation to emphasize masculinist ideas and perceptions of the world.[68]

PLAYS ABOUT MOTHERS AND DAUGHTERS

I am Sondra
daughter of Lille
daughter of Sarah Rebecca
who came to this country when she was sixteen
and never saw her mother again
daughter of Tzivia
daughter of a woman from Austria

("The Matrilineage")[69]

Many rituals and theater pieces concentrated on the mother/daughter bond. This link was seen as basic and universal, all women were one or both. The mother/daughter bond was the "key to all others,"[70] the "others" being all the relations women share with one another other than the mother/daughter one. Adrienne Rich, author of *Of Woman Born*, first published in 1976, stated that "the core"[71] of her book on motherhood was the relationship of mother and daughter. Many feminist theaters, whether or not they were interested in ritual, focused on this bond as the one that predated sisterhood. The women's movement stressed sisterhood as the ultimate bond, and was thought to be a relationship that defied the patriarchy. Robin Morgan, for example, titled her anthology of women's writings *Sisterhood is Powerful* and it was one of the first such books published.[72] But, as Adrienne Rich points out, before "sisterhood, there was the knowledge – transitory, fragmented, perhaps, but original and crucial – of mother and daughterhood."[73] Valorizing the mother/daughter bond was also understood as a corrective to the relentless glorification throughout patriarchal history of the father/son dynamic. Christianity, for example, is based on the father's relation to the son, and to a lesser extent the son's relation to the mother, but absent is connection between mother and daughter. According to Rich the mother and the daughter share a connection that transcends that of the father and the son because they "have always exchanged with each other – beyond the lore of verbally transmitted female survival – a knowledge that is subliminal, subversive, preverbal: the knowledge flowing between two alike bodies, one of which spent nine months in the other."[74] The ultimate crime of the patriarchy was the denigration of the mother, according to this way of feminist thinking, therefore the ultimate resistance was the celebration of the mother by the daughter.

Women who explored the mother/daughter relationships while attentive to the differences of race, class, ethnicity, and religion looked not only at the mother/daughter bond itself, but also at the position of the bond within specific cultures. Often bearing a somewhat confrontational position within their communities (whether within the feminist community because of their race, ethnicity, or culture or within their cultural, racial, or ethnic communities because of their feminist politics), women felt compelled to explore the ties that bound them to their mothers. They saw those ties as a continuation of their culture in themselves and as a clue to their identity. Trinh T. Minh-ha wrote, "An entire history, an entire vision of the world, a lifetime story. Mother always has a mother. . . . To listen carefully is to preserve."[75] Connie Young Woo saw links to mothers as ties with history: "Our grandmothers are our historical links."[76] There is a strong connection between the relationship with the mother and the tie to the culture. Cherrie Moraga wrote in *This Bridge Called My Back* that "being a Chicana and having family are synonymous for me . . . having a sense of my own soul comes from the love of my mother."[77] In fact, Moraga spoke of realizing that she would no longer be able to write on the east coast, where she lived for several years, because she needed to come back to her culture and family in California in order to create. While these are all entirely separate communities, each of these women within them had a strong investment in thinking about not only their own mothers but also the positions of mothers within their respective cultures. The remainder of this chapter will explore how the ties of community and the methods of ritual were used to dramatize and explore the relationships between mothers and daughters.

Two well-known feminist theaters to concentrate on ritual, myth, mothers, and daughters were At the Foot of the Mountain (AFOM, 1974) in Minneapolis and the Women's Experimental Theater (WET, 1977) in New York. These two theaters were perhaps the most professionally oriented of the feminist theaters at this time. All the founders, except Sondra Segal of WET, had previous professional theater experience and both groups had relatively stable home bases. WET was in residence at Women's Interart Theater, as already mentioned, and AFOM was located at the Pillsbury Waite Community Center from 1976 to 1978 and then at the Cedar Riverside People's Center.

Both AFOM and WET had clearly articulated their missions in published statements and both statements emphasized a commitment to ritual and to feminism. AFOM separated its mission into two different statements, one artistic and the other political. In the Artistic Statement, the theater declared that one of its goals was "to create new rituals for our time." The purpose of the rituals was expressed in the Political Statement as the search to "renew hope and celebrate the healing power of women by recreating life-giving cultural myths."[78] WET's Statement of Purpose did not overtly express the wish to create myth or ritual, instead it emphasized the dramatization of women's experience and the creation of a female aesthetic as a productive means for nurturing women in the theater.[79] Despite this, WET's choice of material – the mother/daughter relationship, the bonds between sisters, and the house of Atreus myth, as a trilogy about women's roles in the family – put them within the myth–ritual context.

Organized under the title *The Daughters Cycle*, the trilogy of *Daughters*, *Sister/Sister*, and *Electra Speaks* was created to explore the positions of women in families as mothers, daughters, wives, and sisters. All three works were ritual celebrations of and laments for the power and oppression women experience within the family unit. However, the first play, *Daughters*, concentrated most specifically on the mother/daughter relationship using ritual as its method. The play is defined by WET as "a ritual exploration of the mother/daughter relationship."[80] The strongest and most well-known of the ritual devices employed by WET, the Matrilineage, was used first in *Daughters*, and then as a signature ritual in the two subsequent plays. Sondra Segal conceived of the Matrilineage when she, Roberta Sklar, and Clare Coss were still involved in Womanrite.

In 1976, when Womanrite was deciding on material for a new production, Segal presented her idea for a play on mothers and daughters that would begin with a personal genealogy of each performer based on their maternal lines of descent. The device, called the Matrilineage, was to emphasize that "every woman was a daughter."[81] Women found that the ritual of the Matrilineage affected them profoundly. In production, *Daughters* began with the cast's recitation of their own matrilineage and ended with the cast inviting the audience onstage to recite their own lines of maternal descent. Clare Coss remembers quite clearly how affecting and effective the device was:

> Women would come back with their mothers, their daughters, their sisters. They would come back [to the recitation of the matrilineage] add the names that they had recalled. They would go home and call their mother and their grandmother and find out names. Women who had never thought about themselves through their matrilineage were so excited about it. It was thrilling to have generations come back.[82]

The feminist historian Bettina Aptheker was so moved by the experience of reciting her foremothers she used the experience as the introduction to her book on women's history.[83] Suzanne Messing wrote in the *New York Times*:

> Of course I always knew it; however, when saying it aloud, I suddenly understand it. My mother, my daughter, and I are bound by more than kinship. We are survivors, the last of a clan, the last of who knows how many generations of related women.[84]

Messing then went on to describe how reciting her matrilineage inspired her to delve into her past, ask questions of her relatives, and teach her daughter all that she had learned. She brought her own daughter to *Daughters* and watched her recite her matrilineage.

Like WET's *Daughters Cycle Trilogy*, AFOM's *The Story of a Mother* dealt with the relationships of women within the family. The play was divided into five sections and each section included an opportunity for the audience to participate in a ritual. At predetermined moments the performers stopped the action of the play and asked the audience to participate in "open-ended ritual segments,"[85] that enabled them to perceive the world as their mothers and to speak the articulated and unarticulated thoughts, feelings, and words of the mother–daughter relationship. During the first ritual moment, "Calling Forth the Mothers," the audience were instructed by a performer to understand the world through their mothers' eyes:

> Call for your mother, whatever name you would use, until she appears. See her in front of you. Notice age, standing or sitting, what she is wearing, how her hair is, hands, all physical characteristics, what she is doing. Approach her or let her approach you. Look at her, speak, touch. Ask her: Can I enter you? Slowly enter whatever way is right for you. Turn around. Fit your ... genitals, pelvis, hips, stomach, spine, chest, breasts ... into hers (one at a time). Be aware of yourself as her. ... When you are ready, open your eyes, see the world as she saw it.[86]

Once the audience were transformed into their mothers they were asked to recite a "litany" in their mothers' voices. Beginning with "I always said–" audience members were expected to fill in the blank. Martha Boesing described the effect to Meredith Flynn:

> All those cliches. The place rings with cliches told from the perspective of the person who said them and didn't think of them as cliches at all, who really felt them. I *do* want you to brush the hair out of your eyes. It suddenly takes the cliches and translates them into a very personal event. But in this very litanized formal recital, so it's both very personal and very ritualized at the same time. But the audience is no longer a witness, they literally participate in the event.[87]

The effect of the four subsequent rituals was similar, to create empathy for the roles both mother and daughter have to play in order to survive in the family.

It is important to note the contiguities between *The Story of a Mother* and *Daughters*. Historically, the plays were developed during the same time period; *The Story of a Mother I and II* from 1978 to 1981 and *The Daughters Cycle Trilogy* from 1976 to 1980. Both plays were intended as ritual explorations that depended on audience participation. They alternated ritual segments with units written with the audience participating simply, as WET put it, as "witnesses."[88] The topics explored in both plays were remarkably similar – birth, death, menstruation, relations within the family, and the ways in which the oppressive culture had negatively intervened in the mother/daughter relationship. *Daughters* and *The Story of a Mother* include narratives personal to the actual performers and in many cases use the performers' names in the pages of the script to identify the speakers. In neither play is there a linear or developmental cause to effect narrative. Instead, the plays use repetitions and shifts in rhythms by alternating the number of speakers, the types of exchanges (whether as characters or more archetypal roles), and the mode of address to the audience, to emphasize the pervasiveness of the relationship and its treatment within patriarchal culture.

In *Daughters* there is the recurring "mother/daughter totem" that works with the chorus in a series of calls and responses throughout the play.[89] While never the same lines, the totem establishes patterns of tensions between mothers and daughters from the first image it offers: "Close your eyes. . . . / Spread your legs./ Feel the heat between your legs./ Imagine yourself becoming very wet/ and the muscles of your legs and pelvis/ pulling back/ as you open. . . . / You are splitting open. . . . / Do you wonder why you feel so connected to your mother?" to the last exchange of the Totem and the chorus.

DAUGHTER: I'm afraid.

MOTHER: (*Gazes out the window as though* SHE sees her internal experience externalized. SHE trips off vocally on the phrase MOUTH ON FIRE – a prolonged scream).

DAUGHTER: I'm afraid.

MOTHER: (*Her focus returning*) Don't be.[90]

The Story of a Mother uses the rituals already described and a collage of single lines on a specific theme delivered by all the performers to establish tensions. In the third section of the third unit, titled "The Shampoo," a series of images is offered through single lines.

R: The water is not too hot.

P: Nobody likes a dirty child.

C: Guys want to respect you.

M: You look pretty enough without doing all that stuff to your hair.

R: When we're all done, we'll put a bow in it for Daddy.

P: You look like a sheep dog with all that hair in your eyes.

C: It is not sexy. It's stringy.

M: What kind of junk are you putting on your head? It stinks.[91]

Both plays offer dynamic exchanges among the performers that are not dialogue, yet serve to keep the plays' actions in motion.

Despite the fact that *Daughters* and *The Story of a Mother* are willing to look at the negatives of the mother/daughter bond they end on a celebratory note and the final images are positive and communal. In *The Story of a Mother* the performers offer bread to the audience while singing "We will walk through the streets of this city which sleeps,/ which sleeps, my daughter,/ you and I./ You carry my heart,/ I'll carry you, my little daughter,/ on this parade through the city."[92] In *Daughters* before the final recitation of the Matrilineage, a single daughter sits in front of the audience, addressing them as her mother, and reads a "fragment from a letter to my mother" that ends "I want us to rock together and give comfort/ on each other's laps/ bringing the world down to a low hum/ so you and I can stand up straight/ and start all over again."[93] The plays end with the idea that the bond is both empowering and ultimately positive.

Other theaters at this time produced scripts that were similar in many ways to the ones AFOM and WET created. Often using direct research with a potential audience and participation with the actual one there was a similar investment in the audience/community as the focal point of the play. One such play was *Persephone's Return*, first performed by the Rhode Island Feminist Theater (RIFT, 1973) in the fall of 1974. It was an important moment in the group's history not only because of its concentration on mothers and daughters but also because it radically changed the group and its relation to the community. The play had a double plot line, the mythic tale of Demeter and Persephone as an explanation of how the matriarchy was supplanted by the patriarchy and exploration of modern day stories of the effects of the patriarchy on women through rape, marriage, and control. The play was shaped by the conception that myth and experience were inextricably linked as the "Afterword" stated:

> The mother/daughter bond, severed by the powers of the patriarchy (men), seemed universal and personal to us all. The myth is the main theme of the play, one that we continually returned to as we pulled from the myth what related to our own present day lives, and from this generated the modern scenes.[94]

The relentless work on mothers and daughters brought about substantial changes in the RIFT company. At the time of the production of *Persephone's Return* the collective was still mixed, five women and three men. After this production, however, the collective voted to become all women so that the women could "experiment with their own material in an all-inclusive 'women's space.'"[95]

The play began with a ritual dance centered on the audience. Titled the "People's Dance," the performers approached the audience, embraced them symbolically, and turned to embrace one another. The men left the stage and the Mother was summoned, beginning the "Woman's Dance." This was divided into five sections "the power circle, undulations, menstruation, the fertility cycle, and the final power circle."[96] At the end of the dance Demeter emerged, beginning the narrative. The following scenes move in and out of modern exchange, primarily between heterosexual couples, and mythic ones among the Greek pantheon.[97] An encounter between a rapist and a woman segues into the Persephone and Hades story.

> RAPIST: Do you live by yourself? Where? (*Struggles.*)
> WOMAN: No, no, somebody help me. (*He throws her to the floor covers her mouth with his mouth. They freeze for a second. She then screams. On the scream everyone exits.* RAPIST *to the underworld where he puts on his* HADES *mask.* WOMAN *puts on* DEMETER'S *mask.*)[98]

Hades' endeavors to keep Persephone in the underworld despite her longings for her mother becomes the story of the unhappy relationship of two modern-day characters, Hal and Petra. Ultimately Hal forces Petra to have sex with him despite her unwillingness. Thus, a connection is created that begins with archetypes, the rapist and the woman, becomes mythic, Hades and Demeter, and ends with two contemporary people, Hal and Petra.

The ritual enacted through the Demeter myth, and through the perceptions of women's lives as constricted and endangered by society, served as a passive way for the audience to experience itself as a community. The ritual of *Persephone's Return* achieved this by valorizing the elements identified as specifically female – birth, menstruation, relationships with other women, and motherhood – and previously devalued by the patriarchy. The play ends on a positive feminist, communal note. All the women performers gather together to build a fire and this begins the "Future Dance," a "hope for an androgynous, nonhierarchical (neither matriarchal, nor patriarchal) time, when some images of the past and present survive, instilled with new meanings."[99] While the play emphasizes the cyclical nature of ritual it also offers the notion that rituals can be a part of change and breaking a cycle.

In 1974 Las Cucarachas (1974, San Francisco) performed a piece with Dorinda Moreno, *Chicana*, which Yvonne Yarbro-Bejarano described in 1983: "The piece combined the image of woman as 'Mother Earth,' a symbol of fertility and mainstay of the strong united family, with the 'mujer rebelde' who demands equality with men and participates actively in social and political struggles."[100] Bejarano adds that the piece, a "teatropoesía," a form that combines dramatic texts with poetry, "evoked" the figures of "la indígena of pre-Columbian times, the Native American, La Adelita of the Mexican Revolution, La Llorona, a Brazilian mother accusing her government of repression and genocide, and 'la nueva Chicana.'"[101] While Bejarano's description does not specifically mention the mother/daughter relationship it is obvious that notions of motherhood are crucial to *Chicana* placing it firmly in the context of the feminist inquiry into that dynamic.

New Cycle Theater (1977) in Brooklyn was another feminist

Figure 6 Karen Malpede's *The End of War* (1977) as done by New Cycle Theater

theater based solidly in myth and ritual, but that rarely included the audience directly in performance. Unlike RIFT, the theater did not function as a collective and Karen Malpede served as the playwright for the theater. New Cycle Theater placed itself firmly within a biological understanding of woman. According to the Mission Statement the "theater takes its name from the cycles of life (birth, rebirths, death), the seasons, the phases of the moon, and the cycles of the woman's body."[102] While New Cycle never did a play concerned solely with the mother/daughter connection, all of the plays the company produced centered on a woman's capacity for reproduction and her relation to that capacity. Writing on *A Monster Has Stolen the Sun* (1981) a reviewer noted that the "central focus of the play is woman's creative power to make new life."[103] *The End of War* (1977) closed with a ritual enactment of birth and the connection, through the birthing process, of all people. Galina, a revolutionary, gives birth in jail and calls a woman and a man to help her. Malpede describes the action:

> Voline places himself behind Galina and holds her up. They begin to move in the rhythm of birth. Elena comes to her and begins to breathe with her, rubbing her belly. The image is of the three of them, Voline, Elena, and Galina, as near equal participants in the birth-effort.[104]

Malpede's *Rebeccah*, performed in 1976, was produced before her company New Cycle Theater was founded but many of the participants in the production would go on to become part of New Cycle. Emphasizing the woman's relation to birth and renewal and echoing "the ancient seasonal rites,"[105] *Rebeccah* tells the story of a woman who transcends historical time and loses her son in a pogrom, her daughter in the Triangle Shirtwaist fire, and emerges from the Holocaust to give birth to a new settlement. The play was intended to demonstrate "how a new community can be built out of the garbage of this civilization."[106] Karen Malpede's work with New Cycle consistently drew upon myth, ritual, and the importance of the mother. Her plays were often performed in a circle, allowing the audience to see each other as they witnessed the performance, clearly implicating them in the staged spectacle.

The Cutting Edge (1975, New York City) shaped their work similarly to AFOM and WET. In 1976 they collectively developed a play about mothers and daughters, *Croon*. The company "interviewed mothers and daughters, taped the discussions over a period of time," and used the material to build a series of scenes eventually refined into a play.[107] In the program notes Andrea Balis, Artistic Director of the Cutting Edge and director of *Croon*, wrote that the group "started from the feelings that there were things all mothers wanted to say to their daughters and couldn't and there were things all daughters need to say to their mothers and never will."[108] Performed by two women who alternate the parts of the mothers and the daughters, *Croon* used comedy to explore the complex relationships women share. The two performers acted out sketches around such issues as sex, adolescence, dishwashing, men, sibling rivalry, careers, death, love, and guilt. It was assumed by the director, and presumably the rest of the collective, that "everyone will hear something that they either have wanted to say or have wanted to hear."[109] While the play maintained a more traditional separation of audience and performer, the company proceeded from the idea that they were offering a service to women by realizing the unspoken in the mother/daughter bond.

The Women's Repertory Theater of Long Island created a "dramatic presentation for voice and dance" based on the poems of six women.[110] The short seven-page script has four roles: the Mother, Young Woman I and II, and the Child, a 12-year-old girl. The mother, described as "monolithic," speaks of her experiences of longing and waiting for daughters who speak of themselves as divorced from her with feelings of ambivalence.[111] "My mother the bag already lives out of reach./ Only my letters touch her with paper kisses."[112] The two young women identify themselves as mothers, as well, and admit that they love their daughters similarly to how the Mother loves them. The Child enters and responds to their testaments of love with "Oh ma, leave me alone."[113] From there the play centers on generational splits – the Child's love for her grandmother and the two young women's discomfort with that bond, viewing it as a potential betrayal. At the end of the piece three adult women surround the Child and exit through the audience while reciting declarations of love. "Now with a lover's lack/ I measure space and time only/ by the miles, the waves, and the railroad tracks/ the price of minutes running out/ on telephones, a disembodied voice/ that haunts only the ear/ while arms and womb lean over/ a terrible void."[114] The play is interesting especially because of its inclusion of the grandmother and for its attention to the role of daughter as mother. Most of the plays coming from feminist theater groups tended to concentrate primarily on the daughter's view of the mother, in other words, women in single roles rather than women occupying more than one role at a time.

When Lilith did a mother/daughter play they approached it quite differently from WET, AFOM, New Cycle Theater, or Cutting Edge. Since Lilith had never been committed to ritual theater the issue was approached from the perspective of a single individual, Michele Linfante, who wrote from her own experience the only mother/daughter play Lilith ever performed. First produced in 1980, *Pizza* was largely autobiographical and centered on Linfante's own relationship with her dying mother and her mother's proposed visit to San Francisco.

After Terry Baum left the company, Lilith settled on family as the topic for their next play but despite the decision they were struggling with the shape and focus of the play. Linfante, during this time, was deciding whether or not to go home and take care of her sick mother.

> Here I was, the Italian girl, clearly my brother didn't want to have anything to do with it, so what is Michele going to do? Was I going to go home and take care of my mother or stay with my career and write this play?[115]

Linfante's family decided to send her mother to her in California. She clearly remembers talking to Terry Baum, who identified Linfante's situation as the solution to the problem Lilith was having with the topic.

> It was, in fact, Terry who put her finger on it. I'll never forget that day. She said this is the play, this is the play. I'll never forget that feeling in the core of me that this was the play. I started writing about my mother coming to visit me.[116]

Linfante's mother never made the trip but the play did get written.

The play unfolds in Grace's apartment as she struggles to come to terms with her mother, her mother's illness, and the impending visit. The apartment scenes alternate with a series of flashbacks about Grace's childhood in the family pizza parlor as her mother develops Parkinson's disease and how the illness changes their relationship. The memories are triggered every time Grace opens a box of pizza. From the beginning Grace and her mother, Lena, disagree and it is clear that Grace has a strong mother figure. But when Lena begins to forget things and the doctors have no diagnosis she begins to lose her strength and begs Grace to help her. Unable to help, Grace leaves home for New York City. Her community opposes the move because, as her mother's friend tells her: "A girl ought to stay home and take care of her mother."[117] Later Grace leaves New York and moves to California and she continues to feel as though she had deserted her mother. She alternates between feeling suffocated by her mother and feeling linked to her. At the end of the play Lena shows up at Grace's apartment, but she is not the elderly and dying mother, but a young and vibrant Lena. After she convinces Grace that she is her mother they sit down to eat the pizza Grace has ordered. "You are my Ma, aren't you?" she asks with some doubt. "That's what I've been telling you," Lena answers. "You got some with sausage?"[118] *Pizza* was later developed in 1982 into a full-length play. The play was not a ritual but it proceeded from the company's agreement that the mother/daughter bond was an important one for every feminist theater to explore.

In 1981 Valentina Productions (1980, San Francisco) created a teatropoesía piece, *Voz de la Mujer*, mentioned earlier in this chapter. One of the primary themes of the production was motherhood, although not limited to the mother/daughter bond – Yvonne Yarbro-Bejarano described it as an "exaltation of motherhood."[119] Anita Mattos performed and wrote a segment, titled "Pantomima," of the production which Barbara Brinson Pineda characterized as a "mime of a woman's coming of age through the birth of two children and being abandoned by their father."[120] Bejarano notes that the piece had many similarities to *Chicana* which demonstrates the centrality of the experiences of women as mothers within both the cultures of feminism and Chicanas.[121]

Some theaters never did a specific play about mothers and daughters yet had an investment in the bond that influenced their work. For Spiderwoman Theater (1975) in New York City the issues of community, culture, and mothers are complexly interwoven. The theater itself is named for the grandmother/goddess of the Hopi who was the first to teach her people how to create designs and to weave. Thus creation and expression are linked to the mother and Spiderwoman interprets this to mean that story telling belongs to women. "I really understood story telling. Everyone in my family told stories and told them with such relish. There were times when you knew the story but you waited for that moment."[122] While Spiderwoman has never done a play that is only about motherhood or the Miguels' mother, they have created many works

140

that deal with their family and their experiences as children in a white supremacist society. In *Sun, Moon, and Feather* (1981) they examined their bonds as sisters and their childhoods in Brooklyn, with "a father who did snake oil sideshows and a mother who wanted to be white, civilized, and Christian."[123] *The Winnetou's Snake Oil Show from Wigwam City* includes a section on the Miguels' mother who was born with a caul and therefore considered special. In 1988 Spiderwoman said they were beginning the process of developing a show about their mother.[124] Certainly *Power Pipes* (1991) dealt with a sense of motherhood in their exploration of goddesses and spirituality.

Split Britches' first piece, *Split Britches*, emerged from Lois Weaver's desire to mark the existence of some of the women in her family from the Blue Ridge Mountains in Virginia. Starting from the assumption that these lives were worthy of exploration, Weaver and two other members of Spiderwoman Theater, Pam Verge and Peggy Shaw, developed the piece over two years, 1980–81. The piece owes less to the ritual celebrations of AFOM or Cutting Edge than to Spiderwoman's dynamic play of parody and pastiche. The mother/daughter dynamic can be seen in the play because it is insistently interested in the lives of the women who preceded the playwrights/performers and whose legacies are outside the dominant culture and therefore at risk of being forgotten or erased. As Vivian Patraka wrote in an introduction to the play:

> When you create the past you create the future by enlarging the circle of who one can associate with and the vision of what people can create and act upon. They include characters outside the public (male) gaze of history and challenge its standard determinants of class, age, gender, and sexual preference: *Split Britches* is about women too old, too poor, too dumb, too lesbian, or too insistent on controlling their own lives to be visible.[125]

Both "slides" (actually performers in still tableaux changing their positions as lights change) and a narrator's voice explain to the audience the relationships among the three women and their relationships with the larger world. The ways in which their sexuality, class, and gender marginalize them with their culture are foregrounded. While in many ways removed from the myth/ritual context explored previously, there is a shared emphasis on women who went before, whose struggles enabled the struggles that followed.

In many cases individual women, not members of a particular feminist theater but invested in many of the same ideas and concerns, grappled with notions of motherhood and its relation to different cultures and historical moments. Anita Mattos, a Latina performer, director, and writer, worked for many years in political theater in Puerto Rico and the United States. In Puerto Rico she did folkloric puppet theater concerning nationalist issues. When she moved to the U.S. she performed with Teatro Latino from 1979 to 1982 and Teatro de la Esperanza in San Francisco from 1984 to 1987. She also directed the first staged reading of Cherrie Moraga's *Giving Up the Ghost* (1986) in 1987 and co-directed its production at Theater Rhinoceros in 1989.[126]

Mattos believes that her sensibilities about theater and creation have been formed by her experiences of being a single mother in a theater dominated by men unconcerned with issues of child-care and the position of mothers in this society. "Women's work is not valued and the women's work that is most devalued is the work of the mother."[127] In 1990 Mattos was involved in creating a piece titled *Mothers, Madwomen, and Poets*. The first section was about the mothers of the five members of Teatro de la Esperanza and how they are all experiencing profound illnesses, both mental and physical. She was trying to figure out "what makes women crazy."[128] Another section of the piece told the stories of many Latina poets who committed suicide. Like Martha Boesing who understands theater as ritual as a way to heal, Mattos, too, thinks the healing force of theater is crucial. "Healing has to be part of it or I'm not interested in it."[129] Most significantly, Mattos' sensibility of what it is to create is centered on female biology and images of motherhood:

> I am into focusing on the process as it happens. . . . I call it a matrix. I believe in creating a matrix in which creative work can be done. It is interesting that the word "matriz" in Spanish means womb because that's where that came from, the womb. The womb is not passive but it's benign. What's cooking in there is the ultimate work.[130]

Most of her twenty years in theater have been with male dominated, ethnically oriented theaters such as Teatro de la Esperanza. However, she worked with Valentina Productions, the

San Jose chapter of Women in Teatro (WIT), and in 1980 they performed a collage piece of women's writings, *Voz de la Mujer*, at the Eleventh Annual Chicano/Latino Teatro Festival.[131]

Naomi Newman, of A Travelling Jewish Theater (ATJT) in San Francisco, refocused her long-time commitment as a feminist to create a piece about Judaism and women in 1986. Tired of collaborating with her male colleagues in ATJT, Newman decided to create a piece of theater to "free the voices inside of me. I wanted the piece to speak from a place of my own experience."[132] Gradually three voices emerged: that of an artist in her fifties, a grandmother/mother in her sixties or seventies, and a very old bag lady. These three characters together became *Snake Talk: Urgent Messages from the Mother*.

While Newman was in the process of creating *Snake Talk* her friend, the poet Deena Metzger, pointed out to Newman that "these voices [that Newman had identified] were my personal, contemporary versions of the triple goddess or the three fates, found in nearly all mythologies of the ancient world as Creator, Preserver, and Destroyer of life."[133] Newman also saw the three characters as her personal vision of three "stages" of womanhood; maiden, mother, and crone.[134] In the play there is a homage to friendship, which is Newman's acknowledgement of Metzger's contribution and friendship.

In 1988 Newman reworked *Snake Talk* in collaboration with Martha Boesing whom Newman had met on a trip to Nicaragua in 1984. Boesing had received a Rockefeller grant to write with a company other than AFOM and Newman convinced Boesing to use the grant to work with her at ATJT. Boesing lived with Newman for three months during which time they reconceptualized the scenic approach, created new material, and reorganized the pre-existing material. Newman comments on this time: "It really created a new play although a lot of the writing stayed the same."[135] Through Boesing's work the piece, according to Newman, became tougher and "more grounded in daily life."[136]

In performance, the stage is divided into three areas.[137] Stage left is the poet/creator Else's space marked by a table, a chair, and a book (her journal). Center stage belongs to Rifke, the mother/preserver. In her space is a wooden table and bench with a chopping bowl and chopper that belonged to Newman's mother. The Hag, crone/destroyer, is stage right. The Hag speaks from under a ladder where she hides her belongings collected from the street. Newman wears a black dress and she adds/takes off costume pieces as she shifts from character to character. The moves are usually marked by harmonium music and singing.

The poet/Else concentrates her monologues on her poetry and the contradictions inherent in being a woman artist. "People are always telling me to calm down. I wonder if they ever told Beethoven to calm down?"[138] Rifke/the mother contemplates the state of the earth and laments the position of women, directly addressing the audience. She criticizes the position of women in the Jewish tradition and religion:

> What they did to women in the Bible, it shouldn't happen to a dog. . . . All the men in the Bible have books named after them. None of the women in the Bible have books and few have names. Half the world's wisdom is out the window. Oy, they raped them. Oy, they stoned them. Oy they de-holied them.[139]

Rifke then invites the audience to join her in reciting the "Oys" as a way to release anger over the treatment of women. She stresses that this ritual is only the beginning, the next step is to act, and suggests specific strategies. For example, she sings an old folk tune about a rabbi teaching children the alphabet but rewrites it so that it is about a mother teaching her children the alphabet. "I would like to know," she demands, "who took the mother out of this song and who gave the alphabet exclusively to the rabbis?"[140]

The third character, the crone/destroyer, speaks of aging and dying. The snake teaches her about the cyclic nature of life and she is the figure of doom who people pass by quickly because she reminds them of mortality. "I look like graves."[141] The Hag also proposes that she, and all women, were "the snake" at one time and the Biblical use of the snake as the devil is a perversion of matriarchal power.

The emotional and political climax of the play is when Rifke tells a story of abusing her daughter. Catching her daughter dancing "like a goy," to Marian Anderson's singing of *Ave Maria*, Rifke screams that she is Jewish and must not act like a "shikseleh."[142] She locks her daughter in the closet and ignores her screams and pleading. For Rifke, her daughter's prayer-like dance is an insult to the Jewish people who recently perished in the Holocaust. When she unlocks the closet and holds her daughter the audience see her shake in sorrow for an act she cannot undo and are intended to realize, according to Newman, that violence encourages violence.[143]

144

Newman bases her theater piece on life experience, Jewish tradition, and a pre-patriarchal, matriarchal organization of the world to create contemporary feminist thought. She speaks to women by emphasizing their connections while pointing up the differences. She uses the idea of the nature of women being tripartite, but she also stresses the particular nature of being Jewish in the predominantly Christian culture of the United States. Newman uses the ritual to explore her personal place in the world, but also to connect her to other women. She has moments when the audience may participate, she allows them time to complain and later in the performance hands out oranges, saying "Someone is taking care of you."[144] Newman's reworking of the piece with Martha Boesing is significant because Martha Boesing firmly believes in the power of ritual theater to heal and to bring women together. In Newman's case, however, ritual theater is informed by ethnic, cultural, and religious affiliations.

The investment in the mother/daughter bond existed across boundaries of race, class, and sexuality. However, the bond took on different meanings in each setting and each production reflected the particular investments of the theater and its members. What is significant is that mother/daughter plays were seen as productive vehicles for representing the community and its interests. The next chapter continues the examination of the community/theater relationship through the reception of feminist theater and how the theaters changed as the community changed.

5

REPRESENTING THE PATRIARCHY AND EXPERIENCE

Plays about violence against women

Identifying and working from women's lived experience was by and large seen as a positive and empowering move on the part of feminism. As this experience was defined it became the basis for theorizing political action and change. It quickly became apparent that not all experiences were empowering or recuperable. Around the issue of mothers and daughters feminists found enormous inspiration, not only as a counter to the father/son dynamic so revered in Western history but also as something unique to women and therefore auspiciously feminist. However, when issues about rape and violence against women began to emerge it quickly became apparent that some areas of women's experience were deeply and negatively imbedded in the patriarchy and that they had to be eradicated, not changed. The mother/daughter relationship was a positive one that had been distorted and corrupted by patriarchal forces to suit their ends. The emphasis was therefore on change not abolition because it was considered an empowering connection between and among women, one that would prevail. But when it came to rape or battery the focus of action and critique was on eliminating them as a potential part of women's experience. Violence against women in the form of rape or battery can be understood as patriarchal rather than feminist experiences because they are ones that, should a feminist vision of the world prevail, would disappear. Women's experience was thus differentiated among those to be preserved or recuperated and those to be eliminated or reviled.

Defining rape and battery turned out to be complicated processes. As Susan Brownmiller noted in the introduction to her groundbreaking book on rape, when a group of my women friends discussed rape one evening in the fall of 1970, I fairly shrieked in dismay. I *knew* what rape was and what it wasn't. Rape was a sex crime, a product of a diseased, deranged mind. Rape wasn't a feminist issue, rape was . . . well, what was it? At any rate, I certainly knew something about rape victims! The women's movement had nothing in common with rape victims. Victims of rape were . . . well, what were they? *Who* were they?[1]

Brownmiller articulates through her personal experience the way rape was regarded by the larger movement. The experience of rape was something ancillary, involving women perhaps, but nothing to do with feminism. By the end of the decade feminists would radically alter rape laws, the treatment and views of rape victims, and enshrine rape and battery as important focuses of feminist political action. In order for this to happen, though, they had to define rape and battery, its effects on women, and its role in the cultural and social systems. These understandings were both utilized and developed by feminist theater groups who also came to realize that violence was a feminist issue. This chapter examines how feminists came to define and link rape and battery and how those definitions emerged and developed in the performances of theater groups.

DEFINING VIOLENCE AGAINST WOMEN

Rape, as an issue, did not arise because certain feminist leaders viewed it as "the issue" nor did it arise because it was a designated topic on a consciousness-raising list. Instead rape became an issue when women began to compare their experiences as children, teenagers, students, workers, and wives and began to realize that sexual assault, in one form or another, was common.

(*Rape: The First Sourcebook for Women*)

Susan Brownmiller ends the introduction to *Against Our Will: Men, Women and Rape* by saying: "I wrote this book because I am a woman who changed her mind about rape."[2] In the introduction, titled "A Personal Statement," Brownmiller explores how it was that she came to write such a book and why it was necessary. She begins by testifying that she has never been raped herself and that the question "have you . . ." is the one she had been asked most often. She explains that while she had never been raped, she gradually came to realize that she was implicated in the issue of rape. "It . . . did not occur to me that acceptance of these attitudes [traditional ones on rape] gave me a feeling of security I needed: it can't happen *here*."[3] From there she discovered that while she had not been raped she was essentially no different from the women who had been. Therefore, she concludes: "I learned in ways I preferred to deny the threat of rape had profoundly affected my life."[4] The process she describes, from ignorance and denial to recognition and connection, resonates with consciousness-raising. Through testimony Brownmiller identifies how and why she was ignorant about the issue and documents the emergence of her changing attitudes. The attitudes she discovers are developed through a collaborative process, working with other women in discussion. Brownmiller's description of her own experience echoes that of the larger movement and the way rape came to be theorized and understood.

Brownmiller was not the only theorist/activist to follow this trajectory. All the early influential works on violence, more specifically rape and battery, begin with the idea that all women, including and especially the authors, are personally implied. The women do so by offering themselves as "typical" women and then describe how their lives have been circumscribed by rape. It is not the physical experience of forced penetration, however, but the threat of the experience, the idea and existence, that delimits their lives. Susan Griffin, for example in her work on rape now in its third edition, positions herself in the book's opening paragraph in the 1971 essay, "Politics":

> I have never been free of the fear of rape. From a very early age I, like most women, have thought of rape as part of my natural environment – something to be feared and prayed against like fire or lightning, I never asked why men raped; I simply thought it one of the many mysteries of human nature.[5]

The first section in *Rape: The First Sourcebook for Women* is the transcription of an actual consciousness-raising session, held in 1971. There are nine participants of whom two actually come out and say "I was raped."[6] However, all the women relate a personal tale that testifies to the impact that the idea of rape has had on them. Similarly, in *Radical Feminism* there is an account of a consciousness-raising session, held in 1970, that differs little from the one in *Rape*.[7] The emphasis on personal narrative as a guarantee of authenticity continues in more recent works. In her controversial book *The Morning After: Sex, Fear, and Feminism on Campus*, Katie Roiphe writes at the end of her introduction:

> This book comes out of frustration, out of anger, out of the names I've been called, out of all the times I didn't say something I was thinking because it might offend the current feminist sensibility. But there is something else – my grandmother and her card games, her hands turning over card after card, dealing faster and faster, memorizing numbers. It is out of the deep belief that some feminisms are better than others that I have written this book.[8]

While Roiphe's book is in many ways antithetical to the books discussed earlier, she participates in the discourse on similar terms – authenticating her work and ideas with personal testimony, assuring readers that what is contained in the book is true because it is, at least in part, an account of lived experience.

The theories of rape, and later of battery, that emerged from the discourse of testimony and consciousness-raising took two related paths. One direction established that rape was an experience common to all women, and that as potential victims only chance separated the woman who had been raped from the one who had not been. The other trajectory worked from the notion that rape was not an isolated instance of violence but a method of enforcing a system of oppression. These two characterizations are obviously intertwined; if all women are potential rape victims then there must be something more going on than unrelated, individual occurrences. Concomitantly, if rape is a method of enforcing an oppressive system then its victims, both potential and actual, must have something in common.

In January 1971, in New York City, the Radical Feminists organized a "Speak Out" on the issue of rape. The poster for the event announced that rape was "a political crime against women" and that women would "testify about our experiences."[9] Out of that event grew a conference on rape held in April of the same year and organized by the same group. The Radical Feminists, who would later publish a book based on the two events, determined something crucial from the Speak Out and conference. "It is no accident that the New York Radical Feminists, through the technique of consciousness-raising, discovered that rape is not a personal misfortune but an *experience shared by all women* in one form or another."[10] The Speak Out depended almost entirely on testimonies and what was derived from the testimonies was the principle that any and all women risked rape simply because of their gender identification.

Gender was a highly polarized matter when it came to rape. Women were its potential targets and sufferers and men were its potential perpetrators and beneficiaries. Thus women needed to unite in order to resist and abolish the practice. In order to move women from Brownmiller's initial position ('I've never been raped') to one that made each woman aware of her vulnerability, a homogeneous characterization of men and women emerged. One writer described the gender positions in relation to rape:

> *everyman*: has probably raped or beaten a woman; or enjoyed rape fantasies . . . or at least a man he works with or socializes with, who he thinks is an ok type, has raped or beaten a woman.
> *everywoman*: fears rape, or lives inside limits imposed by that fear: no late night walks, no living alone, no hours of solitude by the river.[11]

While simplistic, the formula makes two points; it demonstrates the different ways men and women are positioned by rape – men can fantasize or passively condone it without threat or harm, women conversely are controlled by its threat and the fear that emerges from the threat – and it demonstrates how women's behavior is dictated by the existence of rape. Their choices are circumscribed by physical threat and limited by the need for self-preservation.

> That *some* men rape provides a sufficient threat to keep all women in a constant state of intimidation, forever conscious of the knowledge that the biological tool must be held in awe for it may turn to weapon with sudden swiftness borne of harmful intent.[12]

The comparison foregrounds how women are linked by the threat of rape and that it is common to all their experiences.

Women were also believed to be linked not only by the threat of rape but also by what they would experience if they were raped. "The pattern that emerged from their individual experiences was not a common pattern of assault . . . but a common pattern of responses that they encountered: 'You're lying,' 'It was your fault'."[13] The police and courts were notorious in their treatment of rape victims. If the women were courageous enough to report the crime (and many did not, often out of shame or because they did not think they would be believed) and to see the matter brought to trial, the women would usually find themselves under scrutiny. Their sexual histories were usually the focal point of the defence in order to prove that the woman had behaved or lived in such a way to encourage her rapist. Battered women experienced similar reactions, often being counseled to examine how and why they had provoked the abuse. Del Martin points out: "Victims are treated as if they created the situation in which they find themselves and are held responsible for their problems, irrespective of other contributing factors."[14] Feminists pointed out that since women were usually powerless and isolated in violent situations there was almost no way they could protect themselves from this particular attitude. Women could derive power from working together in order to change these negative attitudes or situations – collective action was the only sure means of securing change. But that course of action could be determined only by analyzing women's actual lived experience.

Testimony, as exemplified in the "Speak Out," served specific purposes. The editors of the Radical Feminist volume on rape write that the women shared their experiences to "counter the myths that (1) women cannot be raped against their will, (2) women really want to be raped, and (3) women make false accusations."[15] Previously rape had been, at best, something shameful to be hidden and, at worst, something a woman brought upon herself. Susan Brownmiller, in her four "deadly male myths of rape," characterized prevalent mainstream attitudes: "All women want to be raped. No woman can be raped against her will. She was asking for it. If you're going to be raped, you might as well relax and enjoy it."[16] These "maxims" demonstrated the idea that violent physical abuse was construed by the dominant order as a consequence of being a woman. Rape was either a joke, "relax and enjoy it," or a punishment, "she asked for it." The overall message, as Brownmiller and others understood it, was that any woman would be at fault, that somehow she would be seen as bringing her fate upon herself. Rape, according to this analysis, was an effective mechanism of control virtually indistinguishable whether as threat or as act.

For rape to be an issue central to all women it had to have direct impact on each woman's life. The threat and the act had to be elided in order for it to speak to women as something they shared. Not only was rape endemic to women's lives, it was positioned as "an illustration of a more general problem: sexism."[17] Barbara Mehrhof and Pamela Kearon put it even more simply in their early piece on rape: "Rape is an effective political device."[18] Intent became central to the analysis. It was not coincidental that women who were raped were made to feel responsible by society, a punishment for something they had done. Somehow they had misbehaved, had they not they would not have been raped. The attitude was reinforced by making rape something shameful so that women did not dare voice their experiences. Alone, they would believe that somehow, since they were the only ones suffering, they were responsible. Society can then blame the victim, often with her collusion, as Susan Brownmiller points out: "to make a woman a willing participant in her own defeat is half the battle."[19] While feminist analysis used the threat of rape as a common element of women's lives it also foregrounded the ways in which it was part of the oppression of women and how it worked to perpetuate women's secondary status. Not always necessarily seen as natural, it was always seen as an effective enforcement of the patriarchal system.

That the patriarchy needed to rely on rape in order to oppress seemed proof that violence was ingrained and inseparable from it. This position allowed the women who later used the work of rape awareness in the field of spousal abuse to link the analysis of battery into the analysis of rape. The two were different manifestations of the same goal: the oppression of women. One author identified "wife-beaters" as the "home guard."[20] The acts were not identical, but they were linked. Battery was, however, more closely associated with the institution of compulsory heterosexuality. "Rape is regarded [by patriarchal society] as an act of sexual behavior provoked by the woman, not as an assault which demonstrates the male's contempt for and control over her. Battery is still the prerogative of men whose property women and children are."[21] Just as a woman who allowed a man into her apartment, for example, was believed to be at fault if he subsequently raped her, a wife (using the term loosely) was believed to be in collusion with her situation. Thus, the movement from individual situation to cultural and political analysis was fraught as it indicted the family as well as other bastions of culture. One theorist described the difficulties of the situations:

> Wife-beating . . . is a complex that involves much more than the act itself or the persona; interaction between a husband

and his wife. It has its roots in historical attitudes toward women, the institution of marriage, the economy, the intricacies of criminal and civil law, and the delivery system of social service agencies.[22]

The long list of ideologies, institutions, and systems foregrounds the difficulties feminists faced. Strategies built from the analysis of rape were invaluable. While violence was often positioned as an essential element of patriarchy, women working in the arenas of rape and battery were constantly looking for ways to bring about change.

Despite the differences between rape and battery as acts, as discourses they were contiguous. They functioned effectively to position women as (un)willing collaborators in their own abuse. Fearing the stigma of being labelled a rape victim or battered wife, women remained silent, protecting and perpetuating both acts. Consciousness-raising, whether in formal groups or informal discussion and reading, was the primary method of deriving theory and action, as well as relating to women who had experienced rape or battery. The process was often described as bringing women out of isolation, making them aware of larger implications of their situation, encouraging them to recognize and interpret it as cultural and political, and working from there for change.[23] The process could be discerned in a variety of expressions from formal, academic analyses to the public testimonies of women.

TAKE BACK THE NIGHT

Take Back the Night is a supportive environment for women to share their experiences of rape and violence without being blamed. We will mourn the victims of violence, celebrate the survivors, and draw attention to the issue of violence against women in general. Come light a candle and Take Back the Night.

(Take Back the Night Candle Light Vigil Poster)[24]

One legacy of consciousness-raising was the notion that stories had to be told publicly. Valuing what had been devalued, individual women were encouraged to describe their experiences, thoughts, and feelings to other women. In New York City in 1971 there was a "Speak Out," and similar ones were held in many cities including, for example, San Francisco in 1972 and 1977, Portland, Oregon in 1977.[25] Personal stories were included in most books on rape, presented as long quotations preserving the sense of authenticity and direct address. Public forums to facilitate and enable testimony began to develop. Testimony became theatricalized, a part of the spectacle of a feminist march or demonstration. While the "Speak Outs" did make public what had been an intensely private experience they also made the experience something that was performed or re-enacted in the telling.

The best known form of public demonstration that has also had the most longevity is the Take Back the Night March. The idea for the first march came when Starhawk, a leader in the spiritual and eco-feminist movements, was asked by the organizers of the 1978 conference Feminist Perspectives on Pornography to create a ritual to serve as the "climax of the weekend . . . a march through the North Beach section of San Francisco. . . . it took place in Washington Square Park, at the end of the march."[26] Starhawk worked with Hallie Iglehart, Nina Wise, Ann Hershey, Lee Schwing, Helen Dannenberg, Diane Broadstreet, Lennie Schwendinger, and Toni Marcus as the primary creators and performers of the event, and though she notes that other women were involved the nine women named are primarily responsible.[27] Laura Lederer, who is credited with the conception of the 1978 conference, saw the march and ritual as serving a specific function and making clear feminists' position on the treatment of women.

> Take Back the Night was a profound symbolic statement of
> our commitment to stopping the tide of violence in all arenas,
> and our demand that perpetrators of such violence – from
> rapists and batterers to pornographers – be held responsible
> for their actions and be made to change.[28]

While Take Back the Night received its initial impetus from the anti-pornography movement it was clearly marked from its initial inception as tackling the larger issue of women and violence. It is not surprising that it cropped up in various forms across U.S. campuses as a protest against violence, primarily rape, because it had not been intended as a ritual specific to pornography but more flexibly on violence on various fronts.[29]

Take Back the Night was not the first ritual of its type in which Starhawk had been involved. In 1976 Hallie Iglehart and Starhawk created a ritual to end a conference on violence against women. Only twenty minutes in length it involved hundreds of women. Iglehart wrote later:

We felt it was essential to transform the violence we were dealing with and to direct our anger in a focused ritual way. ... We also wanted to create an experience that would emphasize the connection between the conference and our everyday lives.[30]

The basic elements of Take Back the Night were present in this early ritual – the bonds among women, the relationship of experience to political action, and the belief in the efficacy of ritual.

The march's overall structure and intent clearly emerged from spiritual and ritual feminism. Hallie Iglehart wrote in 1983 about collective rituals that they were "a powerful community-creating resource." Thus, she added, ritual can be used "to raise and regenerate our power and direct it towards social and political action."[31] Take Back the Night participated in and used ritual similarly to feminist theaters. Intended as a public display of feminist community, rituals served to remind women visibly that they were part of larger communities than the women who were part of their daily lives. At the marches (and the first Take Back the Night March had 3,000 participants), women saw, reinforced, and performed their bonds with other women.[32]

Andrea Dworkin delivered what Laura Lederer called "an exhortation to march."[33] Dworkin's speech set the mood for the march to come. It concluded:

Tonight we are going to walk together, all of us, to take back the night, as women have in other cities all over the world, because in every sense none of us can walk alone. Every woman walking alone is a target. ... Only by walking together can we walk at all with any sense of safety, dignity or freedom. Tonight, walking together, we will claim to the rapists and pornographers and women batterers that their days are numbered and our time has come. ... Tonight, with every breath and every step, we must commit ourselves to going the distance: to transforming the earth on which we walk from prison and tomb into our rightful and joyous home. This we must do and this we will do, for our own sakes and for the sake of every woman who has ever lived.[34]

The end of the speech reaffirms bonds and similarities among women. It also provides a common sense of purpose that was picked up in the ritual that followed.

As the women arrived at Washington Square Park, where the march ended, they were chanting, "Wipe the slate clean,/ Dream a new dream."[35] Holly Near was singing and the Witches formed a "birth canal" through which all the marchers had to pass to enter the park.[36] The ritual was led from the back of a truck by Starhawk and some of the other women. Behind them a women's acrobatic group, Fly By Night, were doing what Starhawk described as an "aerial dance."[37]

Starhawk found that the physical design prevented many women from perceiving the ritual as such and that many took it for a more conventional, less participatory performance. "It is the first time I have done a ritual so theatrical, where the bright lights cut us off from the crowd, who become 'audience.'"[38] Despite the lack of audience understanding, the ritual begins. The event primarily consists of an invocation to dance while the leaders of the ritual chant about the sanctity of women's bodies and express the power of women. The conclusion urges the participants to

> Open your eyes and look around you . . . see our strength in one another's face . . . know that we are strong. Know what women of old knew . . . that the night must belong to us. Know that we are women who take back the night. Know that the night is ours.[39]

Starhawk adds that the women present exploded in: "Cheers, laughter, screams, kisses."[40] From Dworkin's exhortation to march to Starhawk's celebration of the finished march, the ideas that women hold these experiences in common is foregrounded.

Ritual events as protests or consciousness-raising around violence against women were not uncommon and Take Back the Night was by no means the only ritual. The year before the first Take Back the Night was created in San Francisco, Suzanne Lacy formulated two events in Los Angeles.[41] The first, titled *Three Weeks in May*, took place over an extended period of time. Not one unified event, the "performance structure" was determined by Lacy while individual events within the structure had a great deal of autonomy. The activities/events included "speeches by politicians, interviews with hotline activists, self-defense demonstrations, speakouts and art performances" as well as a rally against rape held at City Hall.[42] One of the most notable elements of the entire event was the two maps of Los Angeles Lacy used to document the location of rapes that occurred during the three weeks and the service and support agencies for rape victims. The maps were placed in city hall as well as local malls. Sue-Ellen Case notes:

> Lacy's maps confronted hundreds of women – intersecting their personal shopping – with the objective facts about violent crimes against women committed in the city at that time. . . . The objective–subjective blend of the political and the personal created a theater of feminist consciousness-raising.[43]

The over thirty events were covered by print and broadcast journalism, thus the audiences were much broader and larger than they otherwise might have been.

Seven months later, this time in collaboration with Leslie Labowitz, Lacy created another performance piece against violence. Organized as a protest against the media and political handling of the murder victims of the serial killer dubbed the "Hillside Strangler," "*In Mourning and In Rage* . . . offered an alternative to the case through the news, one which included a strong feminist analysis of violence."[44] The piece opposed the notions of randomness put forward by mainstream sources and instead pointed to the political uses of female terror. The ideas fueling the work resonated with Susan Brownmiller's summary of rape: "It is nothing more or less than a conscious process of intimidations by which *all* men keep *all* women in a state of fear."[45] The work also foregrounded the ways in which the media could play off this by sensationalizing their reports, including details about the victims' lives, in order to encourage a fearful atmosphere.

The piece was "performed" by a variety of women, including performance artists, activists, and politicians. The ritual began when:

> Sixty women formed a motorcade of cars bearing funeral stickers and "stop violence against women" stickers. They followed a hearse to city hall, where news media reporters waited with members of city council. Out of the hearse climbed ten tall women robed in black mourning dress. These women each spoke of a different violence perpetrated against women as they removed a scarlet red cloak. Women from the. motorcade chorused after each statement "In memory of our sisters, we fight back!"[46]

The various politicians in attendance then pledged their support and the ritual concluded as women danced to a song Holly Near performed, "Fight Back," composed specifically for the ritual.

Similar to the two rituals in Los Angeles was one created in honor of International Women's Day 1978 and performed in Portland, Oregon. This one centered on actual testimonies. Each testimony included specific details of the women's experience. They offered brief stories of women who refused to be beaten or raped. Titled *We Fight Back*, the ritual was performed by eight women around a statue in downtown Portland. The women wore masks and put a wreath of flowers and a knife at the foot of the statue. Each speaking in turn, one woman would tell a woman's story that was scripted according to a formula that gave the woman's name, relationship to her attacker, her action against him, her legal status, and geographical information.

> My name is Evelyn Ware. I am 29 years old. My husband beat me repeatedly. He continued to beat and harass me even after we got divorced. I shot him. I was found not guilty on grounds of self-defense. California.[47]

After each of the thirty-three stories the rest of the women would chant: "I am a woman. I fought back."[48] The chanting culminated in a paraphrase of Adrienne Rich. "When a woman fights back, she creates the possibility for more resistance around her."[49] The ritual itself ended when, after placing the wreath on the head of the statue, the women took off their masks and recited in unison: "We are women. We fight back."[50]

Take Back the Night, *Three Weeks in May, In Mourning and in Rage* . . . , and *We Fight Back* were all rituals in keeping with the principles outlined in the previous chapter. They looked for and found similarities among women, integrated the events into women's daily lives, and served to foreground ways in which women could seize or have seized power for themselves. Kay Turner wrote in an issue of *Heresies* that "doing the ritual is more important than knowing the ritual. The eficacy [sic] of the ritual is always in the acting of it, in becoming bodily involved with the elements."[51] These four rituals, performed in open public spaces, were not about women's willing participation in "elements" they controlled but how women's experience includes forces hostile and dangerous to them.

Take Back the Night both in its original form and its subsequent life on college campuses allowed women to envision themselves full participants in society, no longer prevented from being out at night. As Andrea Dworkin said before the 1978 march, "we have to take back the night every night or the night will never be ours."[52] Contained in the ritual, the political action is the threat it seeks to resist. Ostensibly if the ritual were to succeed it would become obsolete. Similarly, *Three Weeks* and *In Mourning* mark the degradation and literal erasure of women. Confronting people in mainstream venues – malls, the streets, city hall, television – where they might not expect the message or the performance was an act of aggression based on the notion that what was at stake was the abolition of the subject of the ritual. "We Fight Back" marked and celebrated those women who had taken matters into their own hands.

The experiences explored by the four rituals are not solely patriarchal. The initial experiences, that of the acts of rape or battery, were patriarchal ones that feminists wished to obliterate. Where they cease to be patriarchal and begin to be feminist is in the symbolism of uniting women, speaking out, and fighting back. However, if feminist resistances were successful future generations of women would not have any experiences of violence to which to testify. Unlike the strategies and bonds forged around motherhood, the bonds that emerged from the connections among women identified by the theories and rituals around violence were viewed as temporary and transitory. They were empowering not in their implied permanence and enduring strength but in their goal and effect which, once achieved, would eliminate the theories, rituals, and goals entirely.

Theaters participated directly in these ideas. Groups made plays from testimonies, their own and others', volunteered at shelters, and explored the relationships of women to violence. Their perform-ances were contemporaneous with the production of other rituals and theories. Rather than seeing the theaters as separate from these activities, their work was embedded in it unimaginable without the labor in the other areas and indebted to it.

PLAYS ABOUT VIOLENCE AGAINST WOMEN

ESTHER (*Stands quietly. Makes decision. Locks door. Opens curtains, leaves one light on. She slowly strips to her slip. Sits on bed, waiting.*) We hear: *footsteps on the fire escape.*
ESTHER: It is my imagination. It is always my imagination. The trains are

not running, the power is off, the mail has stopped. I cannot breathe. It is my imagination. Nothing is happening. Nothing at all.
We hear: *glass breaking at window as curtain falls.*

(*Abide in Darkness*)[53]

Many women became feminists in a state of rage or found themselves growing in anger once they began to analyze women's situations critically. The anger was both outward, "I won't let you treat me that way anymore," and inward, "How could I let myself be treated that way?" According to Susi Kaplow, one of the organizers of the 1971 Speak Out in New York, however, these two forms of anger are indispensable to feminists.

> Anger becomes a tool which you can control, not only to help you make personal changes but to deal with the world outside as well. You can mobilize your anger to warn those around you that you're not having any more bullshit, to underscore your seriousness, to dare to drive your point home.[54]

Anger was also a productive emotion from which to create theater. For some women the desire to do theater came from anger, for others the anger grew while doing theater as they discovered more about the treatment of women, especially around the issue of violence.

In 1969 Caravan Theater (1965, Boston) produced their first feminist play. *How to Make a Woman*, created through improvisation by five women and three men during a four-year period, concentrates primarily on the ways in which women are constructed and positioned by society throughout their lives. The dramatized moments are by implication typical – learning how to walk with "lady-like" steps, receiving her first purse, or typing his résumé – and the audience is supposed to understand such moments as unavoidable rites of passage for a woman in patriarchal society. When Mary, the woman who is "made" by the processes within the play, is raped the event is also positioned as inevitable. The other women onstage physically mimic Mary's actions during the rape; the "other two women are moving sympathetically, victimized, to ground, as is Mary."[55] Visual connections are made among women – what happens to one, happens to all.

While raping Mary the "Hunter" repeats over and over that he loves her. After he climaxes he justifies his actions to her.

I'm sorry, but it's often like that. You'll get used to it. You'll learn to love it and like it as I do. I didn't want to hurt you, but you needed the training. . . . I've been very helpful to you today. I've opened up a whole new world of instinctual pleasures. I understand women, at first they're very shy about such things. They need to be opened up. It's a biological truth. In a day or two you'll have forgotten this unpleasant moment. I love you. I really do.[56]

Later he adds: "Men are like that."[57] Rape is inevitable, the Hunter implies, but it is an experience necessary to becoming a woman in the patriarchy. Later in the play another male character, the Wolf, beats Mary as she repeats over and over "Want..want..want..want" and the Wolf repeats the word "Lovely."[58] After he beats her, the Wolf seduces Mary but does not allow her to reach a climax. The play intentionally offers no solutions for women's oppression, preferring instead to work those out in post-show discussions.

The first production of the Westbeth Feminist Playwrights Collective (New York City, 1970) was *Rape-In* (written 1970, produced 1971). Dolores Walker, one of the playwrights of the evening of one-acts, done as a cabaret, told Linda Killian bluntly, "*Rape-In* was an angry show."[59] The show used humor, anger, and horror sometimes in combination, sometimes alone. In Gwen Gunn's piece *Across the Street*,

a young woman, long humiliated by the whistles and sexual invitations of construction workers, turns her rage into effective action by taking one hard hat up on his suggestion. After he returns from her apartment, he tells his co-workers of his horrifying experience: "they had an orgy on me. They used me in disgusting ways, like I was nothing."[60]

Humor was obviously the vehicle for the expression of anger while in Dolores Walker's play the anger is induced in the audience by the passivity and victimization of the female protagonist. In *Abide in Darkness* Ellen stops by Esther's apartment to borrow some sugar. Throughout the play Esther paces nervously while putting on more and more layers of clothes. There are four locks on her door and she has no phone or mailbox. Obviously something has happened to her to bring her to this situation but the play is oblique on this point. Esther says:

I am sorry. I did not mean to be rude, asking you who you were, but since IT happened, I am very careful. I do not have a phone, I do not use this as my mailing address. I am very careful. Since IT happened.[61]

Ellen asks Esther what she means and Esther replies, "Do you like my rug?"[62] Not surprisingly, Ellen is put off by Esther's strange behavior and leaves despite Esther's efforts to detain and befriend her. After Ellen is gone Esther stands alone repeating: "It is my imagination. It is always my imagination."[63] As the lights fade there is the sound of a window breaking.

Two other plays in the *Rape-In* cabaret, *Crabs* by Sally Ordway and *There's a Wall Between Us, Darling*, were about anger turned outward as revenge. Charlotte Rea describes *Crabs* as having "the woman remain true to her role of giver – 'She' gives him the crabs that she got from his best friend."[64] The character also rebels against having to serve as his secretary so he can advance in his career. In *There's a Wall Between Us, Darling* a woman literally immures her husband in the cellar "with his dog, pipe, books, and slippers" for "ruining her career."[65] The cabaret combined different positions around and representations of anger to provoke the audience into that state. Combining laughter and fear, the one-acts served to express and invoke anger, and hopefully action.

Rape was an important element in Alive and Trucking Theater's (A&TT, 1971, Minneapolis) first production. Created collectively, the play incorporated improvisation into its structure. The opening scene varied as it was an improvisation about the creative process but it always ended with the identification of the title for the play *Pig in a Blanket: A Tender, Poignant Drama of Young Love*.[66] The play ranged over a variety of subjects all illuminating some aspect of women's experience or social conditioning. From careers to heterosexual relationships to Ken and Barbie, the play used humor to explore sexist culture. Scene 5 (of eight) in Act 1 depicts a gang rape. Despite the choice to present it as a "stylized enactment," at some performances women would become upset and stop the scene.[67] While there are many potential reasons for the audience's reactions, the mode of presentation, for example, it is obvious that personal involvement and a sense of ownership played a part in the reaction. The audiences did believe that they had the power to intervene, an assumption by no means common to audiences.[68]

Another Minneapolis-based group, Circle of the Witch (1973), had a scene about rape in their first production, a cabaret-style piece, *Sexpot Follies* (1974). Their view of rape coincided directly with the position of the larger feminist movement, that rape covered more than the act of forced sexual relations. The play's rape scene began as hooded masked figures advanced menacingly on the emcee. These figures then

> freeze as rape statistics are quoted over a loudspeaker. Each rapist then removes a hood identifying an institution which rapes women – government, mass media, education, the nuclear family, institutionalized religion – then describes how it operates.[69]

The sketch ended with each institution transformed into a non-oppressive, non-exploitive alternative by the example and influence of the "alternative family."[70] The moment in the play cleverly illustrated the intertwining of individual, physical rape with rape as a trope standing for all the ways in which women are oppressed.

Oppression and how it is enforced comprised most of the inspiration for At the Foot of the Mountain's first production. *Raped: A Woman's Look at Bertolt Brecht's "The Exception and the Rule"* (1976) took shape after the women read all the available material on the subject of rape, including Brownmiller's book. Realizing that no extant play expressed the ideas they were discussing and reading, the members of the troupe decided to adapt a text to their own ends. They selected Brecht's *The Exception and the Rule* because of its critique of capitalist power relations and its treatment of the oppressed. Brecht's materialist analysis combined with AFOM's feminist one was useful because, according to the company, "it deepened our understanding of the historical and international terrorism of rape."[71] In Brecht's play inequitable power distribution is the rule, while compassion and kindness are the exceptions. The Merchant hires the Coolie to carry his wares across the desert, abuses him terribly, and finally in paranoid fear imagines the Coolie's retribution and kills him. The tribunal acquits the Merchant because the system cannot imagine a situation where the Coolie would not attempt to kill the Merchant. The Coolie is ultimately held responsible for his own murder.

AFOM drew a parallel from Brecht's Marxist analysis to the patriarchal system that holds women responsible for their rapes. Meredith Flynn writes that in *Raped* "women are seen as the unwilling or duped victims of violent, institutionalized, or casual male sexual activity."[72] However, "male sexual activity" was not the boundary of rape as it was explicated by Martha Boesing and

AFOM. It had a larger meaning as a metaphor for the oppression of women. As Susan Brownmiller wrote in the introduction to *Against Our Will* about her own process of consciousness-raising on rape: "I learned in ways I preferred to deny that the threat of rape had profoundly affected my life."[73] Rape was not merely the act of forced sexual intercourse but a terroristic control of bodies through the threat of potential violence.

The collaborative process began with disclaimers, according to Martha Boesing, because none of the women involved felt she had ever been raped. But, Boesing went on to point out,

> by the time we opened the show each of us had shared one or more rape stories. Some of us were victims of emotional rape; some of us were incest victims; some of us had lovers who refused to take "No, not tonight" as an answer, some of us had experienced mind rapes. For example, in college a creative writing teacher whom I adored said to me: "You're bright. You ought to do something you can do well. But you can never be a writer. It's a genetic problem. Women's minds are filled with trivia. They can never be great artists." I didn't write again for ten years. That's a rape story.[74]

Starting with these stories and a new broad definition of what it is to be raped, Boesing and AFOM set out to script a performance that would present these experiences.

After the collectively created and ritually performed play had been firmly established in their repertoire, AFOM was invited to perform at a Midwestern women's conference. The group realized that many of the women present would already be familiar with the production. In an effort to present something new they encouraged the audience to stop the show at any moment to share their own rape stories.[75] Describing the first performance that included the audience, Phyllis Jane Rose said, it was "absolute electrification of this spontaneous thing because it suddenly made you a part of a community."[76] The Women's Experimental Theater (1977, New York) had similar experiences in performances of *Electra Speaks* (1980). At one point Clytemnestra has a monologue about violence against women in which reason, motherhood, and misogyny are linked.

> Nurtured by woman as food, he creates
> he creates his institutions

religion family law
philosophy education
at night he sucks her tittie
by day he wreaks his vengeance
this baby man hates his mommy . . . .
he fucks his mommy . . . .
he fucks, he rapes his mommy
he rams it down her throat . . . .
he fucks the shit out of her
he kicks her pregnant belly . . . .
he hates her . . . .
he begs for her forgiveness
why this baby, this boy, this baby man
he's just a mass of contradictions
claims reason for himself
insititutionalizes his hatred
gives her his seat on the bus[77]

Sondra Segal notes that women were so affected they would send messages backstage during the performance. "I would get intermission notes passed to me from women who would say that until hearing that [the 'baby man' speech] they had not understood that they were abused. . . . In hearing it they understood that they had been."[78] *Electra Speaks* shared with *Raped* the use of performance as a public opportunity for women to testify to their violent experiences, although in different ways, adding another layer of women's experiences to the performance. Rape, in AFOM's production, moved from an individual experience hidden in shame to a political act of terrorism to be shared and denounced. The new definition bonded women together, as Phyllis Jane Rose, artistic director, testifies, and made rape a male political strategy of control rather than a private tragedy.

Spiderwoman Theater's (1975, New York) first two plays were about violence and anger. The topic resonated strongly and it was through feminism that Muriel Miguel discovered her anger and her anger led her to examine Native American issues through her feminism.

I said to myself I better start looking at this more as a woman because I have all this rage and all this anger. If I stay in the movement I'm going to be killed or at least beat up, I was *so* angry. I was so angry that if a man looked at me on the street

165

Figure 7 Women's Experimental Theater's *Electra Speaks* (1980) by Clare Coss, Sondra Segal, and Roberta Sklar, with Segal as Electra

I was ready to walk up one side and down the other. I was just beside myself.[79]

When Miguel got a grant from New York State she decided that Spiderwoman Theater would use the money to create a play about violence. The show explored "violence against women, violence between women, and the violence we're led to inflict on ourselves."[80] For the women of Spiderwoman the issue of violence was not as clear cut as it was for many other theater groups because for them violence was produced through the intersection of white supremacy and male dominance. As their flyer put it:

> Throughout history women have absorbed the horror of wars, street violence, domestic brutality, and personal intimidation. Hence we ourselves have become part of the violence and have been denied a constructive outlet for expressing our horror. We use our stories to create drama which offers support for women involved in the struggle against violence.[81]

As Native Americans their peoples had been subjected to a brutal genocide and as women they had witnessed rape and battery.

The show, *Women in Violence* (1976), was a raw, angry work that found women complicit, to a certain degree, with the violence in their lives. The complicity charged by Spiderwoman was not similar to the one levied by the mainstream; Spiderwoman never said women deserved or wanted to be beaten, nor did they say that women brought such treatment upon themselves. What they did say was that women often perpetuated violence. Spiderwoman was wary of the feminist movement seeing feminism as more responsive to the concerns of white women than to those of women of color. White women, as far as many women of color were concerned, were not entirely to be trusted. As Paula Giddings wrote in 1984, for example, white women were often full partners in the violent attacks on civil rights workers in the south.[82]

Spiderwoman tackled violence differently from other feminist theater groups. *Women in Violence* juxtaposed "slapstick and pornographic comedy" with "the violence of our stories."[83] During the creation/story telling process the group focused in on their "personal clowns." Muriel Miguel describes her clown as coming from deep within her, connected to her strategies for coping with the world.

> I already knew what my clown was, I already knew that I was a trickster. I already knew how I took absurdity and turned it around to laughter, how I would take something that was really bad and keep pushing it and pushing it till it got absurd. I knew I did this. I knew that it was a mechanism that I took to protect myself from the world. We explored that and all of us came up with different clowns, it was amazing. I was a lion; gold in my hair, this mustache, these whiskers, and I had a long tail. One of the things I would say was "I didn't say it, my tail said it."[84]

Lisa Mayo played the perfect woman in white face with blue eyes, blonde ringlets and the silhouette of the perfect woman in a long black dress. "At the end she took everything off and was in a beige leotard outfit. People were absolutely shocked."[85] The other two women in the show, Lois Weaver and Pam Verge, were a bag lady and radical nun.

In 1975 Spiderwoman Theater presented *Women in Violence* as a work in progress to theater friends in New York, mostly women from the Open Theater, including Joyce Aaron. The audience was extremely supportive and encouraged the company to continue to work on the piece. Aaron felt that the piece lacked a beat or connective tissue.[86] To give the play the drive Aaron felt was missing Spiderwoman added a series of violent racist jokes.

> We would build them. . . . It started with "Why do Puerto Ricans wear pointy shoes? To kill cockroaches in corners." "How can you tell an Arab at the airport? He's feeding bread to the plane." Finally as the audience was still laughing the performers would deliver the final blow: "What's the difference between a Jew and a pizza? The pizza doesn't scream when you put it in the oven." We kept smiling, it got worse, we slaughtered them.[87]

Miguel recalls that some people would miss the connections made in the piece among violence, humor and racism. One prominent white woman in theater told Miguel not to use a Jewish joke at the climax. When Miguel asked what they should use, the woman replied, "a Polish joke." Miguel added, "It just proved our point."[88]

Spiderwoman's second play also dealt with violence but it used the text of Aristophanes' *Lysistrata* as the starting point, over which they laid their own stories, comedy, and music. The result, *Lysistrata Numbah* (1977), used the classical tale of women's refusal to have sexual relations with men until the men stopped all wars to explore the themes of male domination over women and the violence against women as domesticated war. Each performer told a story of abuse: a botched abortion or a battering husband. One woman told about the public humiliation of having a rum and Coke poured over her head by an angry man. "In Spiderwoman's version [of *Lysistrata*] . . .: war is violence *per se*, it is also the violence of men towards women. The Acropolis stands for the power of the state and all power abuse."[89] On the humorous side there was a satire of Piaf's "La Vie en Rose," jokes on masturbation, cosmetics, and "touchy-feely" women's theater. The play ended with the coalition of women crumbling and a critique of the emphasis of the women's movement on consciousness-raising and discussion standing in for true change and polemical argument. In both plays the critique of violence was multi-faceted and in many ways out of step with the larger feminist movement. The work was obviously indebted to the feminist analysis of violence but the introduction of race added complications and complexities ignored in the theories and analyses solely produced by white women.

Emmatroupe (1975, New York City and named for Emma Goldman) created a mixed media piece that treated rape in a ritualized and stylized fashion. *A Girl Starts Out ... A Tragedy in Four Parts: virgin joy, rape, attempted suicide, decision to abort* (1978) is a mythic/archetypal telling of a girl's transition to womanhood. It blended dance, visual and symbolic imagery, music, and a written text adapted from Andrea Dworkin's *Our Blood: Prophecies and Discourses on Sexual Politics* and George Eliot's *Felix Holt*. In *A Girl Starts Out* rape became less an institutional control of women and their bodies, more a rite of passage, an inevitability in all male–female relations. According to Eleanor Johnson, one of the founders of Emmatroupe, the intention of the piece was to create

a new expressionism voiced through language, image symbol, myth, and story. The scenario is one of female persecution, but its mode steps outside the pornographic: the female character is victimized as women in life are victimized, but the actor's body is not sexualized for a male viewer and rape is never sentimentalized, *romanticized*, or glorified.[90]

Unfortunately, Johnson does not go on to describe how Emmatroupe accomplished this through their staging choices and Ruth Wolff's discussion of the production in her positive *Ms.* review is equally unhelpful although she does note that no men appear onstage and that the style of the production is "mythic, "archetypal," and "far less verbal" (than other performances she had seen that dealt with the subject).[91] Erika Munk, who did not like the production, wrote about the performance style:

The main character – "conceived and acted" by Michele Manenti – mimes the story, with the help of figures who are sometimes "witnesses," sometimes musicians, puppeteers, and chorus. The first scene is typical. A hooded figure beats a drum, women in grey and black bear masks dangling from a pole, and red cloth is slowly pulled off a crumpled figure who rises to perform "madness." Her movements are at once abstract and sentimental; the dancer begs, *insists*, that we not only sense but share her sufferings.[92]

Emmatroupe's concern with the portrayal of the act of rape is an important one. Placing rape on stage was a chancy proposition and, in representing it, it was possible to make it pornographically erotic. Many groups such as Circle of a Witch chose to formalize, so that what is on stage are the ideas behind rape rather than the act itself, or else to let someone stand in for the woman, as in AFOM's *Raped* in which the Coolie's murder represents the violent act of rape. Whatever solution a particular group chose there was always awareness of the difficulties of representing rape and violence. *A Girl Starts Out* shares with *Raped* and *Sexpot Follies* a construction of violence and rape as enduring, immutable, and unavoidable.

Rather than approach the subject of violence against women through rape, Rhode Island Feminist Theater (RIFT, 1973, Providence) developed a play on the subject of battered wives. When RIFT created *Internal Injury* in 1978 it was one of the first feminist theaters to deal with the topic. The play is fairly realistic and follows the narratives of three white women, played by Barbara Conley, Sherilyn Brown, and Carol M. Sullivan, in monologue, duologue, and chorus. Helen is middle-class and middle-aged with a daughter and has been beaten for years. After much soul-searching she finally leaves her husband. Peg, young, pregnant, and working-class also leaves her husband, only to return. At the end of the play it is learned that she has died due to "injuries from falling downstairs."[93] The third woman is Josephine, a young artist who marries her abusive boyfriend and gives up her art for him. The play was created collectively after four months' research with battered women, and on the books and articles about them.[94]

Internal Injury attempts to understand why battered women behave the way they do and why, most importantly, they do not simply leave, aside from the material reasons such as lack of money or the dearth of available shelters and ignorance of social services and legal systems. At one point all three characters ritually chant three lines taken from *Battered Women*: "The more he beats me, the sicker he is: The sicker he is the more he needs me: The more he needs me, the more I love him."[95] The feminist focus on women's actions and survival strategies was intended to encourage bonding among women, especially between battered women and women who have never experienced this kind of violence. According to Julie Landsman, *Internal Injury* starts from the powerful abuse of violence against women and then

> skillfully moves on to envelop themes within the thought patterns of women understood and felt by all women, as well as battered wives. The play becomes, then, as penetrating to all women as it is to those whose lives are being carefully enacted onstage.[96]

According to the director, Joanna Miller, "we are trying to reach people not alienate them."[97] The reaction Landsman describes was crafted by RIFT neither to castigate women nor to blame all abuse on the dynamics of heterosexuality. Like Emmatroupe, RIFT was very concerned with the glamorization of violence. Violence was never graphically or realistically enacted onstage, instead women "are beaten by unseen assailants who draw no blood."[98] Despite the concentration on the different issue, battery rather than rape, the emphasis remained the same – all women were at risk from the experience of violence and they were as oppressed by the threat as by the act.

In 1979 It's Just a Stage (IJAS, 1974, San Francisco) changed its name from It's Just a Stage: A Lesbian Theater to It's Just a Stage: A Woman's Theater.[99] With the new name the group created *The Mountain is Stirring* (1980) about violence against women. The change radically altered the demographics of IJAS' audiences. The issue of violence against women, particularly battery, was, at that point, perceived as a straight woman's issue and Iris Landsberg believes that the audiences were almost entirely heterosexual.[100]

Departing from their usual cabaret/revue style, the piece alternated a traditional play with non-verbal physical theater using slides, masks, mime, and original music.[101] The narrative part of the show concerned Elaine, a waitress, battered by her husband. Elaine vacillates between staying with her husband because of the physical threat, her fear of being alone, and her desire to leave the brutal abuse behind. Through the help and support of her friend, Ruth, Elaine is able to leave her husband and create a new life. Juxtaposed with the realistic story line were scenes of physical theater staged by Iris Landsberg. At one point she performed a "masked bound woman struggl[ing] to free herself from her bonds."[102] Landsberg commented on this scene that IJAS, because they expected people to be more affected by the realistic narrative, were surprised that it was the physical theater that "tore people up."[103] The group also used the play as consciousness-raising and a source of information. In post-show discussions IJAS brought in speakers from various women's organizations to explore the issues raised by the play.[104]

Some groups extended their communal involvement into the local Take Back the Night Marches. For three years, from 1979 to 1981, the Theater of Light and Shadow (TLS, 1977) in New Haven performed poems and short plays on the town green at the culmination of the marches.[105] They also explored the issue of violence in their own venue. TLS' last production was staged in the winter of 1983, *The Women Here Are No Different* by Nancy Beckett. The play explored life in a shelter for battered women. Despite the popularity of the show and the resulting requests to perform it for a number of area community groups, TLS could not pursue these opportunities to broaden the play's audience because the group itself was beginning to unravel. By August of the same year TLS would be defunct.[106] TLS' experience with *The Women Here Are No Different* recalls those of At the Foot of the Mountain and It's Just A Stage in that all three groups found that plays about violence against women resonated strongly for communities of women suffering and working against abuse. These plays had enormous potential to be seen by people other than those who regularly attended their theaters.

One group, Living Lessons Inc., founded much later than most of the groups examined here, began specifically to address the issue of violence. Angela Lockhart, an African–American woman who had once been in an abusive relationship, wrote a play drawn from her own experiences and those of her multi-racial cast, all battered women without professional theater experience. First presented in October of 1990, *Please Listen to Me* was originally produced for "a conference held in observation of National Domestic Violence Month. Since then she and her theater company . . . have staged it for social workers, probation officers, and United Nations delegates."[107] The play served to empower both the performers (as one said: "*I feel if you are all letting me tell everyone, then what happened to me must have been wrong,*") and the audiences; Rubin comments that after "one performance two women came up to an actor, admitted they were being abused and asked her where they could get help."[108] While this play is ten years later than the plays of the majority of the feminist theater groups discussed here it is obvious that *Please Listen to Me* uses many of the same strategies and critiques that groups had in the 1970s and 1980s.

Another legacy, however indirect, are the rape plays specifically written to be performed on college campuses to raise students' consciousnesses about the issues around violence. One such play, *Until Someone Wakes Up* (1992), was created by Carolyn Levy and twenty-one of her students at Macalester College in Minneapolis.

Levy had been the artistic director of the Women's Theater Project in the Twin Cities from 1980 to 1988. The mission of the organization was to "[produce] new plays by women about issues of importance to women and [bring] those plays out into the community in the Twin Cities and beyond."[109] The processes at the Project had been collaborative and Levy wanted her students to experience this mode of creation. While searching for a topic to work on with the students Levy read Robin Warshaw's *I Never Called It Rape* about date rape. The book galvanized Levy.

> I . . . learned that one in four college women has been or will be the victim of rape or attempted rape. . . . But I read on and learned that women are not alone in being victims: men are raped, too. I found that if I looked hard at the society and culture in which we are living, if I really examined forces at work on our students as they grow up, then the rape statistics were not a surprise.[110]

From this point Levy worked with a variety of students in diverse situations; workshops, classes, interview sessions with rape "survivors", counselors, and shelter workers, as well as other forms of community research, in order to cull a script from the personal experiences of everyone involved.[111]

Ultimately the show was produced with a cast of eight and was always billed as a work-in-progress, allowing them the freedom to make changes during the run of the show. *Until Someone Wakes Up* performed first on the Macalester campus and then toured the state. Like many of the plays discussed earlier, the date rape play utilized humor to bring out the anger and inequities of the situation. One scene presented an incongruous juxtaposition, placing the rhetoric around date rape ("what did she expect, she went out with him") within an unexpected scenario, the restaurant.

173

WAITER: Would you like some coffee?

WOMAN: Yes, please.

WAITER: Just say when. (*Starts to pour.*)

WOMAN: There. (*He keeps pouring.*) That's fine. (*He pours.*)
Stop! (*She grabs the pot; there is coffee everywhere.*) What
are you doing? I said *stop*.

WAITER: Yes, ma'am.

WOMAN: Well, why didn't you stop pouring?

WAITER: Oh, I wasn't sure you meant it.

WOMAN: Look, of course I meant it! I have coffee all over my lap!
You nearly burned me!

WAITER: Forgive me, ma'am, but you certainly looked thirsty. I
thought you wanted more.

WOMAN: But –

WAITER: And you must admit, you did let me *start* to pour.

WOMAN: Well, of course I did. I wanted some coffee.

WAITER: See, there you go. A perfectly honest mistake.[112]

The audiences were very moved by the play, often using the
resources presented during the play and in post-show discussions to
get help for themselves.

Another such play is a short script that Anne Davis Basting
created for the University of Minnesota, which depends on audience involvement and serves as education on the issue of date rape.
The play consists of two scenes, the first presenting a situation in
which the "rape is the result of alcohol or drug use, mixed
messages, and misunderstandings on the part of both participants."[113] The second scene is played after intense discussion on the
part of the audience, cast (still in character), and counselors who
are present to provide expert opinions or to redirect information
or comments from the characters. The second scene is a revision
of the first in which the mistakes and miscommunications of the
first are clarified and eliminated. "Judging from the feedback
during and after the performances, the form has proved extremely
effective for raising awareness of the potential for acquaintance
rape, ways to avoid it, and steps to take if a student has experienced
sexual violence."[114] Both these plays emphasize the pervasiveness
of date rape and both work to empower the audiences to identify,
avoid, and deal with it.

Violence was a vital subject for feminists and this is evident from
the work in feminist theater. Four of the groups discussed here

began their theaters with plays about violence and many plays not directly about violence contained scenes that grappled with the subject. For example, *Persephone's Return*, discussed in the previous chapter, was primarily about the mother/daughter bond but contained a rape scene that supported the contention that the patriarchy had supplanted the matriarchy in a variety of ways, one of which was through physical violence. Theodore Shank asserts that "violence in relation to women has been the single most important subject of women's plays in the second half of the seventies."[115] The inference here is that women's theaters were more concerned with their negative experiences under the patriarchy than their positive experiences in the feminist community. The emphasis shifts from placing feminist experience in the center, to re-centering patriarchal experience as normative. However, I think it has been demonstrated that while explorations of violence were crucial and a frequent starting place, they were not intended to be the culmination of all feminist theater work, or the entirety of their legacy.

Whether or not individuals onstage or in the audience had experienced physical violence or abuse first-hand was not the issue. The central concern and focus was that all women shared the potential for that experience. In this case it was unlike mother/ daughter plays in which seeing the experience staged was central, although for some women seeing the representation of rape and its issues was empowering, instead, what was important was the emphasis on the potential for that experience – that all women in society were at-risk and none of them could escape the consequences of being at-risk. Attitudes commonly held at the time asserted that if a woman experienced the violence of that act she would be held responsible as the initiator. The doubled threat of violence and culpability bound women in common cause. However, to some extent, that attitude no longer exists. While there is a great deal of work to be done in the area, women are no longer as strongly held to be responsible for the violence directed at them. This shift is entirely due to the labor of feminists, and theaters played a role in that change.

The plays placed the responsibility for violence against women on the society that overtly and tacitly approved such actions as useful methods for oppressing women. While the dramatic approaches could be critiqued for biological determinism or a monolithic point of view, they could also be understood as producing a systemic critique of rape and violence as strategies of oppression. While there has been a great deal of change during the twenty years of plays discussed here, many of the ideas and methods have remained constant.

6

THE COMMUNITY
AS AUDIENCE

Distrusting traditional theater practices that sought to divide performance from audience, house from stage, feminist theater creators and performers looked for ways to emphasize the similarities and blur the distinctions between audience and performer. Patriarchal culture was believed to operate divisively, separating women from women and teaching them to distrust their own experiences and impressions. Feminist theaters, working within the context of the specifically feminist community, intended to counteract that effect by bringing women together to celebrate or validate their experiences and impressions. To achieve this experience, performers and audiences had to abandon previous models of theater dynamics for new ones they would create through feminist performance. Roberta Sklar and Sondra Segal described the unique relationship of feminist performer and audience as a mutual and ongoing struggle. "Performer and audience member became partners in a process that moved towards change on both sides of the performing line."[1] Conceptualizing performance as a process requiring performers and audiences to work together radically altered the dynamics of the event and was part of the project to represent the experiences of the feminist community.

The inclusion of the audience in the performative event was not exclusive to feminist theater. In the 1960s and 1970s experimental theater, beginning with the Living Theater, had advanced on the audience, addressing it directly and often inviting the spectators to participate.[2] Sally Banes describes the New York experimental theater scene: "the stages were so small that the play literally spilled into the audience. At Judson Church . . . the action . . . often took up more of the space than the spectators did."[3] Harry J. Elam, Jr. noted in a 1986 *Theater Journal* article that the acknowledgement of the audience, and that audience's links with the performers, were important tenets of the revolutionary Chicano and African–American theaters of the 1960s. Concentrating on El Teatro Campesino's *Quinta Temporada* and LeRoi Jones' *Slave Ship*, Elam demonstrates that both plays worked in performance to remind the audiences of a mutual commitment to a revolutionary struggle for change.[4] While the oppression against which feminist theaters and radical theaters of color were struggling was often very different and only analogous in a limited sense, these examples do demonstrate that there was, throughout theater committed to social and political change, a discarding of fourth wall boundaries for a redefined audience/performer relationship based on blurred distinctions between the two previously separate groups. For feminist theaters, the melding of audience and performer came from a feminist belief in bonding women into a community to resist the divisive patriarchy. The emphasis was thus on ideas held in common by a larger group that included both audience and performer. When Susan Suntree described the rehearsal and performance processes of the Women's Ensemble of the Berkeley Stage Company (winter 1975–76), for example, she stressed this very bond as a goal of the performance. The audience was not an abstract concept or a group of people added to the end of the process, but an indispensable and omnipresent element of creation. In rehearsal for *Antigone Prism* the performers' role as audience to one another was emphasized as similar to the actual audience in performance. "We never lost sight of our desire to communicate to an audience in performance, the audience was always there."[5] Similarly, the ensemble adopted performance strategies that would achieve the same results. The performers entered through the audience, socializing before the performance began. The actual performance occurred in a long playing space resembling a corridor with audience arranged on two sides. This way the spectators saw not only the performance, but each other, continually reminded of the presence and participation of a large group of women. After each performance the performers served wine and cheese to the spectators requesting comments and impressions from them.[6] The Women's Ensemble operated within a system that worked to de-emphasize difference and distance and to emphasize identification and proximity.

Antigone Prism was based on the performers' personal relationship to the Greek myth of Antigone, concentrating on Antigone's courage and her "belief in her own values and experiences."[7] The emphasis was on a ritual of self-recreation. Each woman was expected to reach inside herself to create herself anew from her own life experiences. *Antigone Prism* is also typical of the common emphasis on Greek myths and drama in feminist theaters. Sondra Segal, when asked why WET had turned to Greek myth for their play about family, said it was because it was the Greeks who were the basis for Western culture.[8] Rosemary Curb cites five theaters that turned to ancient Greece for their inspiration between 1977 and 1979.[9] The move was also authenticating, to legitimize the feminist community through the reproduction of the foundations of patriarchal culture. Simultaneously, it also served to reclaim for women the myths used to found and legitimize the patriarchy.[10]

The valorization of ritual in the Women's Ensemble was typical of many feminist theater groups as a method through which to connect audience and performer. *Antigone Prism* is an example of one kind of inclusion, a passive reminder to the audience through visual means that they are part of the larger community of women. Another aspect of ritual was the active involvement of audience in the performance process either through question and response, contribution of stories, or as focal point of dance and movement. It's All Right to Be Woman Theater (IARTBW, 1969) set aside one part of every performance to enact "Dream Plays." Audience members were encouraged to come forward and share their dreams. As the individual related her dream (men's dreams were never dramatized) the performers would mime it onstage. The group would first portray one of their own dreams to encourage the audience to participate. This exchange was based on the belief that "what happens to us or what we feel or dream is important enough to share with each other and with other women, that is, in fact, the most important thing we have to share."[11] IARTBW, similarly to the Women's Ensemble, performed their work in a circle made by the audience.[12] The circle was intended to draw the audience together in a feeling of communality.

As Susan Bennett noted in her book on the audience: "The spectator comes to the theater as a member of an already constituted interpretive community and also brings a horizon of expectations shaped by the pre-performance elements."[13] It is generally accepted by feminist theater scholars and practitioners that the audience assumed by traditional theater is, as Roberta Sklar told Charlotte Rea, "a male-oriented theater."[14] Jill Dolan would later call the white, middle-class, heterosexual male audience member the "ideal

. . . spectator."[15] Feminist theater endeavored to replace that ideal with a female spectator. As has already been documented this intent radically altered the material of performance. But it also altered the composition of the audience; the theaters not only replaced the male spectator with the female in a theoretical sense, but often barred him from attending performances, replacing him in a literal sense as well.

Women's Experimental Theater (WET, 1977, New York) was very invested in the critique of the relationship between the feminist theater audience and performer. They preferred, whenever possible, to perform for an all-female audience because it afforded possibilities not available in the mixed gender group. As the women in WET wrote: "An all-woman audience has the space for unfettered response, and it can take off in celebration of itself. And it does. This is one of the great rewards of creating and performing women's theater."[16] Clare Coss said that Sunday nights were reserved for women only; if a man came to the show he was given a ticket for another performance.[17] The presence of men, WET believed, gave rise to what they called the "Worried-Woman Syndrome."[18] Excluding men meant that the women in the audience would not be concerned with the men's reactions and therefore could have a fuller experience. "It was very freeing for people not to have to be worried about what anyone else thought."[19] The most influential factor affecting the production choices WET made was the all-woman audience. They believed that men would probably not be able to understand the performance because of its all-woman orientation and that their negative reactions would adversely influence women's reactions.

Twila Thompson, a member of Women's Collage Theater (1976, New York), said her group also preferred all-women audiences believing that women would be more concerned with what the men thought than what they themselves felt.[20] The group did not usually have the option to exclude men from the audience as the majority of their performances were on tour, so Women's Collage separated their audience into gender-specific groups. They preferred theater-in-the-round or a three-quarters arena, dividing the audience into four groups; women, men, women, men. The two performers acknowledged the divisions in performance by using the male sections as the male characters. This allowed them to gauge the different responses of men and women to the show. Thompson said that it was rare for the men to comment either negatively or positively about the seating

Figure 8 Women's Collage Theater's *Sirens* (1976) with Barbara Tholfsen (left) and Twila Thompson (and puppets)

but that women "were worried that men would be offended."[21] Some of the post-show discussions ended up being entirely about the seating arrangements.[22] Alive and Trucking Theater (A&TT, 1971) in Minneapolis also separated audiences by gender "and were amazed to hear the different reactions to scenes."[23] The group believed that the separation furthered the consciousness-raising possibilities of the play.

Performance was not the totality of the feminist theater event, it was more than what occurred between when the lights dimmed and the audience applauded. Instead, it began with the research in the community, continued with performance, was further developed in post-show discussions, and was extended by workshops with the audience. The previous chapters examined moments of performance concentrating on their positioning within the feminist community and through representative topics, such as the mother and daughter bond and violence against women. This chapter delves into other elements surrounding that event: research within the community, the devices employed by the theater to define their audience, audience reactions, post-show discussions, and workshops.

WORKING WITH THE AUDIENCE

This section concentrates on the ways in which theaters initiated contact with their audiences other than in the actual moment of performance. Some companies researched their topics with actual women and offered to teach the women the skills they had learned because they felt it was incumbent upon them to do so. This pooling of resources, extrapolating rather than interpolating their material from the community, occurred because theater companies wished to strengthen and emphasize their participation in feminism and in notions of feminist communities.

Before the members of the community were constituted as audience, theaters generating their own material usually conducted a period of research around the play topic. The practice of researching for performance by using women as the primary source, both company members and women outside the theater, was based on the feminist belief that women were the best resources for information on women. Cultural myths, books, and accepted wisdom about women were viewed with suspicion and thus the only potentially accurate research materials available were the women themselves. Empirical evidence was believed to guarantee authenticity when feminist theaters could cite women as their primary sources. The Women's Experimental Theater wrote that *The Daughters Cycle Trilogy* was "developed with the research participation of over two hundred women."[24] In the hierarchy of authoritative sources of information, the testimony of women was considered superior to the books, articles, and traditional ideas about women. This attitude, obviously shaped to some extent by consciousness-raising, privileged autobiography over biography thus encouraging women, audience and theater members to interpret their own lives as meaningful and remarkable. The books Phyllis Mael cited in "The Catalog of Feminist Theater" as influential on feminist theater were being published as feminist theaters were producing, so that the theaters, while benefiting from the growing body of work by women, were also part of the production of that work.[25] The huge volume of feminist books, articles, and research that apply feminist theory to a wide range of topics and disciplines, and indeed feminist theory itself, emerged contemporaneously with feminist theater. With the absence of feminist published material it was inevitable that feminist theaters turned to first-hand experience as a way to create performance. Even when more feminist material became available, Adrienne

Rich's 1976 book on motherhood for example, it was still important to gather testimonies of actual women. Gradually, however, by the mid- to late 1980s published material began to replace first-hand research with women. Witness Carolyn Levy, discussed in chapter five, who was inspired in the early 1990s to do a play about date rape after reading Robin Warshaw's *I Never Called It Rape*. Obviously there were new possibilities once a body of feminist work was readily available.

The Daughters Cycle Trilogy was shaped through research with potential audience members from the women's community. WET told *Ms.* that "we set up workshops of women with exercises that would evoke the sister connection in the family. Then we gathered the data: images, lines, questions."[26] One exercise, used continuously throughout the information gathering on all the plays of the trilogy, seated the participants around a table as if at a family dinner. One woman would sculpt the bodies at the table into positions and then each participant would have to speak from that position.[27] From the women, from the potential audience, came the play itself; the material to be dramatized and the understandings of family relationships for women.

In 1977 when AFOM started to develop *The Story of A Mother*, they drew on each other for their information but saw it as incomplete, awaiting the contributions of the audience. One company member wrote in the newsletter at the time:

> We are working to do this [explore the mother/daughter relationship] through a dramatized ritual event, a journey of sorts on which you as an audience member will be invited to come witness your own relationship to your own mothers and daughters. . . . As we work on this drama every day, we discover more about it and witness it emerge as a healing ritual event. In January and February we will take parts of it to groups in the community who perhaps have no experience in theater, but who will bring their own life-experiences to the piece and respond accordingly. Thus we hope to create *The Story of A Mother* in concert with the community, tapping the shared feelings of all mothers, daughters, and families around this central bond.[28]

It is clear that the theater envisioned the piece from the start as something that came out of, rather than into, the community. Perhaps part of the intention or role of *The Story of A Mother* was to participate in the formation of a community, a community identified through feminist notions of the mother/daughter bond.

At the Foot of the Mountain received two grants to develop *The Story of a Mother*, one from the National Endowments of the Arts (their first NEA grant) and a second from the Humanities Commission. The Humanities grant stipulated that AFOM tour the play to community groups. Deciding to fulfill that requirement a little differently than the Commission had intended, they took it as a work-in-progress to parents' and senior citizens' groups. While these were not specifically feminist communities AFOM were especially interested in the opinions of the older women whose experiences would probably not be available elsewhere. Post-show discussions were used to change and further refine the piece. Not only did this practice give AFOM access to information they might not have had and give them first-hand accounts of motherhood to ensure authenticity, it also strengthened their bonds with different communities, giving those communities a stake in the production of *The Story of A Mother*. The company's play became the audience's play as well.

Another, more practical, reason why groups turned to women's testimonies was that there was little published material to consult. By the mid-1970s the works of many influential feminist authors, such as Kate Millet, Shulamith Firestone, Mary Daly, Nancy Chodorow, or Helen Dinerstein, were or soon would be available, but these works tended to be analytical and theoretical providing frameworks for practitioners and spectators rather than personal narratives and first-hand testimonies. The Rhode Island Feminist Theater's (RIFT, 1973, Providence) work on violence against women is an excellent example. Information by women about women was just beginning to be widely available as feminist theater groups were established. When RIFT developed their play *Internal Injury* in 1978 there was little material available on the subject of battered wives. While they read what was published they also used "real stories"[29] of battered women or, as another review put it, "personal contact with Rhode Island battered wives."[30]

Privileging interactions with women who had lived experience with the topic under consideration often brought theaters into contact with facets of the feminist community previously unknown to them. Just as AFOM's *The Story of a Mother* involved the theater with senior citizens and parents who they might not otherwise have met, members of RIFT became involved in the politics of battered women. One woman from RIFT volunteered at Sojourner House, a Providence shelter for battered women, while another took a counselor training course. Had they not collaborated to create the play they might never have focused on the issue personally.[31]

Audiences and theater members also met formally outside performance in workshops designed to share knowledge and skills. These were considered as much a part of feminist theater as the performance or the post-show discussion. As a body of feminist work and knowledge emerged, feminist theater practitioners felt compelled to share the knowledge. Through workshops, women, long denied training in many practical skills traditionally identified as male, could share with one another their acquired information. The sharing made it clear that ability could be taught and was representative of the attitude that the women performing were not intrinsically better or more talented than the women in the audience but possessed more information. RIFT was one theater that emphasized workshops as a place for the audience and the theater group to meet as equals in feminism but with unequal information. "Workshop sessions and discussions are integral parts of RIFT's work as it seeks to further break down the barriers between audience and performers."[32] Unlike the workshops of the Women's Experimental Theater, these were not specifically designed to elicit information as the potential basis for a play. Instead, they were places for RIFT to offer its training to the community. Imagining equal knowledge and skills on both sides of the performing line made it possible to imagine a new relationship of performer and audience. The hope was that the perception of each group by the other would be based less on mystification and lack of information and more on a desire to serve and speak out on topics of mutual interest and experience.

Members of Circle of the Witch (1973) in Minneapolis, in a summary of their own history and goals, wrote that they understood "theater's purpose not just as entertainment, but also education and challenge, not just in the traditional one-dimensional sense: the flow goes both ways between audience and performers."[33] While workshops were a natural way to extend the "flow" beyond the confines of performance, as the Washington Area Feminist Theater (WAFT, 1972) found, they were also an excellent way to reach out into the community to recruit new members. One workshop early in the group's existence was intended to provide women with training in technical theater but finished up as a seminar in scenography because two participants were interested in designing. The two women ended up designing and building the sets for the next three WAFT productions.[34] Alive and Trucking Theater also recruited members through workshops. "[W]e held weekly workshops open to the public, as a way of working with people who were interested in the group."[35] Finding members through the audience helped ensure that the new members shared a political orientation and investment in feminism with the theater.

Workshops and research moved beyond the simple sharing of practical skills, however. They were also a venue for continuing the work of the performance, giving practical strategies for achieving, or beginning to achieve, the changes and attitudes encouraged in the play. Orange County Feminist Theater (no founding date) had a variety of workshops on "sex-role conditioning, women's health, language, dating, alienation."[36] Calliope Feminist Theater (no founding date) in Hartford, Connecticut offered "theater games in order to provide women with an understanding of the creative process, and to help them 'develop their own senses of creativity.'"[37] It's All Right To Be Woman Theater had a workshop on "physical consciousness-raising for women" as well as one on self-defence.[38] Cutting Edge taught "improvisation, piece construction, and movement as well as masks and a workshop exploring the relationships of insides and outsides called 'Women and Facade.'"[39] Spiderwoman Theater has a workshop they usually offer while on tour on their storyweaving technique in which they share physical exercises to put women in control of their bodies and techniques for turning life stories into theater. Arrangements to take the workshop are usually made by the host venue. Women are asked to tell stories from their lives and the members of Spiderwoman Theater gradually move participants from telling their individual stories to working together to enact stories emerging from the group. Key phrases from the stories, rather than the plots, are emphasized, in order to convey the experience of the story and its place in the teller's life and not merely the sequence of events. To this physical gestures are added and the group eventually works together to realize a single story, which by that time has been transformed into a collective one.[40]

Despite the careful choice of material and the conscious definition of audience, theaters could not control their audience's reactions, nor could they always agree with them. Theaters were committed to listening to their audiences but they could sometimes disagree with what they had to say.

THE AUDIENCE AS CREATOR/THE AUDIENCE AS CRITIC

I leave here with knots in my stomach and a glow throughout my body. You broke down so many defenses; the arguments you provoked I have spouted and thought so many times: the split you develop I feel in every day life. It is a comfort to know that others fight this way always, and that, yes, it hurts. Yet it is so nice to know that there are others who desire a similar kind of world and who manage to fight, go crazy, and still keep on. Thank you so much.

(Women's Collage Theater Comment Book)[41]

No one would deny that the experience of witnessing feminist theater was a profoundly affecting one. For women who were struggling to articulate their own feminism or to fight against the oppression that had been, until then, an unnamed and unarticulated part of their lives, the chance to see that struggle represented and then to hear other women testify to the resonance of that struggle was very powerful. They were often incoherent in their gratitude to the theater. If they felt that the experience had been misrepresented or wrongly construed, they could be incoherent in their anger. For many of the women already involved in theater the first experience in the audience forced them to re-evaluate their involvement in experimental or other non-feminist theaters, sometimes leading them to found feminist theaters of their own.

Roberta Sklar, Clare Coss, and Karen Malpede all described the importance of It's All Right To Be Woman Theater for their work. Phyllis Jane Rose resigned her position as head of the directing program at Southern Illinois State University to work with At The Foot of the Mountain because she realized that she could best combat oppression by leaving the institutions that were perpetuating that oppression.

River Journal crystallized for me the lesson of experience: that women and men habitually relate hierarchically. . . . Here I was chairing the directing program in the theater department of a large university and I caught myself daily, hourly, wearing these masks [of the seductress or the mother]. . . . After

187

directing *River Journal* I chose to quit my job. It seemed hypocritical to spend energy to avoid the traps of these masks when I could participate in their destruction. I moved to Minneapolis to work with At the Foot of the Mountain and helped to transform it into the feminist theater collective it is now – passionate, struggling, angry, joyous, questioning.[42]

Ritually envisioned political ideas brought Rose to make a commitment to feminist theater, a commitment that grew from politics and ideas she felt were explicated powerfully and uniquely by feminist theater.

For feminist theater practitioners who could not point to a particular theater group or moment of realization, there was still a need to perform feminist theater. Michele Linfante said: "I couldn't deny that women's theater needed to be done and something about it lured me strongly."[43] The pull Linfante described was connected to the way performers felt welcomed by the audience as they presented their work. Necessity was generated by an audience that, as Joan Mankin describes it, "was pulling it right out of you. The women in the audience especially wanted to hear it so much, it was so important. They were listening to every word and catching everything you said."[44] All the feminist theater performers remember enthusiastically the experience of performing. The excitement and interest in the house generated similar emotions and investment onstage.

Feminist theaters did not perceive themselves as theater based on a model of seduction or mystification. The theaters did not perceive their audiences as unwilling masses to be led or ignorant pupils awaiting instruction. Rather, feminist theater was based on the premise of providing relief, solidarity, and strength to women engaged in the daily struggle against oppression. Writing on the nontraditional theater that came into being during and after the 1960s, Susan Bennett commented: "Many of these emergent theaters have self-consciously sought the centrality of the spectator as the subject of the drama, but as a subject who can think and act."[45] The relief that feminist theater provided for its audiences came through the support it gave them. One woman wrote in the Comment Book of the Woman's Collage Theater:

Thanks for the show. . . . Although I'm a feminist it is good to hear that other women have the same feelings, have the same thoughts, go through the same anger and hopeless conclusions. I hope I can affect people the way you do.[46]

This was perhaps the most common reaction both recorded in the Comment Book and remembered by the practitioners, a sense of gratitude at having individual perceptions reinforced and validated. The knowledge that individual and isolated contact with oppression and sexism was not a personal but a political experience appropriate for public discussion reaffirmed what women had experienced first-hand.

Testifying to the importance of post-show discussions, one woman wrote that the

conversation at the end allows me to reorient, re-group, say what's going on and then hear other people's places, states, feelings and try on their points of view and come back with what feels original within me.[47]

These discussions took advantage of the live aspect of theater. The ideas generated by the performance could be discussed and developed by continued contact with the performers. The immediacy of performance was continued; the live, performing bodies joined the live audience and participated in live discussion. The pooling of responses also allowed for change and development. When sharing occurred a new solidarity often emerged; the airing of multiple points of view demonstrated for women the mutuality of their experience. Women did not have to feel alone as they fought to resist the destructive ideas of dominant society. In this way the theater experience was not merely delight at representation but a chance to pool resources and ideas and renew commitment to the struggle.

This was certainly Anne Herbert's experience at Naomi Newman's *Snake Talk*. Herbert wrote, and then sent to Newman, an essay about what the show meant to her. She saw Newman's show seven times before she wrote her piece, and mentioned in it that she planned to see the show several more times. "*Snake Talk* and Other Planets That We Make Among Ourselves" was written not only because Anne Herbert was so affected but also because she was not the only one who felt a strong commitment to the show. "When I went to see *Snake Talk*, I felt like I had regrown an arm that I had forgotten was amputated. The missing part that came back in that room was my future."[48] The "wisdom"[49] she found in the play gave her hope for the future, her's and the planet's. The sense of renewal that Herbert took from *Snake Talk* validated her belief that there was a difference between her perceptions of the world and mainstream reality. "When I go to *Snake Talk* again the power of experience is not so much what Naomi says but that her speaking from her source clears my heart and I can hear what my source has to say – my own snake talk."[50] For Herbert, *Snake Talk* was about the wellspring she believed existed within people to protect against loneliness by providing the wisdom destroyed by life in a harsh world.

By refusing to see oppression as the idiosyncrasy of a particular individual or institution but rather as specific practice of culture and society, the possibility of change emerged. Knowing that change was possible was important but seeing it represented and dramatized could be invigorating and empowering. One woman from Seattle at a performance of the Women's Collage Theater's show, *Sirens*, wrote:

> I knew it would be good to come and it was. Thanks, it made me feel proud of women and myself – of what we've done, of what we are trying to do. The feeling of denying that their reality – "patriarchy" etc., you know what I mean – is not the only reality as they would have us believe. The power and release of seeing our own reality to the extent that we can, when we can, creating it when we can – I mean, this means something. Somehow it means something to realize that it means something and keep trying when/how we can.[51]

The moment of recognition testified to here demonstrates how significantly the experience of being part of the audience/ performance community had the potential to strengthen and empower many women. By groping for words to express her reactions to the realization that representations of women in the dominant discourses are contradicted by the experienced reality of women, this woman facilitated her ability to struggle. If she could understand her experience and see it represented then she could fight against the systems that erased it. The pride she described is part of the process of enabling and is evidence of the support feminist theater provided for women. Her reaction to *Sirens* is almost identical to Anne Herbert's to *Snake Talk*. Both women found an alternative construction of "reality" that more closely mirrored their own perceptions.

The euphoria the woman from Seattle described – her recognition that it "means something to realize that it means something" – was a reaction shared by many of the women who saw their experiences represented in a way that resonated as accurate. The identification of those lived experiences often served to foreground the extent to which those experiences had been previously missing. Many women experienced feminist theater as a transforming moment, as a near-religious feeling. Certainly this was encouraged by the use of ritual and the stress on community. The often celebratory nature of the shows themselves could move women; as one woman in the audience of the Women's Collage Theater show *Sirens* put it,

> [b]y the end of the play I had and have a very strong sense that I know you, I know your faces, I have been playing with you and screaming, singing, ripping, dancing, killing and hugging with you all my life.[52]

The long list of forceful actions testifies to the power that performance could have to affect women.

Post-show discussions provided a venue for the expression of reactions, feelings, and dialogue. Most groups believed, as the Rhode Island Feminist Theater did with *Persephone's Return*, that the "play . . . is not the entire production."[53] There was always a post-show discussion to provide an open dialogue between the audience and the performers. RIFT's talks were not meant to be informational, since background materials were provided in the program, but rather to encourage "an exchange of mutual growth and consciousness-raising."[54] The discussion groups were sometimes carefully structured into three types, male, female, and mixed. It is not clear whether or not the individual spectators could choose the group they wished to join. However, what is crucial is that even in situations where audiences did not participate directly, as they did in the open-ended rituals of *The Story of A Mother*, for example, a forum for hearing their voices was usually provided. Most groups could not imagine *not* initiating a dialogue with their audiences.

As it has been demonstrated, feminist theater could be very powerful, could often evoke strong reactions, and had the potential to change lives. But the same investment that led audience members to praise also led them to critique as well. The reactions could be just as strong when women felt that the theater had misrepresented feminism, abused their power, or not fulfilled their mission correctly. Feminist theater had endeavored to create a brand of theater that defied the more common audience/performer dynamic and in doing so found that their audiences, once included as part of the spectacle, took their involvement seriously. The Theater of Light and Shadow in New Haven (TLS, 1977) received a strongly worded letter from a loyal audience member criticizing them for presenting material she felt was demoralizing.

> Women are well aware of the pain and suffering we live with. What I would like to see is alternatives, answers, and models for new behavior. We are looking for and need information on how to change our lives for the better. At least we need positive celebration of those parts of our lives that are good.[55]

Not only did she find the production wanting in terms of its specific content but also in the way it reflected the overall mission of the theater. TLS had failed to adhere to the more common practice of presenting material that relentlessly focussed on the lighter side of women's experience. The letter ended: "Feminist women's culture, as much as possible, must educate, energize, and entertain. I am sorry to say none of these things happened for me through your performance."[56] Two of the theater's members, Debra Flynn and Nancy Lee Kathan, responded to the letter seriously, trying to explain their position. The criticized plays had been presented as consciousness-raising for women not already committed to feminist theater, by "dealing with life in a way many of us (already converted feminists) have consigned to the past."[57] There was nothing unusual in the exchange: most women believed that feminism belonged equally to the audience and the theater and that each was accountable for the feminism onstage.

Feminism was a movement without a central leadership, without a specific constitution, and without party cards. It is true that some women took leadership roles on certain issues, such as the founding of the National Organization for Women in 1966 or the passage of the Equal Rights Amendment (ERA, a constitutional amendment preventing discrimination on the basis of gender which had been introduced in the 1920s and despite intense effort on the part of women during the 1970s, was finally defeated in 1982), and that certain women's names, including those of Gloria Steinem, Betty Friedan, Kate Millet, or Florynce Kennedy, were characterized by the mainstream media as the leaders of the Women's Movement. Yet most feminists felt that the media "created 'stars' and denied the grassroots character of the movement" and, while it is undeniable that some women were more prominent than others, there was the strong sense throughout the Women's Movement that these women had no more credibility or influence than any other woman who called herself a feminist.[58] When consciousness-raising groups were founded, local actions undertaken, or books and articles published no one believed that they had to check with these women before making a statement on behalf of the Women's Movement. To be a feminist was no more than to identify one's self as such and that meant that there were always serious disagreements as to what was and was not feminism. There were different kinds of feminism and arguments among feminists about the different approaches. Peta Tait in her book on an Australian feminist theater group described her experience at one kind of feminist discussion – the collective meeting. Her memories of this kind of exchange are similar to many women's memories of post-show discussions and demonstrate the kind of individual ownership women felt about feminism.

> The collective meeting was not the same kind of environment as the consciousness-raising group satirized more recently in, for example, Wendy Wasserstein's play *The Heidi Chronicles*, which shows a stereotypic meeting of American women, where everyone is warmly welcomed and sits around making new members comfortable. The Women's Movement groups of the 1970s are almost always mistakenly shown as this kind of conciliatory and amiable socializing. While this did happen, my own experience of women's collectives in the 1970s was of argumentative meetings which were frequently confrontational, as women struggled to transform their personal experience into political action. At the same time women contributed perceptive insights through these exchanges. Also some women held political beliefs which made them disdainful of other women and their values. Above all, such meetings were exciting, intellectually stimulating and amongst the most significant arenas of political action in the 1970s.[59]

Feminism belonged to everyone and most feminists believed that every woman was accountable to every other woman. Despite the fact that a feminist theater group or playwright had put significant labor into a performance piece there often was the assumption that authorship did not necessarily confer absolute authority over the material.

The challenges and dissents described above were familiar to

Spiderwoman Theater. As Native Americans who had always felt somewhat external to the feminist movement, they saw it as motivated primarily by white concerns. Thus, when they encountered the accusations that they were not fulfilling the needs of a woman's culture, that they lacked the positive images of women that many feminists felt the theater owed the movement, or that they had to represent some kind of feminist demographic, Spiderwoman often responded angrily or impatiently.

> People would come up to us and say, "How many lesbians are in this group?" After a while you get so angry, so tired of it, and say, "How many do you want?" Or they'd come up and say, "Are some of you women married? Are there mothers in the group?" It was like you were everything to everyone. Or they would say, "I'm so angry at you, this should have ended this way. This should have happened and that. I'm so angry, you people didn't give hope." I'd say, "Well, that's your story, it's not my story. If you want to do it, you start a woman's group and you do that, but we're not going to go off in the sunset and hold hands. Forget it."[60]

Miguel and the other members of Spiderwoman found the prescriptive attitudes of many feminists constricting and racist. Implicit in the critique was the assumption that all-white groups that created theater did so based on the celebration and positive images of women who they envisioned as being like themselves. These were then the models for feminist theater and subsequent groups often followed in their footsteps. The tendency to universalize ignored the problem that many of the early groups relied on the unquestioned assumptions born of their white privilege. Miguel described this as having "to be perfect for all those women who say that one size fits all." But she countered: "That's what our pieces mean, one size *does not fit all*."[61]

Harriet Ellenberger in "In Search of Lesbian Theater" endeavored to define, among other things, the experience of being in the audience for lesbian theater and, more generally, feminist theater. She reacted against the model of audience offered by political theater artists, such as Peter Schumman of Bread and Puppet Theater, as a "somewhat recalcitrant mass which must be seduced into thinking about important things for its own good."[62] She compared this understanding to her own impressions while watching the production by Wicked Women's Theater (no founding date,

Northampton, Massachusetts) of Jane Chamber's *A Late Snow* in June of 1983. The audience in this case did not need to be seduced into thinking, they were willing and eager to take advantage of the opportunity to consider the representation of their lives:

> They were not passive, they were actively testifying, themselves becoming actors by responding to the actors, laughing, shouting out interjections, murmuring assenting phrases during some particularly right-on speech from the character who argued that lesbians must come out publicly if our lives are ever to become less impossible.[63]

As Ellenberger pointed out, it would be very difficult to force an audience into that kind of consideration. Enthusiasm can be manufactured but the care and attention in that enthusiasm came from a strong desire to be represented. Ellenberger's lesbian audience at a lesbian play wanted the opportunity to consider their lives and experiences. "We wanted to. We needed to. It was a rare opportunity; it was a relief. It was the kind of experience that lets us know we aren't crazy."[64] The reactions Ellenberger witnessed went beyond gratitude for fulfilling a necessity – there was also a

Figure 9 Audience in the "front room" of the Front Room Theater Guild (1981)

195

deep respect. The audience for *A Late Snow* participated to the fullest – groaning and hissing, cheering and agreeing – and this active participation recognized the importance of seeing their own stories and experiences. They demonstrated respect by being fully present to the performance.

Patricia Van Kirk had similar experiences with the audiences for Front Room Theater Guild (FRTG, 1981). Her audiences also responded energetically, and *A Late Snow* was one of the most popular shows the theater ever did.[65] But the dedication of FRTG's audiences was demonstrated not only during performances but also on the streets. "We made lesbians more public in a theatrical sense and they came and supported us incredibly. I still have people who come up to me and thank me on the street and it has been years."[66] The effect of witnessing what one understands as personal experience or community reality is a powerful one, representation acted as validation.

Iris Landsberg of It's Just a Stage (IJAS, 1974) also experienced the connection with and the vitality of the audience. The sensation of performing this specific type of community theater is unlike any other. For her it was about "people being able to identify their lives, women being able to look and say yes, I know that. Putting out some pieces and women being shocked and cheering that it was finally out there."[67] The recognition and community situation also created a proprietary sense in the audience. Audiences began to inform the theater of what they wanted to see and often made the artists feel besieged with requests and demands. "We used to get letters from women telling us what the pieces should be about. That's how they related to us. 'You should do a piece about sports.' 'You should do a piece about ———.'"[68] The place of the theater in the community was unstable. As the theaters redefined how theater audiences and theater performers interacted they called into question how theater was determined and created.

The notion of accountability, of shared responsibility for the images and representations onstage, and audience investment could lead to serious disagreements as to the proper subjects, approaches, and group composition for a feminist theater. Audiences, whether as a whole or as individuals, often felt compelled to work with the theater to create performances acceptable to feminist politics at the moment. The most obvious example of this sort of investment is the controversy surrounding the San Francisco Mime Troupe's (SFMT) first and only production concerned solely with feminism, *The*

Independent Female, or A Man Has His Pride, in 1970. Joan Holden wrote the play inspired by a British labor play that used ironic melodrama to make its political points. *Independent Female* reversed the political terms, as the British play had done, and what was politically desirable was cast negatively as threatening and unacceptable. Feminism became a threat to society, lesbians a threat to the family, and men the salvation of San Francisco.

Gloria Pennybank is forced to choose between her fiancé, an up and coming businessman who promises to treat her "like the most precious thing a man owns,"[69] and her job, where she has a chance to lead a strike for equal pay for all the women at Amalgamated Corporate Life. A co-worker, Sarah Bullitt, warns Gloria that marriage to John will make her no more than "personal property."[70] Gloria's mother supports the marriage and is confused by the strike. John, the fiancé, explains that these circumstances are the result of women's liberation, "the high sounding term with which a clique of unwomanly power-mad females masks its plot to destroy the family and enslave the male sex."[71] John fails to stop the strike and he precipitates Mrs. Pennybank's conversion to the cause when he kills Sarah, who dies exclaiming "shot in the back because she refused to live on it."[72] The play ends with a choice for the audience, they must decide for themselves the true ending of the play.

Will HEADSTRONG YOUTH'S impetuous course be halted? Will MANKIND recover its pride? Will RESPONSIBLE LEADERSHIP withstand this assault? Or does the implacable, rebellious spirit of INDEPENDENT FEMALE portend this society's ultimate collapse? Young ladies and gentlemen, the future lies in your hands.[73]

The audience, it is hoped, will choose to pick up where the play leaves off.

The version described here is the printed version, the one that the Mime Troupe produced and toured. But there was an earlier version. In this other version Sarah was a much harsher character and did not have the quotations Holden later added to give the history of and legitimation for the women's movement. But the most radical difference was the ending. In the original play the strike failed and Gloria was reunited with John. Some of the women in the Mime Troupe "were really allergic to the irony and suggested we needed to hear from the women's movement."[74] So in May 1970, the SFMT invited an audience of about one hundred women from different Bay Area consciousness-raising groups to serve as a special preview audience. Holden recalls the reception the feminists gave the production: "They were the worst preview audience I have ever experienced. They didn't laugh once. They were glacial. They hated the play. They erupted and started screaming they'd tear down the stage if we did it."[75] After battling for hours the objections boiled down to three things: the ironic tone, the characterization of women through stereotypes, and the negative ending. While Holden and the SFMT were unwilling to capitulate on the use of irony, which was for them the obvious spine of the play, they were willing to work on the other two objections. By the end of the evening, according to Holden, there "were some women who really understood what we were trying to do and so they volunteered to be a committee to talk to us about it."[76] This "committee" decided that they should re-work the women characters and the ending. "They thought women really wanted a positive ending, that they really deserved a positive ending."[77] Holden eventually agreed with the women, although she still thought "a bad ending makes people angry, not thinking everything is nice."[78] The revised version of the show was an instant success in Los Angeles and opened in San Francisco in Golden Gate Park. Holden feels that more women than was usual for the SFMT saw the show because of its feminist content. She also was interested to note that people would react to the show by talking about their anger and that everyone wanted to tell their stories. In places where the women's movement had not made a significant impact the play "acted like C-R."[79]

The San Francisco Mime Troupe was not and is not a feminist theater group. The anecdote, however, serves as an interesting illustration of the way audiences might invest in the importance and meaning of theater and the belief shared by many theaters in the importance of what the audiences had to say. Although *Independent Female* was produced by a theater outside feminist communities it was obvious through their invitation to the consciousness-raising groups that the contributions of the feminist community were often sought after and valued when a play was intended to be understood as feminist. Also, if anything, the investment by the audience increased when the issues were to be taken outside the communities to a larger audience. What is significant is the sense of joint ownership, implying that both the women and the theater owned the play.

Obviously, the relationship between the audience and the performer is in some ways the primary focus of every theater. The difference in the feminist theater relationship was that together they were struggling over the substance and form of feminism, sometimes in harmony, sometimes antagonistically. The audience was not a passive partner in the exchange – willing to speak loudly whether in praise or criticism. However, this does not mean the audiences themselves were always in agreement. More often than not they disagreed among themselves, as well as with what they saw. While the theater groups had undergone many changes by 1987 they had begun to disappear from the landscape – often to become something else or for the members to create feminist theater in other ways. Despite this, what had not lessened was the extreme reactions performances could elicit.

In 1987, at the Women and Theater Program (WTP) Conference in Chicago, the new multi-cultural ensemble of AFOM presented *The Story of a Mother II*. Before *The Story* began the conference participants were asked to write their names down and place them in a tambourine. The women in the ensemble each told compelling personal narratives about their mothers' struggles with patriarchal institutions. After this they drew each name out of the tambourine and said, "The name of the daughter is . . ." and read the name, then "the name of the mother is . . ." and waited for a response from the audience member named.[80] Jill Dolan says that she was unaware the names would be used in this way and that, as far as she knew, no one was told that they would be expected to participate.[81] While the stories told by the women in 1987 were different from the ones told in the 1978 version, the rituals remained unchanged. One woman, interviewed by Anna Deveare Smith for Smith's performance piece on WTP as part of her "On the Road" series, told Smith about her experience as a spectator of the original *The Story of A Mother*:

> I had seen the original production of "Story of a Mother"/ when the Foot of the Mountain/ had done it in '73/ so I knew/ all about the psychological probing stuff/ and I'd reacted *real* negatively to it when it happened/ in Minneapolis but there were just lots of women who were real/ moved by it/ I mean what happened at the end of the Minneapolis performance/ is that they bring out this kind of mega Mother I mean this/ giant figure a kind of totem of the mother and women in the/ audience were given the opportunity to take *ribbons* and place/ them on the figure of the mother and *speak* to her and tell/ her

> what was on their minds/ God/ women came out of the
> audience in *droves*/ saying the most touching/ moving things/
> about their mothers/ and. . . . [82]

Later in 1987 the discomfort with the rituals had increased but there
were still some women who felt invested in them. The point is that
not all women in 1978 were interested in participating and felt
extremely uncomfortable with the ritual possibilities, while in 1987
not all women rejected the rituals, but at both times the audiences
were specifically invested in what appeared onstage before them.

Jill Dolan and some of the other women present, however,
thought that the rituals were implicitly coercive, with required
participation construed by the theater as willing participation.
There was no room in the ritual moments for dissent or refusal.
AFOM assumed that the mother/daughter connection was always
a positive and empowering one to women but, as Dolan describes
from the conference,

> some spectators . . . were uncomfortable assuming their
> mothers' bodies because their mothers were alcoholic or racist
> or otherwise inappropriate role models. In the atmosphere of
> exaltation that [AFOM] established, however, there was no
> room to explore this ambivalence. [83]

The argument that ensued focused on the questions of universality
and the concept of implicit racism. Many of the women present felt
that the similarity of the script to the original, the absent presence
of Martha Boesing, the hovering custodianship of Phyllis Jane Rose,
and the assumed commonality was highly problematic given the
interpretations AFOM wanted to impress upon their audiences.
"After a decade of theorizing, practicing, and refining our politics,
this reverential stance towards ourselves as women seems simplistic
and conservative."[84] This was not the stance of the entire membership of the organization. Many women believed, and still believe,
that AFOM was of signal importance as a leading company and
deserved to be treated better. The performers felt attacked by the
predominantly white audience and charged their critics with racism
because these women argued that the women of color were manipu-
lated by the white women of AFOM. The members of the company
also felt that the complaints about the coerciveness of the ritual were
racist. Rebecca Rice told Anna Deveare Smith in an interview for
the piece on WTP:

By performing "Story of a Mother" I was rewarded with a negative/ response,/ and it said to me once again,/ you're making a mistake/ you knew better than this/ when "Story of a Mother" was done before it was done by a/ predominately white group/ we're moving into not only something more personal/ but we're moving into the language and language forms/ of our different mothers./ It's more threatening/ and it calls up a lot of feeling/ that's where the crap hit the fan/ and when you get into that stuff the demons start to fly/ they're going to fly and crash and scream and roar/ if I had to paint a picture of the energy in that room it would/ have been full of reds and blues and yellows and bright greens.[85]

What this rancorous post-show discussion played out were the conflicts among differing feminist ideologies, animosity between theorists and those opposed to theory, and the problem of racism and its history in the feminist movement. Feminism had changed since the show was first produced in 1978 and the foundations of universality and commonality were eroded by questions of the differences implicit and explicit in race, class, and sexuality. What had not changed, however, was the investment in feminism on the part of the audience and the performers. The debate was painful and divisive; seven years later it was still being discussed in the organization and served as a powerful turning point in its history.[86] Susan Bennett writes on theater audiences that they "bring to any performance a horizon of cultural and ideological expectations. That horizon is never fixed."[87] This contention is certainly borne out by the instances of spectating cited in this chapter. Women expected to see their experiences on stage and when they did not they expressed their disagreements with the group. This could be productive and yield a new text impossible to imagine without the audience intervention, as in the history of *Independent Female*, or it could be negative, emerging either from racism or homophobia, as in the reactions that Spiderwoman Theater often received, or from conflicting notions of feminism, as in the clash between AFOM and WTP. However, all these instances are proof that feminist theater is a powerful catalyst for feminists, that the reactions it elicits are profound, and that meaning and representation are controversial categories within feminism.

CONCLUSION
Changes and legacies

Theater is interactive with the world, it does not exist separate from its audiences. [Feminist theater] was very much a reflection of the women's movement in this country and it still is.

(Roberta Sklar)[1]

I realized that time and conditions were changing for people, that they weren't all going to be working in a happy little collective. Perhaps some of what needed to happen was that the people going out there as actors learn some tools.

(Harriet Schiffer)[2]

This book is primarily concerned with work that was done in the 1970s, although some of what was discussed here was done in the 1980s. However, the work included from the 1980s relates directly to the theater groups that had started around 1969. Wherever one places an end date and however one formulates a "period" for the feminist theater groups it is not inaccurate to say that by the end of the 1980s few groups remained. The absence of a large number of theater groups that can be labeled or label themselves "feminist" is not indicative of the end of the intersection of feminism and theater. Instead, it is about change. Changing ways to do theater, made possible in large part by the work done in the groups, and changing notions of what constituted theater as well as growing and diverse ways to identify oneself as a feminist contributed to new, diverse, and innovative examples of feminist theater.

Many were quick to see the Equal Rights Amendment as a "crucial symbol" of second wave feminism in the U.S.A. and its defeat as evidence that the "second wave had petered out."[3] The 1980s witnessed growing conservatism and a shift away from the demonstration- and specific goal-oriented politics that had begun with the Civil Rights Movement in the mid-1950s. It is undeniable that the 1980s brought about enormous shifts in the strategies, practices, and emphases of many politically oriented groups. What can be denied is that the 1980s saw an end to feminism whether completely or as a broad-based movement. While easily identified markers of grassroots communities in many cases disappeared, some bookstores, festivals, and discussion groups remained. However, these spaces and strategies were often inadequate to address the growing interest in and emphasis on the differences among women and new and different ones emerged. Thus feminism changed radically and in the change became harder to quantify. Flora Davis points to the mainstream media as a primary contributor to the idea that feminism was no longer of vital concern because of its inability to see the changes feminism had undergone.

> The press exaggerated the very real problems that activists were facing and often suggested that the women's movement was on its last legs. Granted it wasn't easy to gauge the strength of feminism in the 1980s. The women's movement was wonderfully diffuse – there were now women organized as feminists almost everywhere. . . . The media, defining the movement narrowly as a few organizations with nationwide memberships, failed to see what was in front of their eyes.[4]

While some used the increasing diversity and diffusion of feminism as evidence of its marginalization and disappearance others saw it as a radical shift signifying new strategies and tactics. As Steven Buechler writes, "the movement's diversity and ongoing character preclude any single statement of movement outcomes and necessitate recognition of multiple outcomes."[5] But as shifts occur it is possible to assess previous incarnations of feminism without signaling or assuming an end to feminism.

The multiplicity of possibilities for feminism and theater was demonstrated in the previous discussion of the many ways spectators and theaters could interact as members of a larger feminist community. The idea behind post-show discussions was to foster dialogues about feminism in general and the issues of the performance in particular that moved beyond the bounds of the performance. Workshops were intended to disseminate skills beyond the confines of the specific group and into the community at large. Audiences could then be more than participants in the creation of theater, they could also assist the theater in putting what it had learned and discovered to a wider audience. Teaching women self-defense, acting, movement, story telling, and creativity bolstered the self-worth of the audiences and gave them practical skills and agendas to apply to their own lives. These ideas and activities throw one particular question into relief: what is/was the lasting effect of feminist theater? Or, in other words, what is the legacy of the theater movement that from 1969 through to about the mid-1980s was comprised of perhaps as many as 160 groups?[6] This conclusion will examine why the groups may have disappeared and what happened to the people, ideas, and labor of that movement. This is not intended as a where-are-they-now blurb on each woman and group mentioned in the previous chapters but as an analysis of the possible effects of feminist theater on the current theater scene.

There is a general agreement that the changes in the political situation in the United States during the 1980s severely limited the arts funding available to the feminist theater groups. While funding had never been easy, many agencies had always been reluctant to fund theaters that were openly feminist or lesbian, and the conservative mood ushered in with Ronald Reagan's election to the Presidency in 1980 made it extremely difficult to obtain funds as the available money shrank and the grantors turned to less radical arts projects. However, growing conservatism alone cannot account for the demise in theater groups anymore than it fully accounts for the shifts in feminism as a whole. There were other, larger factors besides the economic situation that signaled an end to the existence of feminist theater groups as a movement.

One of the strongest reasons was one that every woman mentioned: burn-out and fatigue as evidenced in feminist organizations across the board; what Flora Davis calls "the graying of the women's movement."[7] The collective structures favored by the groups meant that every woman was supposed to share equally the burden of running the company. In many cases this came to mean that a few of the women would unofficially do all the work or that the company was so small that the work, even when fairly distributed, was considerable. When a single woman was responsible for both business and artistic leadership she usually perceived herself as solely responsible for keeping the theater alive. Barbara Tholfsen characterized the end of Women's Collage Theater as directly linked to her own physical and mental state. "I did too much. . . . I just took on too much. I did practically everything.

Once I lost energy, that's really what happened, the theater fell apart."[8] Tholfsen's experience is representative of many in feminist theaters. Lilith's history after Terry Baum's departure from the company is marked by the departures of fatigued and stressed members. Iris Landsberg attributes the end of It's Just a Stage to frustration over their financial situation and exhaustion.[9] Another factor that contributed to the "graying" was that things had changed enough that younger women were not facing the same kinds of discrimination women before them had and they were not as inclined to do theater based on feminism in similar ways to their predecessors.

Feminism encouraged women to eschew behind-the-scenes labor, or at least traditional behind-the-scenes labor, for positions traditionally closed to them. This often meant that the administrative duties were the least desired and the most neglected. Roberta Sklar perceived a direct link between this disinterest in the administrative side of a business and the eventual end of the groups. The conventional positioning of women within society was part of the oppression women in feminism were trying to change, but the resistance to the labor associated with those positions was often labor necessary to keep the theater afloat:

> A problem that I saw in a decade or more of feminist theater in this country is that people did not come forth who wanted to handle that part of the work. I'm going to say something that is based on nothing but my own feelings and perceptions. I think the structure of feminism didn't allow this to happen. . . . Women are supposed to do all that and wash the floors themselves. . . . Nobody wants a male genius to wash the floors when he could be making genius things. . . . Feminist theater never got that stripe of people doing service, everybody wanted to be the cook, nobody wanted to do the shopping.[10]

While it is healthy for a theater's business and artistic structures to be in close participation as a way to maintain the political commitment and to integrate the operations of the theater, having the two identical structures guarantees that both sides will suffer. Sklar's observations are echoed by Kimberly Roberts of the Theater of Light and Shadow in New Haven. By 1983 "[f]ewer and fewer people were interested in the business end. There was no less commitment to theater and feminist theater, but just less interest in administration. Everything fell on a few shoulders."[11] The end result was always the same, the people who carried the load of creation and administration experienced despair and depression and found themselves less and less willing to do the labor for little or no pay. Harriet Schiffer notes about her experiences running Lilith that even when there was a strong and creative person handling the business end an absence of funding made that job very difficult and that the person had to stay in touch with the creative part of the theater. To split them entirely, Schiffer comments, is always a mistake.[12]

The feminist theater movement enjoyed fifteen years, more or less, of activity. During that time women turned to theater to express their politics, communal bonds, and artistic visions and viewed material factors such as funding, business managers, or production and design resources as of secondary importance. They used spaces never architecturally intended to serve as theaters, performed in their street clothes, and advertised by word-of-mouth. This was all accomplished in the context of the feminist community because it provided the audiences, material, and emphases. The greatest strengths and the most debilitating weaknesses of feminist theater came from its community base. Some of those strengths have already been explored. The community gave the theater a clearer meaning and purpose than most theaters enjoy. The audiences and performers were engaged in a mutual struggle against oppression, generating new cultural forms. This gave meaning and weight to the performance events that still resonates for feminists in theater today, even those who never saw a performance by a feminist theater group.

The community could also limit what a theater might achieve. In many cases theaters were not encouraged to go beyond what was commonly accepted as proper subjects for feminism to investigate, nor were they encouraged to present other than positive role models. Indeed, positive role models would go on to become one of the most hotly debated issues in feminist theater, as feminist practitioners and critics asked themselves repeatedly and with great difference of opinion whether or not theaters and playwrights had a responsibility to present role models that demonstrated women's strengths and possibilities. Patricia Van Kirk's goal was to make Front Room Theater Guild a professional theater because she thought "lesbians deserved a professional theater."[13] However, while the community supported and appreciated the theater it also held the theater back. When Van Kirk cast men in male parts she met with great disapproval and condemnation.[14] This experience is by no means unique to FRTG or lesbian theater.

Feminist theaters also found that when they did succeed in abandoning the community context they lost their sense of purpose and their artistic/political vision. For *Daughters of Erin* (1982) Lilith Theater made a commitment to pay all the members of the company a wage competitive with Equity salaries, to bring in a professional director, and to cast the show from both the company and the professional acting pool. The group had begun to splinter at that point primarily because no one could make a living off the theater so they spent a great deal of time and energy to raise the money necessary to accomplish the project. Lilith decided it would act primarily as the producer for the show rather than as the performing company.[15] As Sue-Ellen Case remarked to Joan Mankin, the theater "went against everything [it] had ever been."[16] Mankin remembers that in an in-house critique session she and Carolyn Meyers got a lot of negative criticism from the performers about how they handled the show and their power. "Then we . . . had nothing left. We just spent all our money on the show and everyone left, all the people that we hired."[17] The experience of *Daughters of Erin* threw the theater company back on to its original premises – concentration on process, connections with the women and community, and exploration of vital issues – and their final productions were exhilarating experiences for those involved. But Lilith was never able to reactivate their funding sources and by 1986 the theater no longer existed.

The forms and shapes of the theaters came directly out of the communities. Many women in the larger women's community and feminist theater groups believed that underneath superficial distinctions women were the same. When theaters took on projects of integration or dedicated themselves to a multi-cultural enterprise they initiated their own obsolescence. Many of the theaters and communities were formulated through the similarity of the experiences of white, middle-class women. Bringing in women who did not share their aesthetics or their experiences destabilized the artistic visions of the companies. The groups, by and large, did not have the mechanisms to negotiate such differences because they were grounded in the ideas that a consensus that would satisfy all the members of the group could eventually be reached. There were no provisions for differences that could not be bridged or issues that would not be resolved without enormous changes.

Ensemble work requires a very delicate balancing act between the group and the individual member. Trust is always a major issue and often women of color and lesbians experienced moments of oppression and discrimination that made them profoundly wary of the other members of the group. Terry Baum's desire to make the lead character in *Sacrifices* a lesbian brought the homophobia in Lilith to the surface and AFOM's change to a multi-cultural ensemble foregrounded problems around racism. These problems confronted women with differences that could not be contained within the structures they had constructed and eventually forced them to dismantle their organizations.

The changes and confrontations described here were not isolated in feminist theaters. These shifts were symptomatic of the changes feminism as a whole was undergoing. Identity politics emerged as one critique by women of color of racist feminist practices. Based on the differences of race and ethnicity, these feminists posited that their experiences were radically dissimilar from the white middle-class model and could not be explicated within it. This politic is clearly illustrated in *This Bridge Called My Back* edited by Cherrie Moraga and Gloria Anzaldua in the late 1970s and published in 1981, but it can also be dated back to 1974 with the emergence of the Combahee River Collective and the publication of their "Statement" in 1977, a manifesto of black feminist politics and organizing. *Bridge* was an articulation by women of color of their views on their experiences, their feminism, their history, and the interactions between their different cultures, races, and ethnicities. Some of the work was a critique of the women's movement in its current incarnation as predominantly white. The writers documented their anger and pain at being rebuffed, sometimes politely but more often rudely, when trying to participate in feminist organizations. Mitsuye Yamada commented that a majority of women of color, specifically Asian Pacific women, joined ethnically focused groups because of a "pervasive feeling of mistrust towards the women in the movement."

> Instead they have become active in groups promoting ethnic identity, most notably ethnic studies in universities, ethnic theater groups or ethnic community agencies. This doesn't mean that we have placed our loyalties on the side of ethnicity over womanhood. The two are not at war with one another; we shouldn't have to sign a "loyalty oath" favoring one over

the other. However, women of color are often made to feel that we must make a choice between the two.[18]

White women did not usually experience the same interactions of racism and sexism that women of color did and therefore rarely created structures that were responsive to the complex concerns of multiple oppressions. Anti-racism has always been a tenet of feminism but in their eagerness to combat the sexism with which they had had first-hand experience many white women glossed over the insularity of their experience and were often inclined to present it as a universalized sisterhood.

These critiques by women of color, accompanied by ones from lesbians, splintered the previously tight focus on a transcendent model of feminist thinking and activism. As feminism had focused primarily on the bonds women share in common, it now re-focused some of its energies on unacknowledged racism, classism, and homophobia. In order to achieve this women looked for ways to form coalitions across those differences and make them the bases for the means of productive change. While this move was generally positive, it did have negative consequences for many feminist organizations, including feminist theater groups.

Joan Mankin described the situation of Lilith after the 1982 *Daughters of Erin* and in doing so summed up the position of feminist theaters in feminist communities as the politics changed.

> The issues weren't so clear – somehow before the subjects had just seemed to present themselves. We just reached a point where it didn't seem to be that clear and since we didn't have one continuing artistic vision it seemed to get really splintered. Now I don't know if one was the cause of the other . . . maybe that was a symptom of what was happening in the women's movement.[19]

This was the situation that confronted many feminist theaters. As the community began to lose much of its coherence and to flounder for new organizing principles, the theaters that were inextricably linked to them began to founder as well. Sondra Segal spoke of the doubt and confusion that she experienced as WET ended its operations. "I don't know what I have to say that women want to hear."[20]

Currently three of the feminist groups discussed here are still operating with a measure of success. Spiderwoman Theater still tours and creates shows although they are turning their attention more and more to Native American issues with a feminist perspective;[21] Split Britches also continues to produce works, recently celebrating their tenth anniversary;[22] and Horizons: Theater From A Woman's Perspective, founded in the Washington D.C. area as Pro Femina in 1976, is still very active. Recently they moved to a permanent space in Arlington, Virginia. They produced Jane Martin's play about abortion, *Keely and Du*, in 1993.[23] This cannot help but raise the question, is this the entire legacy of feminist theater? Are the three groups still in existence the only trace of a movement that spanned the United States for more than a decade? On the contrary, the legacies of the feminist theater groups are far more rich and diverse than the survival rate of the groups might indicate.

The theater groups have left their mark on theater and feminism in a variety of ways. The most obvious is the phrase "feminist theater." Earlier than some other artistic activities feminist theater groups demonstrated that there was and could be a political aesthetic enterprise that could exist within the second wave feminist movement and maintain its autonomy. This seemingly obvious conclusion should not be underestimated. The fact that people assume that feminism and theater can intersect profitably was originated by the theater groups. While it was often negatively characterized by many of the same stereotypes as feminism itself – shrill, didactic, and man-hating – it brought feminist ideas and images to places that might never have had them. Theaters toured to small towns, community centers, churches, synagogues, colleges, universities, women's centers, schools, and conferences across the U.S.A. Many of the practitioners are still active in theater and brought their politics and discoveries with them to their later careers and activities.

Probably the most enduring legacy of feminist theater for the women who were part of the movement is a commitment to women-centered or women-oriented theater. When asked what she took away from her work with Lilith, Joan Mankin replied:

> I really seek to work with women and I find that I work best that way. . . . I seek out situations where women have the artistic control and the vision. . . . It's the single most important factor of how I look at things and what it says about my role as a woman or myself as woman in the world and the

choices that I make. That seems to be my basic criteria for doing anything and the basic way I approach anything. That has to be. I wouldn't take a role I feel was demeaning or sexist.[24]

Mankin's feeling is echoed by Twila Thompson who "didn't do a lot of auditioning" after she left Women's Collage Theater because "regular theater didn't have the same sense of impact."[25] She has continued to work in socially responsible theater because she is dedicated to work that has political repercussions. Marga Gomez told Roberta Uno that

Lilith taught her about the collective process of creating theater, from writing the material to acting. . . . Gomez attributes her learning about the ethics and morals of the artistic process to Lilith, as well as her acceptance of the personal as political.[26]

The feeling that their work in feminist theaters gave them a high standard to live up to and that nothing would be the same again was shared by all the women interviewed for this book. Some of them despaired that there was not the same kind of radical grassroots movement there had been earlier, but all of them felt that the work they did was significant.

One of the signs of the feminist groups' progeny is the one-woman show. While by no means invented by the women who worked in the feminist theaters of the 1970s and early 1980s, it was a form seized on by women who wanted to remain active in theater with a feminist politic but who could not or would not work with a group. In 1981 Terry Baum wrote *Ego Trip: or I'm Getting My Shit Together and Dumping it All on You* and toured it on the West Coast. She also toured her later one-woman show *Immediate Family* nationally. In the 1980s Michele Linfante wrote a one-woman show in which she played her father, and Pat Bond has created and toured two different shows, one based on the life of Eleanor Roosevelt's lover Lorena Hickok and the other on Gertrude Stein. Harriet Schiffer created her first solo piece in the early 1980s, *Other Things That Fly,* and then a variety of others including, in 1986, *Morning Sickness or Woodsman Spare That Tree: A Piece about Reproductive Ambivalence and the Biological Clock* that grew out of the work Lilith had done on the issues surrounding reproductive rights.[27] Clare Coss wrote a one-woman show *Lillian,* published in 1989, based on the life of the social activist Lillian Wald. Marga Gomez has become a stand-up comedian and in 1990 debuted a one-woman show about her parents, *Memory Tricks*.[28]

One-woman shows became a popular form for feminists because they were flexible to schedule, depended on the availability of a very small number of people, were easy to tour, and most of them had few if any production requirements so that performing in almost any kind of space and under a variety of conditions was feasible. As Harriet Schiffer noted, one-woman shows were also a way for women to bring their work to the attention of theater people who might otherwise have overlooked them.

> When I started doing my solo work it wasn't just because I wanted to do solo work – it's because I knew I was not somebody who was going to be cast as the *ingénue*. I was tired of directors not being able to see me. After two or three years of solo performance these directors who I couldn't even audition for before were coming to me and saying, "I've got a part, why don't you do this?"[29]

The economics of this kind of theater are very simple. Fees are split, at most, two or three ways. Usually the performer does all her own production work and is therefore able to keep the money for herself. In theater groups the money would always have to go to the finances of the group or be split into small amounts for all the members. This often made it impossible for a woman to support herself from her theater work. It is also no coincidence that as the feminist community splintered and the feminist theater groups disbanded, women found it easier to work alone, without having to depend on communities working in concert to produce a work with political content. The potential for burn-out is just as strong but most women felt that more things were under their direct control, reducing the kinds of stress that came from negotiating within a group.

Another legacy of the feminist theater movement has been the producing organizations that have emerged to support women's work. In New York the Women's Interart has existed since 1969 and was initially founded to support "independent women artists and present . . . their work to the public."[30] By 1971 the organization had its own space and was producing theater, sponsoring shows in their gallery, and offering women rehearsal and studio spaces. The first play produced at Interart was Jane Chambers'

Random Violence. The theater has also operated as a home base for WET and Split Britches, as well as supporting the work of a large number of women in the theater, including Glenda Dickerson, Joyce Aaron, Nancy Rhodes, Wendy Kesselman, and Meredith Monk.[31] The organization is primarily liberal in its political orientation, preferring to launch women into the mainstream than to build a separate and alternative theater tradition. Jane Chambers commented in 1974: "For the next two or three years, there is going to be a need for women's theater, where women can learn technical skills."[32] While Margot Lewitin finds that funding is growing increasingly difficult to secure and Interart is more in debt every year she remains committed to the organization.[33]

Brava, in San Francisco, was founded in 1986 to "help emerging and professional women artists gain greater visibility and increase audiences for their work, and to help them increase their professionalism."[34] The organization provides services to women in the arts community, including acting, writing, directing, grant writing, and production workshops, and underwriting for productions. However, their mission is not as generalized as Interart's because they focus on "socially conscious work" that is "feminist and antiracist."[35] To this end they have devised specific strategies to support those commitments. Any panel sponsored by Brava, whether to review work for possible production or in a conference setting, must be at least 50 percent composed of women of color and the majority of the women who serve on the board are women of color.

Ellen Gavin is highly aware of the problematic position she occupies as a white woman heading an organization dedicated to multi-cultural work but she believes that her dedication to Brava's goals and her acknowledgement of the problem makes it possible to work productively. Gavin has supported the creation of autonomous groups within Brava, including a Latina project and a black women's project. They have also sponsored an all women of color workshop on writing. One project Brava supported both administratively and financially was the production of Cherrie Moraga's *Shadow of a Man* directed by Maria Irene Fornes at the Eureka Theater in 1990.[36] This is the kind of interaction between artists and institutions Brava hopes to foster in the future. Ultimately, Gavin hopes that Brava will bring diverse communities to the theater to produce work aimed at fostering a variety of dialogues.

Brava is obviously a product of the changes in feminist thinking. The group's dedication to a multi-cultural vision that engages differences is born out of a sense of the history of feminism that all too often ignored or actively erased differences. It is also an example of the possibilities for a more sophisticated intersection between feminism and theater. Many of the feminist theater groups of the 1970s came from a sense of urgency supporting a utopian vision of a new feminist world. The average existence for a theater was three and half years, scarcely enough time to develop complex and intricate theater experiments and theories, especially when caught in the quotidian requirements of a theater company.[37] Often, after the theaters closed down, the women who founded and ran them used the knowledge and experience gained from their work to push further the boundaries of the possible intersections between feminism and theater.

One example of the potential for feminist theater work based on previous experience is Adele Prandini's production of Judy Grahn's *Queen of Swords* at Theater Rhinoceros in San Francisco in 1989. When It's Just a Stage closed it doors in 1980 Prandini turned to writing and wrote a play *Safe Light* that Alan Estes produced at Rhino in 1984. Beginning with that production she became involved with the theater, eventually working as Artistic Director. She suggested Grahn's play for the 1989–90 season and indicated her interest in directing it. Prandini believes that her ability to deal with the complex text comes directly out of her years of experience with women's theater and the contacts she made during that time. Iris Landsberg, also a member of IJAS, played the role of Helen and some of the designers were collaborators from earlier projects with IJAS.

> That period in the 70s, coming out of the 60s, there was such enthusiasm in this country. . . . There is something wonderful about saying, "Well, we don't have money for costumes, we don't have money for lighting, we don't have money for sets but let's do it anyway." The excitement over *Queen of Swords* is something different because it is having the ability to have the experience to meet the challenge of the project. Twenty years ago I had a lot fewer skills because I had a lot less experience.[38]

Prandini's description of her work on *Queen of Swords* points up one of the most significant contributions of the feminist theater groups. Before the movement there were no recent or extensive histories of women collaborating on feminist projects. As a result of their work in feminist groups the women who had participated walked away with the tools and ideas to continue and to develop their work. More importantly, they also had the associations that make the continued work possible.

There are many other collaborations involving former colleagues from feminist theater both in production and in playwrighting. Some examples include Michele Linfante's and Naomi Newman's collaborations with Martha Boesing, Linfante as a playwrighting student and Newman as an actor under Boesing's direction. Terry Baum and Carolyn Meyers wrote *Dos Lesbos* together. Roberta Sklar directed *The Blessing* written by Clare Coss at the American Place Theater in 1989. None of these collaborations would have occurred if the women had not built up a substantial body of work in feminist theater. That work shaped their sensibilities, as well as building a pool of colleagues with whom they shared a similar history and politic.

Some women proceeded from feminist theaters to graduate programs seeking more traditional training that would give them entrees into the professional theater world while bringing their politics into those settings. Belinda Beezley and Nancy Kathan, of the Theater of Light and Shadow, went on to graduate school in theater, Kathan to the Yale Graduate School in Theater Administration and Beezley to a masters in acting at Cal Arts School of Theater.[39] Patricia Van Kirk enrolled in the University of Washington School of Drama MFA program in directing and there directed feminist works including *Trifles* by Susan Glaspell and *A Mouthful of Birds* by Caryl Churchill.

Like most overtly political theater, feminist theater was a product of its historical moment. Its location within feminist community dictated certain interests, forms, and approaches. As that community dispersed, the performance derived from it began to seem outmoded. Women either shifted their focuses to reorient their theaters toward new ideas and new conceptions of feminism or they closed the theaters and moved on to new ventures. Whatever the solution of individual women and theater companies they took with them the experiences, knowledge, and contacts they had gained during their work in feminist theater groups.

APPENDIX A
List of interviews

The following is a complete list of all the interviews conducted for this book. It will be obvious that some of these interviews were not cited in the body of the work. However, every interview I conducted influenced in some way my thinking on this subject. The interviews are listed in the chronological order they were conducted in order to document how my conception of feminist theater was shaped through time. I have also noted the location of each interview.

Joan Mankin, 19 January 1989, conducted by Sue-Ellen Case, Blue Lake, California.
Margot Lewitin, 14 December 1989, New York, New York, the Women's Interart Center.
Karen Malpede, 15 December 1989, New York, New York, restaurant.
Emma Missouri, 18 December 1989, Northampton, Massachusetts, restaurant.
Helen Krich Chinoy, 18 December 1989, Northampton, Massachusetts, her home.
Twila Thompson, 19 December 1989, New York, New York, her office.
Clare Coss, 19 December 1989, New York, New York, her home.
Roberta Sklar, 20 December 1989, New York, New York, restaurant.
Sondra Segal, 21 December 1989, New York, New York, her office.
Nancy Rhodes, 18 January 1990, by phone.
Barbara Tholfsen, 18 January 1990, by phone.
Michele Linfante, 3 April 1990, San Francisco, California, her home.
Terry Baum, 3 April 1990, San Francisco, California, her home.
Ellen Sebastian, 4 April 1990, San Francisco, California, restaurant.
Pat Bond, 4 April 1990, Berkeley, California, Mama Bear's Bookstore.
Anita Mattos, 5 April 1990, San Francisco, California, restaurant.
Adele Prandini, 5 April 1990, San Francisco, California, Theater Rhinoceros theater.
Naomi Newman, 5 April 1990, San Francisco, California, A Travelling Jewish Theater offices.
Zöe Elton, 6 April 1990, San Francisco, California, restaurant.
Gail Williams, 6 April 1990, San Francisco, California, restaurant.

216

Joan Holden, 6 April 1990, San Francisco, California, San Francisco Mime Troupe offices.

Cherrie Moraga, 6 April 1990, San Francisco, California, her home.

Iris Landsberg, 7 April 1990, San Francisco, California, her home.

Judy Grahn, 9 April 1990, Berkeley, California, restaurant.

Muriel Miguel, 26 April 1990, Seattle, Washington, Group Theater owned apartment.

Patricia Van Kirk, 10 July 1990, Seattle, Washington, my home.

Sue Clement, 16 October 1990, Seattle, Washington, restaurant.

Harriet Schiffer, 30 October 1994, by phone.

APPENDIX B
Interview questions

The following outline is the one I brought to each interview. I did not confine myself to a specific set of questions, preferring instead to provide myself with reminders of the areas I wished to cover. The interviews did not often follow the order of the outline, rather I allowed the circumstances of the interview and the preferences of each woman to decide the order by which we would proceed and the topics we would cover. However, each interview did begin in the exact same way. I always started by asking how that woman got involved in feminism and how she got involved in theater. The two interests were always combined in the same question. I rarely asked all the questions in the outline at every interview but this does indicate my interests and my directions.

Relation to the women's movement
   texts
   people
   events that brought group into being
   alliances to groups
   testimony/C-R
Relations to theater/performance traditions
Relations to/influence of other feminist theater groups
Goals of theater group
Role models
Why theater
Notions of collectivity
   when was it formed
   why was it formed
   how it worked in the day to day and in the larger sense
   decision-making process
   who was central to it
   who participated and why
   how did one join the collective
Conflict and disagreements
   how do you handle them
   is there a procedure
Rehearsal process

how does the casting work
what actors play what parts and why
where
who ran them
how long
process
Process to create works
who is involved
where do the ideas come from
process
Relations to critics
who reviews them
do you get reviewed
what is the critical reception of work
Theater's place in the community
how do you fit in
how does it influence your choices
Funding
ticket cost and structure
box office
grants
who writes the grants
where do the grants come from
why
how is the money spent
Audiences
how did the theater relate to them
what were the reactions to different works
gender breakdown
did they participate
how were they reached
subscribers
advertising
is the theater primary support for members

APPENDIX C
Feminist theaters and producing organizations

The feminist theaters, abbreviations, dates, locations, company members, and productions listed here are drawn from the body of this book. Therefore, the list is not an exhaustive or complete catalogue in any of the above categories. There are many groups for which I could find no founding or closing dates and this I have indicated with a question mark. When the space is left blank it means the group or organization was in operation when this book was written. The date that follows production is the year the group first produced the work. The list is divided into two sections: theaters and producing organizations.

FEMINIST THEATERS

ALIVE AND TRUCKING THEATER (A&TT, 1971–76) Minneapolis, Minnesota
Jan Mandell, Meri Golden
Pig in a Blanket: A Tender, Poignant Drama of Young Love (1971).

AT THE FOOT OF THE MOUNTAIN (AFOM, 1974–91) Minneapolis, Minnesota
Martha Boesing, Phyllis Rose, Rebecca Rice, Nayo-Barbara Watkins, Bernadette Cha, Jan Magrane, Judith Katz, Carmen Maria Rosario, Antoinette Maher, Sherry Blakey Banai
Raped: A Woman's Look at Bertolt Brecht's "The Exception and the Rule" (1976)
The Story of A Mother (1978)
The Clue in the Old Birdbath: An Affectionate Satire of Nancy Drew (1978) by Kate Kasten and Sandra DeHelen with music by Paul Boesing
Pizza (1980) by Michele Linfante
Internal Injury (1982)
Tribes (1982) by Judith Katz
The Story of a Mother II (1987).

BLACK STAR (1978–?) Cambridge, Massachusetts.

BOSTON WOMEN IN THEATER (?–?) Boston, Massachusetts.

CALLIOPE FEMINIST THEATER (?–?) Hartford, Connecticut.

CAMBRIDGE LESBIAN THEATER (?–?) Cambridge, Massachusetts
Sequoia.

CARAVAN THEATER (1965–78) Boston, Massachusetts
Bobbi Ausubel, Stan Edelson
How to Make a Woman (1969) by Leilani Johnson, Joel Polinsky, Sara
Salisbury, Joe Volpe, Aili Singer, Anne Barclay, David Klein, and Barbara
Fleischmann.

CHRYSALIS THEATER ECLECTIC (1978–?) Northampton, Mass-
achusetts
Emma Missouri, Judith Katz, Andrea Hairston
Tribes (1982) by Judith Katz.

CIRCLE OF THE WITCH (1973–78) Minneapolis, Minnesota
Micki Massimino, Joyce Indelicato, Nancy Sugarman
Sexpot Follies (1974).

THE CUTTING EDGE (1975–?) New York, New York
Andrea Balis
Croon (1976).

EMMATROUPE (1975–?) New York, New York
Eleanor Johnson, Judah Kataloni
*A Girl Starts Out . . . A Tragedy in Four Parts: Virgin Joy, Rape, Attempted
Suicide, Decision to Abort* (1978).

FEMINIST AMERIKAN THEATER (?–?) Boston, Massachusetts.

FRONT ROOM THEATER GUILD (FRTG, 1980–87) Seattle,
   Washington
Patricia Van Kirk, Cappy Kotz, Phrin Pickett
This Brooding Sky (1980) by Sarah Dreher
A Late Snow (1981) by Jane Chambers
In Search of the Hammer: The First Adventure of the Three Mustbequeers
(1983) by Cappy Kotz and Phrin Pickett
The Return of the Hammer (1985) by Cappy Kotz and Phrin Pickett
Last Summer at Bluefish Cove (1985) by Jane Chambers
The Clue in the Old Birdbath: An Affectionate Satire of Nancy Drew (1986)
by Kate Kasten and Sandra DeHelen with music by Paul Boesing.

HORIZONS: THEATER FROM A WOMAN'S PERSPECTIVE (originally
Pro Femina, 1976–   ) Washington, D.C.

IT'S ALL RIGHT TO BE WOMAN THEATER (IARTBW, 1969–76)
New York, New York
Sue Perlgut
It's All Right To Be Woman (1969).

IT'S JUST A STAGE (IJAS, 1974–80) San Francisco, California
Adele Prandini, Iris Landsberg
A New Show Revised (1978)
Glimpses (1978)
The Mountain is Stirring (1980).

LAS CUCURACHAS (1974–?) San Francisco, California
Chicana (1974).

LAVENDER CELLAR (1973–75) Minneapolis, Minnesota
Nythar Sheehy, Marie Kent, Pat Suncircle.

LESBIAN–FEMINIST THEATER COLLECTIVE (1977–?) Pittsburgh, Pennsylvania.

LILITH (1974–86) San Francisco, California
Terry Baum, Carolyn Meyers, Joan Mankin, Michele Linfante, Marga Gomez, Vicky Lewis, Bernadette Cha, Kitty Tsui, Elizabeth Rodin, Harriet Schiffer, Charlotte Colavin, Shirley Fields
Lilith Theater (1974)
Good Food (1975)
Moonlighting (1976) by Terry Baum and Carolyn Meyers
Sacrifices (1977) by Carolyn Meyers, Terry Baum, Michele Linfante, and Resnais Winter
Manifesto (1977–78) by Dacia Maraini
Pizza (1980) by Michele Linfante
Trespaso (1980) by Martha Boesing
Exit the Maids (1981)
Daughters of Erin (1982) by Carolyn Meyers and Elizabeth Rodin
Fetal Positions (1983–84)
Breeding Grounds (1984–86).

LIVING LESSONS, INC. (1990–?) New York, New York
Angela Lockhart
Please Listen to Me (1990).

LOS ANGELES FEMINIST THEATER (LAFT, 1969–?) Los Angeles, California
Sondra Lowell
In the Shadow of the Crematorium (1969) by Myrna Lamb
Scyklon Z (1969) by Myrna Lamb
The Cabaret of Sexual Politics (1971–72).

NEW CYCLE THEATER (1977–?) Brooklyn, New York
Karen Malpede
The End of War (1977)
A Monster Has Stolen the Sun (1981).

NEW FEMINIST THEATER (1969–?) New York, New York
Anselma Dell'Olio
What Have You Done For Me Lately (1969) by Myrna Lamb

NEW YORK FEMINIST THEATER (1973–6) New York, New York
Claudette Charbonneau, Lucy Winer
But Something Was Wrong with the Princess (1973) by Lucy Winer
In Transit (?).

ONYX WOMEN'S THEATER (1973–?) South Ozone Park, New York.

ORANGE COUNTY FEMINIST THEATER (1971–?) Anaheim, California
Rosalie M. Gresser Abrams.

RED DYKE THEATER (1974–?) Atlanta, Georgia.

RHODE ISLAND FEMINIST THEATER (RIFT, 1973–86) Providence, Rhode Island
Ada MacAllister, Barbara Conley, Sherilyn Brown, Carol M. Sullivan, Julie Pember
Persephone's Return (1974)
Internal Injury (1978) by Ada MacAllister and the RIFT Collective.

SPIDERWOMAN THEATER (1975–) Brooklyn, New York
Muriel Miguel, Lisa Mayo, Gloria Miguel, Lois Weaver, Peggy Shaw, Hortensia Colorado, Elvira Colorado, Pam Verge
Women in Violence (1976)
Lysistrata Numbah (1977)
Trilogy: Friday Night, Jealousy, and *My Sister Ate Dirt* (1978)
Cabaret: An Evening of Disgusting Songs and Pukey Images (1979, 1985)
The Fittin' Room (1980)
Split Britches (1981) by Peggy Shaw and Lois Weaver
Sun, Moon, and Feather (1981)
The Three Sisters from Here to There (1982)
I'll Be Right Back (1984)
3 Up, 3 Down (1986)
Winnetou's Snake Oil Show from Wigwam City (1987)
Power Pipes (1991).

SPLIT BRITCHES (1981–) New York, New York
Peggy Shaw, Lois Weaver, Deborah Margolin
Split Britches (1981)
Anniversary Waltz (1990).

THANK-YOU THEATER (?–?) Los Angeles, California.

THEATER OF LIGHT AND SHADOW (TLS, 1977–83) New Haven, Connecticut
K. D. Kodish, Nancy Lee Kathan, Belinda Beezley, Deborah Flynn, Kimberly Roberts
Voices (1978) by Susan Griffin
The Clue in the Old Birdbath: An Affectionate Satire of Nancy Drew (1979) by Kate Kasten and Sandra DeHelen with music by Paul Boesing
The Women Here Are No Different (1983) by Nancy Beckett.

VALENTINA PRODUCTIONS (1981–?) San Jose, California
Irene Burgos, Rosie Campos-Pantoja, Cara Hill de Castañón, Anita Mattos, Liz Robinson, and Juanita Vargas
Voz de la Mujer (1980).

WASHINGTON AREA FEMINIST THEATER (WAFT, 1972–78) Washington, D.C.

WESTBETH FEMINIST PLAYWRIGHTS COLLECTIVE (1970–mid-1970s) New York, New York
Dolores Walker, Gwen Gunn, Sally Ordway, Susan Yankowitz, Pat Horan, Chryse Maile
Rape-In (1971). Included:
   Across the Street by Gwen Gunn
   Crabs by Sally Ordway
   There's a Wall Between Us, Darling
   Abide in Darkness by Dolores Walker
Up! An Uppity Review (1972). Included:
   Family Family by Sally Ordway
   Interview by Dolores Walker
   Wicked Woman (1974?)
   We Can Feed Everyone Here (1974?).

WICKED WOMAN'S THEATRE (?–?) Northampton, Massachusetts.
A Late Show (1983) by Jane Chambers

WILMA PROJECT (?–?) Philadelphia, Pennsylvania.

WOMANRITE (1972–77) New York, New York
Clare Coss, Sondra Segal, Roberta Sklar
The Cinderella Project (1973)
Daughters (1976).

WOMANSONG THEATER (1974–?) Atlanta, Georgia.

WOMANSPACE (1972) New York, New York
Muriel Miguel, Laura Foner, Carol Grosberg
Cycles (1972).

WOMEN'S COLLAGE THEATER (1976–82) New York, New York
Barbara Tholfsen, Twila Thompson, Helen Marshall, Gayle Biederman
Sirens (1976)
Ladies Don't Spit and Holler (1981).

WOMEN'S ENSEMBLE THEATER (1975–76) Berkeley, California
Susan Suntree
Antigone Prism (1975–76).

WOMEN'S EXPERIMENTAL THEATER (WET, 1977–86) New York,
New York
Clare Coss, Sondra Segal, Roberta Sklar
The Daughters Cycle Trilogy: *Daughters* (1976), *Sister/Sister* (1978), and
    Electra Speaks (1980)
Woman's Body and Other Natural Resources: *Food* (1980), *Foodtalk*
    (1981), and *Feast or Famine* (1985).

THE WOMEN'S UNIT (1972–?) New York, New York
Roberta Sklar
Obscenities and Other Questions (1972).

PRODUCING ORGANIZATIONS

BRAVA (1986–) San Francisco, California
Ellen Gavin.

WOMEN'S INTERART (1969–?) New York, New York
Margot Lewitin.

THE WOMEN'S PROJECT (1978–) New York, New York
Julia Miles.

THE WOMYN'S THEATER (1976–?) Seattle, Washington.

NOTES

INTRODUCTION: TWO PROJECTS

1 Nancy Rhodes, personal interview, 18 January 1990.
2 Alice Echols, *Daring to Be Bad: Radical Feminism in America, 1967–1975* (Minneapolis: University of Minnesota Press, 1989) 54.
3 Echols, 12.
4 Sally Banes, *Greenwich Village 1963: Avant-Garde Performance and the Effervescent Body* (Durham, NC: Duke University Press, 1993) 6.
5 Stanley Aronowitz, "When the New Left Was New," *The 60s Without Apology*, eds. Sohnya Sayers, Anders Stephanson, Stanley Aronowitz and Frederic Jameson (Minneapolis: University of Minnesota Press, 1984) 22.
6 Charlotte Bunch, *Passionate Politics: Feminist Theory in Action* (New York: St. Martin's Press, 1987) 6.
7 Jessie Bernard, introduction, *The New Feminist Movement*, ed. Maren Lockwood Carden (New York: Russell Sage Foundation, 1974) xi.
8 Judith Hole and Ellen Levine, *Rebirth of Feminism* (New York: Quadrangle Books, 1971) 108.
9 Michelene Wandor, *Carry On, Understudies* (New York: Routledge and Kegan Paul, 1986) 131.
10 The definitions in the U.S.A. that were in part indebted to Wandor were most prominently expressed in Sue-Ellen Case's *Feminism and Theater*, Jill Dolan's *The Feminist Spectator as Critic*, and Gayle Austin's *Feminist Theories for Dramatic Criticism*.
11 Wandor, 133.
12 Wandor, 135.
13 Wandor, 136.
14 Sue-Ellen Case, *Feminism and Theatre* (New York: Methuen, 1988) 131.
15 This position is not to deny or erase the intersections of feminism and theater that occurred before 1969, as there were many important ones especially at the end of the nineteenth and on into the twentieth centuries. However, many of these have been identified by women who were influenced by the theater work of the 1960s and 1970s and wanted to find out if they had a history.

226

16 Jill Dolan, introduction, *Presence and Desire: Essays on Gender, Sexuality, and Performance* (Ann Arbor: University of Michigan Press, 1993) 30.
17 Joan W. Scott, response to Linda Gordon's rev. of *Gender and the Politics of History, Signs* 15.4 (1990) 860.
18 Joan Mankin, letter to the author, 16 October 1994.
19 Rhodes, interview.
20 It is important to note that histories of women in theater did exist when Nancy Rhodes researched and produced her staged readings though it is not surprising that she was unaware of them as the history of women in theater in the U.S.A. was not taught in universities until very recently. One book Rhodes might have used was Rosamond Gilder, *Enter the Actress: The First Women in Theater* (New York: Houghton Mifflin, 1931), although it does not concentrate exclusively on the U.S.A.

1 WRITING THE HISTORY OF FEMINIST THEATER GROUPS

1 Grant application quoted in Karen Malpede Taylor, *People's Theater in Amerika* (New York: Drama Book Specialists, 1973) 325.
2 Malpede Taylor, 327.
3 Malpede Taylor, 327.
4 Charlotte Rea, "Women's Theater Groups," *Drama Review* 16.2 (1972) 83.
5 Marilyn Lowen Fletcher, "A Chant for My Sisters," *Sisterhood is Powerful: An Anthology of Writings from the Women's Liberation Movement*, ed. Robin Morgan (New York: Vintage Books, 1970) 559–60.
6 Rea, "Groups," 84.
7 Karen Malpede, personal interview, 15 December 1989.
8 Clare Coss, personal interview, 19 December 1989.
9 Roberta Sklar, personal interview, 20 December 1989.
10 Charlotte Bunch, "A Broom of One's Own: Notes on the Women's Liberation Program," *Passionate Politics: Feminist Theory in Action* (New York: St. Martin's Press, 1987) 31.
11 Carroll Smith-Rosenberg, *Disorderly Conduct: Visions of Gender in Victorian America* (New York: A. A. Knopf, 1985) 11.
12 Gerda Lerner, *The Majority Finds Its Past* (New York: Oxford University Press, 1979) 170.
13 Smith-Rosenberg, 14.
14 Smith-Rosenberg, 25–7.
15 Sue-Ellen Case, *Feminism and Theater* (New York: Methuen, 1988) 113–14.
16 Chris Weedon, *Feminist Practice and Poststructuralist Theory* (Oxford: Basil Blackwell, 1987) 8.
17 Joan W. Scott, *Gender and the Politics of History* (New York: Columbia University Press, 1988) 4.
18 Scott, 5.

19 Claudia Koonz, "Post Scripts," *Women's Review of Books* 6.4 (1989): 19.

20 Weedon, 79.

21 Scott, 27.

22 Joan Hoff, "The Pernicious Effects of Poststructuralism on Women's History," *The Chronicle of Higher Education* 20 October 1993: B2.

23 Traditional history techniques rely primarily on printed matter or documents (oral or otherwise), produced more or less contemporaneously with the events under examination. Theater movements and performances about which much printed material, particularly dramatic texts, are to be found are popular topics for historical examination. In contrast, theater movements such as feminist theater, which produced few published texts and little contemporary notice, are less likely to be found in histories. My investigation of feminist theater relies primarily on techniques of oral history, supplemented by collections of ephemeral materials from the Sophia Smith Collection at Smith College, the Billy Rose Theater Collection at Lincoln Center, the Women's Collection at Northwestern University, and the extensive feminist theater files in the University of Washington Drama Library. Most of the women I interviewed had been members of theaters that created their own scripts, printed their own programs, and theorized their own performance practices. Little of what they did was ever written down or collected for future study. Many of the materials exist only in the memories of the participants.

24 Paul Thompson, *The Voice of the Past: Oral History* (Oxford: Oxford University Press, 1988) 5.

25 Thompson, 21.

26 Susan Armitage, "The Next Step," *Frontiers* special issue "Women's Oral History Two" 7.1 (1983): 4.

27 Katheryn Anderson, Susan Armitage, Dana Jack, and Judith Wittner, "Beginning Where We Are: Feminist Methodology in Oral History," *Oral History Review* 15 (1987): 114.

28 Renato Rosaldo, "Doing Oral History," *Social Analysis* 4 (November 1980): 97.

29 Rosaldo, 89.

30 See appendix B for the interview format.

31 Michele Linfante, personal interview, 3 April 1990.

32 Muriel Miguel, personal interview, 26 April 1990. Emphasis hers.

33 Terry Baum, personal interview, 3 April 1990.

34 Thompson, 18.

35 Rosaldo, 97.

36 Jill Dolan, "In Defense of Discourse: Materialist Feminism, Postmodernism, Poststructuralism . . . and Theory," *Drama Review* 33.3 (1989): 59.

37 Patti Gillespie, "Feminist Theater: A Rhetorical Phenomenon," *Quarterly Journal of Speech* 64 (1978): 286.

38 Janet Brown, *Feminist Drama: Definition and Critical Analysis* (Metuchen, NJ: Scarecrow Press, 1979) 87.

39 Brown, 88.

40 Brown, 88–104.

41 Historically, in the U.S.A. there are two different but overlapping disciplines that deal with the vast territory covered by the term "performance" – theater and speech (often also in departments of Speech Communication). Theater departments have tended to concentrate on history, productions, and in many cases professional training for careers in theater while speech departments have focused more on public speaking, the oral interpretation of literature, rhetoric, debate, and the study of communication both mass and interpersonal with a particular emphasis on oral communication. The boundaries are often less than clear as many smaller colleges and some universities have departments that house both speech and theater. One could say that from a speech communication perspective theater is one mode of communication while from a theater point of view speech can be understood as one of the constituent parts of theater. However, it is important to note that the descriptions here are general tendencies rather than definitive and discrete distinctions.

42 Janet Brown, *Taking Center Stage: Feminism in Contemporary U.S. Drama* (Metuchen, NJ: Scarecrow Press, 1991) 2.

43 Elizabeth J. Natalle, *Feminist Theater: A Study in Persuasion* (Metuchen, NJ: Scarecrow Press, 1985) 5.

44 Natalle, 5.

45 Gillespie, 285.

46 "It is a genre without a rhetor, a rhetoric in search of an audience, that transforms traditional argumentation into confrontation, that 'persuades' by 'violating the reality structure' but that presumes a consubstantiality so radical that it permits the most intimate of identifications. It is a 'movement' that eschews leadership, organizational cohesion, and the transactions typical of mass persuasion. Finally, of course, women's liberation is baffling because it has no clear program, because there is no clear answer to the question, 'What do women want?'" Karlyn Kors Campbell, "The Rhetoric of Women's Liberation: An Oxymoron," *Quarterly Journal of Speech*, 59.1 (1973): 86.

47 Helene Keyssar, *Feminist Theatre: An Introduction to Plays by Contemporary British and American Women* (London: Macmillan, 1984) xiv.

48 Rea, "Groups," 79.

49 Gillespie, 285.

50 Dinah Luise Leavitt, *Feminist Theater Groups* (Jefferson, NC: McFarland, 1980) 4.

51 Leavitt, 10.

52 Leavitt, 9.

53 Rosemary Curb, Phyllis Mael, and Beverley Byers Pevitts, "Catalog of Feminist Theaters–Part 1," *Chrysalis* 10 (1979): 51.

54 Judith Zivanovic, "The Rhetorical and Political Foundations of Women's Collaborative Theatre," *Themes in Drama: Women in Theater*, ed. Michael Redmond (Cambridge: Cambridge University Press, 1989).

55 Lizbeth Goodman, *Contemporary Feminist Theatres: To Each Her Own* (London: Routledge, 1993) 15.

56 Peggy Phelan, remarks on the keynote panel of "Making Feminism/ Making Comedy," Women and Theater Program Conference of the Association for Theater in Higher Education, Philadelphia, 1–3 August 1993.

57 Keyssar, 18.

58 Gillespie, 284.

59 See Jill Dolan, *The Feminist Spectator as Critic* (Ann Arbor: UMI Research Press, 1988) 1–18; and Sue-Ellen Case, *Feminism and Theater* (New York: Methuen, 1988) chaps. 4–6.

60 Sondra Lowell, "New Feminist Theater," *Ms.* August 1972: 18.

61 Linda Killian, "Feminist Theater," *Feminist Art Journal* 3.1 (1974) 23.

62 Killian, 23.

63 Susan Suntree, "Women's Theater: Creating the Dream Now," *Women's Culture: The Women's Renaissance of the Seventies*, ed. Gayle Kimball (Metuchen, NJ: Scarecrow Press, 1981) 108.

64 Brown, *Feminist Drama*, 1.

65 Natalle, 5.

66 Gillespie, 285.

67 Suzanne Messing, "Unmasking Some Female Branches on a Family Tree," *New York Times* 14 September 1980: 27.

68 Charlotte Rea, "Women for Women," *Drama Review* 18.4 (1974): 82.

69 Suntree, 111.

70 Cornelia Brunner, "Roberta Sklar: Toward Creating a Women's Theater," *Drama Review* 24.2 (1980): 33.

71 Meredith Flynn, "The Feeling Circle, Company Collaboration, and Ritual Drama: Three Conventions developed by the Women's Theater, At the Foot of the Mountain," diss., Bowling Green State University, 1984, 84.

72 Flynn, 96. Boesing also credits the influences of Stanislavski and Brecht in the development of her approach to acting.

73 "Theater," *The New Woman's Survival Catalog*, eds. Kirsten Grimstad and Susan Rennie (New York: Coward, McCann, and Geoghegan, 1973) 67.

74 "Theater," 67.

75 Sondra Lowell, "Art Comes to the Elevator: Women's Guerilla Theater," *Women: A Journal of Liberation* 2.1 (1970): 50.

76 Lowell, 51.

77 Malpede Taylor, 325.

78 Gillespie, 291.

79 Rea, "Groups," 80.

80 Rea, "Groups," 80.

81 Brown, *Feminist Drama*, 87.

82 Natalle, 18.

83 Helen Krich Chinoy and Linda Walsh Jenkins, eds., *Women in American Theater* (New York: Theater Communications Group, 1987) 304.

84 Nancy Rhodes, personal interview, 18 January 1990.

85 Dolan, 201.
86 Rea, "Groups," 82.
87 Twila Thompson, personal interview, 19 December 1989.
88 Natalle, 14.

2 FEMINISM, THEATER, AND RADICAL POLITICS

1 James Miller, *Democracy is in the Streets: From Port Huron to the Siege of Chicago* (New York: Simon and Schuster, 1987) 94.
2 SDS, "The Port Huron Statement," *Democracy is in the Streets*, 333. Emphasis theirs.
3 SDS, 333.
4 Stanley Aronowitz, "When the New Left Was New," *The 60s Without Apology*, eds. Sohnya Sayres, Anders Stephanson, Stanley Aronowitz and Frederic Jameson (Minneapolis: University of Minnesota Press, 1984) 20. Emphasis his.
5 Aronowitz, 21.
6 Milton Viorst, *Fire in the Streets: America in the 1960s* (New York: Simon and Schuster, 1979) 427.
7 Viorst, 430.
8 Viorst, 430.
9 Charlotte Bunch, "A Broom of One's Own," *Passionate Politics: Feminist Theory in Action* (New York: St. Martin's Press, 1987) 40–41; Judith Hole and Ellen Levine, *Rebirth of Feminism* (New York: Quadrangle Books, 1971) 296–99; and Maren Lockwood Carden, ed., *The New Feminist Movement* (New York: Russell Sage Foundation, 1974) 61.
10 Robin Morgan, "WITCH Hexes Wall Street," *Going Too Far: The Personal Chronicle of a Feminist* (New York: Vintage Books, 1978) 75–77.
11 Morgan, 80–81.
12 Alice Echols, *Daring to Be Bad: Radical Feminism in America, 1967–1965* (Minneapolis: University of Minnesota Press, 1989) 93.
13 Morgan, "Women Disrupt the Miss America Pageant," *Going Too Far*, 65. It was at this event that the image of feminists as bra-burners originated. No bras were ever burnt, as far as anyone can tell, at any feminist demonstration. What Morgan does not include in her article is that the demonstrators had every intention of burning the contents of the can but were prohibited by order of the Atlantic City government. (Echols, 93–94.)
14 SDS, 374.
15 Kathie Sarachild, "Consciousness-Raising: A Radical Weapon," *Feminist Revolution*, ed. Redstockings, abridged edn. (New York: Random House, 1978) 144.
16 bell hooks, *Talking Back: Thinking Feminism, Thinking Black* (Boston: South End Press, 1989) 109.
17 According to Kathie Sarachild, whom Alice Echols credits as the chief architect of C-R, "the test of accuracy of what any of the books said would be the actual experience we had in these areas." Sarachild, 145.

18 Sarachild, 147.
19 Pam Allen, "Free Space," *Radical Feminism*, eds. Anne Koedt, Ellen Levine, and Anita Rapone (New York: Quadrangle Books, 1973) 273.
20 For an elaboration of the relation of truth and experience, see Sarachild, 147–49.
21 Echols, 90.
22 N.a., "Consciousness Raising," *Radical Feminism*, 280–81.
23 Open Theatre Ensemble, Karen Malpede, ed., *Three Works By the Open Theater* (New York: Drama Book Specialists, 1974) 11.
24 Margaret Croyden, *Lunatics, Lovers and Poets: The Contemporary Experimental Theater* (New York: McGraw-Hill, 1974) 170.
25 Arthur Sainer, *The Radical Theater Notebook* (New York: Avon Books, 1975) 79.
26 Margot Lewitin, personal interview, 12 December 1989. Emphasis hers.
27 Michael Feingold, "Caffe Cino, 20 Years After Magic Time," *Village Voice* 14 May 1985: n.p.
28 Michael Smith and Nick Orzel, eds., *Eight Plays from Off Off-Broadway* (New York: Bobbs-Merrill, 1966) 9.
29 Joe Cino, "Caffe Cino," *Eight Plays From Off Off-Broadway*, 53.
30 Feingold, n.p.
31 Cino, 54.
32 William Hoffman, ed., introduction, *Gay Plays: The First Collection* (New York: Avon Books, 1979) xxiii.
33 Hoffman, xxiv.
34 Cornelia Brunner, "Roberta Sklar: Toward Creating a Women's Theater," *Drama Review* 24.2 (1980): 27–28.
35 Oscar Brockett and Robert Findlay, *Century of Innovation: A History of European and American Theatre and Drama Since 1870* (Englewood Cliffs, NJ: Prentice Hall, 1973) 713; and Reverend Al Carmines, "The Judson Poets' Theater," *Eight Plays from Off Off-Broadway*, 124.
36 Feingold, n.p.
37 Ellen Stewart, "La Mama Experimental Theater Club," *Eight Plays From Off Off-Broadway*, 163.
38 Smith and Orzel, 10.
39 Stewart, 164.
40 The Obie, founded in 1956, is a yearly award originally recognizing the work done in Off-Broadway venues. It was largely the idea of Jerry Tallmer who was a critic for the *Village Voice* at the time. In 1964 the scope of the awards was enlarged to include Off Off-Broadway. For a further discussion of the award and its relationship to the work done in those venues see Ross Wetzsteon, ed., *The Obie Winners* (New York: Doubleday, 1980).
41 Lewitin, interview.
42 Robert Pasolli, *A Book on the Open Theater* (New York: Avon Books, 1970) 2–3.
43 Jack Poggi, *Theater in America: Impact of Economic Forces, 1870–1967* (Ithaca: Cornell University Press, 1968) 199.

44 Joseph Chaiken, "The Open Theater," *Eight Plays From Off Off-Broadway*, 201.
45 Sainer, 3.
46 Croyden, 176.
47 Eileen Blumenthal, *Joseph Chaiken: Exploring the Boundaries of Theater* (New York: Cambridge University Press, 1984) 26.
48 Viola Spolin, *Improvisation for the Theater: A Handbook of Teaching and Directing Techniques* (Evanston, IL: Northwestern University Press, 1963) 9–10.
49 Spolin, 272.
50 Peter Feldman, "Notes for the Open Theater Production," *Viet Rock, Comings and Goings, Keep Tightly Closed in a Cool Dry Place, and In the Gloaming, Oh My Darling: Four Plays by Megan Terry* (New York: Simon and Schuster, 1966) 200–01. Emphasis his.
51 Sidney S. Walter, "Notes for the Firehouse Theater Production," *Four Plays by Megan Terry*, 207.
52 Sainer, 2.
53 Blumenthal, 83.
54 Blumenthal, 42.
55 Croyden, 189.
56 Blumenthal, 77.
57 Blumenthal, 42–43.
58 Sainer, 2.
59 Open Theater Ensemble, Malpede, 36.
60 Open Theater Ensemble, Malpede, 99.
61 R. G. Davis, *The San Francisco Mime Troupe: The First Ten Years* (Palo Alto: Ramparts Press, 1975) 18.
62 Davis, 53.
63 Davis, 70.
64 Davis, 95.
65 Theodore Shank, *American Alternative Theater* (New York: St. Martin's Press, 1982) 59.
66 Shank, 61–62.
67 Shank, 62.
68 Shank, 73–74.
69 Elizabeth J. Natalle, *Feminist Theater: A Study in Persuasion*, (Metuchen, NJ: Scarecrow Press, 1985) 13.
70 Joan Mankin, personal interview with Sue-Ellen Case, 19 February 1989.
71 Terry Baum, personal interview, 3 April 1990.
72 Roger Hahn, "Profile: K. D. Codish," *New Haven Register* October 1983: 35.
73 Arthur Sainer, "Interart Walks a Tightrope," *Village Voice* 7 August 1984: 85; and Lewitin, interview.
74 Patti Gillespie, "Feminist Theater: A Rhetorical Phenomenon," *Quarterly Journal of Speech* 64 (1978): 286.
75 Brunner, 33.
76 Brunner, 33.
77 Open Theater Ensemble, Malpede, 97.

78 Brunner, 32. Emphasis hers.
79 Sally Banes, *Greenwich Village 1963: Avant-Garde Performance and the Effervescent Body* (Durham, NC: Duke University Press, 1993) 36.

3 COLLECTIVITY AND COLLABORATION

1 Alice Echols, *Daring to Be Bad: Radical Feminism in America, 1967–1975* (Minneapolis: University of Minnesota Press, 1989) 16.
2 Carol Hanisch notes that originally most feminist groups were committed to the stated principle "no leadership, no spokeswoman, no votes, action by consensus." This was an attractive slogan to those women who felt abused and ignored by the leadership practices in male alternative groups. But ultimately she believes that the "denial that any leadership or the necessity for it even existed" was a "utopian denial of reality" because it did not acknowledge that "some people actually know more because of the kind and combination of experiences in their lives." The situation Hanisch described led to some of the more outrageous excesses of feminist groups, such as expelling women who got too much media coverage or wrote feminist books, allowing people to talk only by lot, or forcing them to refuse lecture bookings. Carol Hanisch, "The Liberal Takeover of Women's Liberation," *Feminist Revolution*, ed. Redstockings (New York: Random House, 1978) 164–65.
3 Ted Shank, "Collective Creation," *Drama Review* 16.2 (1972): 3.
4 Shank, 4.
5 While this is a simplification of the conventional theater process, it is a common complaint from playwrights that they are often ignored or disregarded when their plays are put into production. Maria Irene Fornes has been widely quoted on her views of the structure of theater that disregards the playwright. Indeed, Fornes insists on directing her own work, especially her new plays.
6 Michelene Wandor, *Carry On, Understudies* (New York: Routledge and Kegan Paul, 1986) 95.
7 Sue-Ellen Case, *Feminism and Theater* (New York: Methuen, 1988) 68.
8 Dinah Leavitt, *Feminist Theater Groups* (Jefferson, NC: McFarland, 1980) 82. "[T]heir [the performers] personal involvement with their companies and dedication to feminism relate to their valuing a means to the end. Actually there is no end; the process is continuous and there is no thought of setting a production."
9 Rosemary Curb, Phyllis Mael, and Beverley Byers Pevitts, "Catalog of Feminist Theaters – Parts 1 and 2," *Chrysalis* 10 (1979): 64.
10 Leavitt, 80.
11 Emma Missouri, personal interview, 18 December 1989.
12 Anita Mattos, personal interview, 5 April 1990.
13 Carole Spedding, "Words *Plus* Texture," n.d., n.p.
14 Spiderwoman Theater, "Our Source," publicity flyer.
15 Cornelia Brunner, "Roberta Sklar: Toward Creating a Women's Theater," *Drama Review* 24.2 (1980): 40.

16 Harriet Schiffer, personal interview, 30 October 1994.

17 Schiffer, interview.

18 Schiffer, interview.

19 Schiffer, interview.

20 Schiffer, interview.

21 Joan Mankin, personal interview with Sue-Ellen Case, 1 January 1989.

22 The two shows they eventually decided upon were *Moonlighting* and *Manifesto* by Dacia Maraini. Michele Linfante added that taking *Manifesto* was a mistake, they should have taken one of their own works. When they performed it at Teatro Maddalena, the theater founded by Maraini, the audiences were visibly unimpressed. Michele Linfante, personal interview, 3 April 1990.

23 Terry Baum, personal interview, 4 April 1990.

24 Baum, interview.

25 Adele Prandini, personal interview, 5 April 1990.

26 Barbara Tholfsen, personal interview, 18 January 1990.

27 See the discussion, later in the chapter, on Lilith.

28 Patricia Van Kirk, personal interview, 10 July 1990.

29 Van Kirk, interview.

30 Trish Hall, "Reaching Beyond Rhetoric," *New Haven Advocate* 28 November 1979: 27. From the Sophia Smith Collection (SSC).

31 Hall, 27. From the SSC.

32 Mary Beth Bruno, "Closing the Curtain," *New Haven Advocate* 17 August 1983: 41. From the SSC.

33 Linfante, interview. Emphasis hers.

34 "Their [feminist theater's] nationwide and apparently spontaneous formation from coast to coast – without encouragement, leadership, or direction from a national organization – makes them an example of a grassroots movement seldom witnessed in the American theater." Patti Gillespie, "Feminist Theater: A Rhetorical Phenomenon," *Quarterly Journal of Speech* 64 (1978): 284.

35 Linda Walsh Jenkins, "Feminist Theater," *Women in American Theater*, eds. Helen Krich Chinoy and Linda Walsh Jenkins (New York: Theater Communications Group, 1987) 277.

36 Theater of Light and Shadow, "A History of TLS in Names, Dates, Places, and Performances," unpublished ms. From the SSC.

37 Julia Garnett, "A National Women's Festival in Santa Cruz," *San Francisco Chronicle Datebook* 15 May 1983: 41.

38 Letter from the National Festival of Women's Theater Coordinating Committee, 24 December 1985.

39 Alisa Solomon, "The WOW Cafe," *Drama Review* 29.1 (1985): 93.

40 Twila Thompson, personal interview, 19 December 1989.

41 For further information on the conferences and the organization itself see WTP Newsletters; Jill Dolan, *The Feminist Spectator as Critic* (Ann Arbor: UMI, 1988); *Women and Performance*, special issue, "Celebrating The Women and Theater Program" 4.2 (1989); and the Women and Theater Program Archives at the Sophia Smith Collection at Smith College in Northampton, Massachusetts.

42 Honor Moore, "Theater Will Never Be the Same," *Ms.* December 1977: 74.

43 *At the Foot of the Mountain Newsletter*, Fall 1985: 1.

44 Muriel Miguel, personal interview, 26 April 1990.

45 Iris Landsberg, personal interview, 7 April 1990.

46 Mattos, interview.

47 Julie Malnig and Judy C. Rosenthal, "The Women's Experimental Theater: Transforming Family Stories into Feminist Questions," *Acting Out: Feminist Performances*, eds. Lynda Hart and Peggy Phelan (Ann Arbor: University of Michigan Press, 1993) 203.

48 Linfante, interview.

49 Van Kirk, interview.

50 See Leavitt, especially chapters 2–5.

51 Berenice Johnson Reagon, "Coalition Politics: Turning the Century," *Home Girls: A Black Feminist Anthology*, ed. Barbara Smith (New York: Kitchen Table: Women of Color Press, 1983) 362. Emphasis hers. I would like to thank Katrin Sieg for bringing this quotation to my attention.

52 Charlotte Rea, "Women for Women," *The Drama Review* 18.4 (1974): 82.

53 Rea, 83.

54 Detroit, "Women's Collage Theater Comment Book," unpublished, n.p., n.d.

55 Unnamed college professor, "Comment Book," 12 April 1980, n.p.

56 The Lavender Cellar Theater, a lesbian–feminist theater of Minneapolis, was inspired by the Alive and Trucking Theater, a feminist theater in the same city. For a while the women of Lavender Cellar discussed joining A&TT instead of founding a theater of their own, but "did not because that group would have been unable to devote enough attention to lesbian issues." Leavitt, 44. This story was repeated many times as lesbians failed to see lesbian stories and characters produced in feminist theater.

57 Clare Coss, "From Daughter of Alistine Melpomene Thalia: A Play Within a Play," *Chrysalis* 5 (1977): 62.

58 Coss, 62.

59 Baum, interview.

60 Linfante, interview.

61 Linfante, interview.

62 Linfante, interview.

63 Mankin, interview.

64 Linfante, interview. Emphasis hers.

65 Kitty Tsui, "Lilith and the Hired Help," *Heresies* 5.1 (1984): 50.

66 Tsui, 50.

67 Tsui, 50.

68 Tsui, 51.

69 Tsui, 51. 'It was stated that because of my 'problems' it would not be 'right' for me to go on a scheduled tour."

70 Tsui, 51.

71 Linfante, interview. "You always bring them in in the context of the

work and that's the way I think you do combat racism; you work together, you are in alliance together over the years."

72 Miguel, interview.

73 Miguel, interview. Emphasis hers.

74 Miguel, interview.

75 Miguel, interview.

76 Vivian M. Patraka, "Split Britches in *Split Britches*: Performing History, Vaudeville, and the Everyday," *Women and Performance* 4.8 (1989): 58.

77 Alisa Solomon, "Tangled Web," *Village Voice* 19 March 1985: n.p.

78 *At the Foot of the Mountain Newsletter*, Fall 1986: 5.

79 Naomi Scheman, quoted in Robert Collins, "A Feminist Theater in Transition," *American Theater* 4.11 (1988): 32. Emphasis hers.

80 Carol Itawa, president of the AFOM board of directors, quoted in Collins, 33.

81 Diane Odeen, "A Cultural Feminist Theater: The *Stories* Change with the Times," unpublished paper presented at the Association for Theater in Higher Education Conference, Chicago, Illinois, 10 August 1990.

82 *Raped* was also cancelled because Eric Bentley was threatening to withdraw permission to produce the one-act if AFOM did not perform the play exactly as it was written. (Collins, 33.)

83 Collins, 34.

84 Odeen, unpublished

85 Collins, 34.

86 Nayo-Barbara Malcolm Watkins, "Multi-Culturalism: What in the World Is It?" *At the Foot of the Mountain Newsletter*, Fall 1988: 5. Emphasis hers.

87 AFOM, "History and Annual Report," 1990, unpublished.

88 AFOM, "Annual Report," unpublished.

89 Watkins, 4.

90 Linfante, interview.

91 Sondra Segal, personal interview, 21 December 1989.

92 Roberta Sklar, personal interview, 20 December 1989; and letter to the author, 1 August 1994.

93 Brunner, 35. Emphasis hers.

94 Rea, 81.

95 Clare Coss, personal interview, 19 December 1989; and Sklar, interview.

96 For a more in-depth account of *Daughters* refer to chapter four, the section entitled "Plays About Mothers and Daughters."

97 Segal, interview; and letter to the author, 1 August 1994.

98 Roberta Sklar, personal conversation, 6 May 1992.

99 For a more detailed and complete examination of the trilogy, see chapter four.

100 Helen Krich Chinoy, "Women's Interart Theater," *Women in American Theater*, eds. Helen Krich Chinoy and Linda Walsh Jenkins (New York: Theater Communications Group, 1987) 295.

101 Coss, interview; and *Electra Speaks*, program notes.

102 Coss, interview.

103 Segal, interview; and letter to the author, 1 August 1994.
104 Coss, interview.
105 Sklar, interview.
106 Segal, interview.
107 Segal, interview.
108 Segal, interview.
109 Segal, interview.
110 Sklar, interview.
111 Segal, interview.
112 Sondra Segal and Roberta Sklar, "The Women's Experimental Theater," *Women in American Theater*, 307–08.
113 Spiderwoman Theater, "Our Source," publicity material.
114 Womanspace Theater Workshop, flyer, n.d.
115 Bell Gale Chevigny, rev. of *Cycles*, *University Review* (December 1973): n.p.
116 Miguel, interview.
117 Miguel, interview.
118 Miguel, interview.
119 See chapter five for further discussion of *Women in Violence*.
120 Miguel, interview.
121 Lisa Mayo, comments during Miguel interview.
122 Spiderwoman post-show discussion, Seattle Group Theater, 25 June 1989.
123 Miguel, interview.
124 Miguel, interview.
125 Renfreu Neff, "Spiderwoman Theater," *Other Stages* 5 May 1983: 3.
126 Miguel, interview.
127 Christopher V. Davies, "Spiderwoman Spins a Delightful Web of Entertainment Overseas," *New York City Tribune* 30 December 1987: n.p.
128 Joe Adcock, "The Wackiness Shines Through This Up-to-Date 'Lysistrata'," *Seattle Post-Intelligencer* 18–24 February 1983: n.p.
129 Spiderwoman Theater, "Our Repertoire," publicity material, n.d., n.p.
130 Hilary Harris, rev. of *Anniversary Waltz*, *Theatre Journal* 42.4 (1990): 487.
131 Miguel, interview.
132 "Feminist cabaret," New York *Daily News* 6 March 1981: n.p.
133 Solomon, "Web," n.p.
134 Jill Dolan, *The Feminist Spectator as Critic* (Ann Arbor: UMI Research Press, 1988) 72.
135 Eileen Blumenthal, "Spinning Free," *Village Voice* 18 February 1980: n.p.; and Adrienne Scott and Sophia Mirviss, "The Incredible Spiderwoman" *Womannews* April 1980: n.p.
136 Patraka, 58. Patraka's article provides a brief history of Split Britches, as well as an analysis of their work.
137 Miguel, interview.
138 Baum, interview.
139 Mankin, interview.

140 Baum, interview.
141 Linfante, interview; and Mankin, interview.
142 Linfante, interview.
143 Linfante, interview.
144 Baum, interview.
145 Terry Baum, Carolyn Meyers, Michele Linfante, and Resnais Winter, *Sacrifices: A Fable of the Women's Movement*, unpublished.
146 For further information on Maraini and La Maddalena see Grazia Sumeli Weinberg, "Women's Theater: Teatro La Maddalena and the Work of Dacia Maraini," *Western European Stages* 1.1 (1989) 27–29. See also in the same issue, Jane House, "Interview with Dacia Maraini," 39–43. An interesting tangent, especially in relation to chapter two, is that in the interview Maraini cites the Living Theater, who toured Italy in the mid-1960s, as a great inspiration to her work in the theater.
147 Schiffer, interview.
148 Linfante, interview; and Mankin, interview.
149 Linfante, interview.
150 Baum, interview.
151 Baum, interview.
152 Baum, interview.
153 Linfante, interview.
154 Linfante, interview.
155 See chapter four for a further discussion of *Pizza*.
156 Mankin, interview.
157 Linfante, interview.
158 Linfante, interview.
159 Linfante, interview.
160 Mankin, interview.
161 Mankin, interview.
162 Before this production was mounted Lilith produced a rewritten, full-length version of *Pizza* in 1982.
163 Mankin, interview.
164 Mankin, interview.
165 Schiffer, interview.
166 Schiffer, interview.
167 Schiffer, interview.
168 Schiffer, interview.
169 Schiffer interview.
170 Van Kirk, interview. All information on the history of Front Room Theater comes from the Van Kirk interview unless otherwise noted.
171 Van Kirk, interview.
172 *Front Room Theater Guild Newsletter*, Fall 1984: 2.
173 Van Kirk, interview.
174 Patricia Van Kirk, letter to the author, 11 January 1994.
175 *Front Room Theater*, 3.
176 Van Kirk, interview.
177 Van Kirk, interview. Van Kirk notes "we did do one of the Foot of the Mountain's scripts *The Clue in the Old Birdbath* . . . we did not

do any RIFT plays. I did read them but most of the plays then were written specifically for the individuals in their respective companies and didn't seem to translate well to our company" (Van Kirk, letter).

178 Tom W. Kelly, "Cove 'Beneficial to Gay Image' Not to Be Missed," *Seattle Gay News* 25 January 1985: 19.
179 Gillian G. Gaar, "Summertime When the Livin' is Easy," *Washington Cascade Voice* 25 January 1985: 16.
180 *Front Room Theater*, 2.
181 Phrin Pickett and Cappy Kotz, *In Search of the Hammer*, and *Return of the Hammer*, liner notes, sound recording, 1985.
182 *In Search of the Hammer: The First Adventures of the Three Mustbequeers*, program.
183 Van Kirk, interview.
184 Ira Gruber, rev. of *In Search of the Hammer*, *Northwest Passage* November 1983: 16.
185 Rebecca Brown, "Type for Adventure," *Lights* 30 September – 13 October 13 n.y.: 17.
186 Marian Michener, "*Return of the Hammer* in Rehearsal at Front Room Theater," *Seattle Gay News* 3 May 1985: 20.

4 REPRESENTING COMMUNITY AND EXPERIENCE

1 Rosalind Brunt and Caroline Rowan, introduction, *Feminism, Culture, and Politics*, eds. Rosalind Brunt and Caroline Rowan (London: Lawrence and Wishart, 1982) 11.
2 Alice Echols, *Daring to Be Bad: Radical Feminism in America, 1967–1975* (Minneapolis: University of Minnesota Press, 1989) 16.
3 Michèle Barrett, "Feminism and the definition of Cultural Politics," *Feminism, Culture, and Politics*, 39.
4 Barrett, 53.
5 Barrett, 47.
6 Anselma Dell'Olio, founder of the New Feminist Theater, intended to appeal to "the large audience of housewives and businessmen who support establishment theater." Dell'Olio was not working within the feminist community, however, as she believed that "feminist theater can work within the traditional framework and can be commercially successful." Charlotte Rea, "Women's Theater Groups," *Drama Review* 16.2 (1972): 82. Dell'Olio's theater seems to me to be feminist theater in a more generic sense of the word than in the more specific case of feminist theater groups of this period. Hers is the only group that I know of that rejected the feminist community as audience in favor of a more traditionally defined mainstream audience. It is important to mention that, in complete contradiction to what I have said here, Rea notes that Dell'Olio's New Feminist Repertory did two benefits in 1969, one for the Redstockings, the feminist political group that pioneered consciousness-raising, and the other for the New York chapter of the National Organization of Women (Rea, "Groups," 81).

7 Charlotte Rea, "Women for Women," *Drama Review* 18.4 (1974): 82.
8 Adele Prandini, personal interview, 5 April 1990.
9 Roberta Sklar, remarks at a meeting of the League of Professional Theater Women in New York City, from the notes of Sue-Ellen Case, n.d.
10 Michele Linfante, personal interview, 3 April 1990.
11 Emma Missouri, personal interview, 18 December 1989.
12 Missouri, interview.
13 Prandini, interview.
14 Front Room Theater Guild, unpublished mission statement, n.d., n.p.
15 Patricia Van Kirk, personal interview, 10 July 1990.
16 Prandini, interview.
17 *Front Room Theater Guild Newsletter*, Fall 1984: 1.
18 Rosemary Curb, Phyllis Mael, and Beverley Byers Pevitts, "Catalog of Feminist Theater – Parts 1 and 2," *Chrysalis* 10 (1979): 70. Emphasis theirs.
19 Curb *et al.*, 74.
20 Lillian Perinciolo, "Feminist Theater: They're Playing in Peoria," *Ms.* October 1975: 102.
21 Van Kirk, interview.
22 Emily Sisley, "Notes on Lesbian Theater," *Drama Review* 18.1 (1981): 54.
23 Van Kirk, interview.
24 Van Kirk, interview.
25 Van Kirk, interview.
26 Iris Landsberg, personal interview, 7 April 1990.
27 Audre Lorde, "The Uses of Anger: Women Responding to Racism," *Sister Outsider* (Trumansburg, NY: The Crossing Press, 1984) 130.
28 Echols, 90.
29 bell hooks, *Talking Back: Thinking Feminist, Thinking Black* (Boston: South End Press, 1989) 22.
30 Cherrie Moraga and Gloria Anzaldua, eds., *The Bridge Called My Back: Writings by Radical Women of Color* (New York: Kitchen Table: Women of Color Press, 1983) xxiii.
31 Moraga and Anzaldua, xxiii.
32 Yvonne Yarbro-Bejarano, "Chicanas in Theater," *Women and Performance* 2.2 (1985): 49.
33 Barbara Brinson-Pineda, "Voz de la Mujer," *El Tecolote Literary Magazine* 23.4 (n.d.): 7.
34 Yvonne Yarbro-Bejarano, "*Teatropoesía* by Chicanas in the Bay Area," *Mexican American Theater: Then and Now*, ed. Nicolás Kanellos (Houston: Arte Publico Press, 1983) 80. Bejarano lists Anita Mattos as performing with Valentina, noting that Mattos is a member of El Teatro Latino; Mattos in her interview with me identifies herself as a member of Valentina Productions (Anita Mattos, personal interview, 26 April 1990).
35 Mattos, interview.
36 Curb *et al.*, 70.
37 Perinciolo, 103.

38 Curb *et al.*, 74.
39 Margaret Wilkerson, ed., *Nine Plays by Black Women* (New York: New American Library, 1986) xix.
40 Spiderwoman, post-show discussion at the Seattle Group Theater, Seattle, WA, 25 June 1989.
41 Muriel Miguel, personal interview, 26 April 1990.
42 Miguel, interview.
43 Loren Kruger, "The Dis-Play's the Thing: Gender and Public Sphere in Contemporary British Theater," *Theater Journal* 42.1 (1990): 41.
44 Terry Baum, Carolyn Meyers, Michele Linfante, and Resnais Winter, *Sacrifices: A Fable of the Women's Movement*, unpublished ms.
45 All productions were performed in and around the Bay area.
46 Batya Podos, "Feeding the Feminist Psyche Through Ritual Theater," *The Politics of Women's Spirituality: Essays on the Rise of Power Within the Feminist Movement*, ed. Charlene Spretnak (New York: Doubleday, 1982) 306.
47 Podos, 306.
48 Podos, 306.
49 Podos, 307.
50 Podos, 311.
51 Podos, 308–09.
52 Sue-Ellen Case, *Feminism and Theater* (New York: Methuen, 1988) 69.
53 *Heresies* 2.1 (1978); *Chrysalis* 6; *Quest* 1.4 and 4.3.
54 Anne Carson, *Feminist Spirituality and the Feminist Divine: An Annotated Bibliography* (Trumansberg, NY: Crossing Press, 1986).
55 Carole P. Christ, "Why Women Need the Goddess: Phenomenological, Psychological, and Political Reflections," *The Politics of Women's Spirituality*, 74–75.
56 See Merlin Stone, *When God Was a Woman* (New York: Dial Press, 1976); Marija Gimbutas, "Woman and Culture in Goddess Oriented Old Europe," 22–31, and Sophie Drinker, "The Origins of Music: Women's Goddess Worship," 39–48, both in *The Politics of Women's Spirituality*.
57 Kay Turner, "Contemporary Feminist Rituals," *Heresies*, special issue "The Great Goddess," 2.1 (1978): 20.
58 Turner, 25.
59 Turner, 26.
60 Turner, 25.
61 "All of the myriad varieties of patriarchal oppression – co-opting and replacing the Goddess, imposing patrilineal descent and ownership of the woman's womb, restricting and mutilating woman's body, denying women education and legal rights, forbidding her control of her body, and portraying that body as a pornographic toy – all of these acts are motivated by one desperate drive: to prevent woman from experiencing her power." Spretnak, introduction, *The Politics of Women's Spirituality*, xii.
62 Meredith Flynn, "The Feeling Circle, Company Collaboration, and Ritual Drama: Three Conventions Developed by the Women's Theater,

At the Foot of the Mountain," diss., Bowling Green State University, 1984, 192.

63 Roberta Sklar, "Reflections," *Women in American Theater*, eds. Helen Krich Chinoy and Linda Walsh Jenkins (New York: Theater Communications Group, 1987) 326.

64 Sue-Ellen Case, "Judy Grahn's Gynopoetics: *The Queen of Swords*," *Studies in the Literary Imagination* 21.2 (1988): 51.

65 Joanna Russ, "Why Women Can't Write," *Images of Women in Fiction*, ed. Susan Koppelman (Bowling Green, Ohio: Bowling Green University Popular Press, 1972) 19.

66 Russ, 20.

67 Judith Antonelli, "Feminist Spirituality: Politics of the Psyche," *The Politics of Women's Spirituality*, 402. Antonelli proposes "hystory" as an alternative spelling because it "indicates the linguistic connection to the womb." She offers this in place of the popular "herstory."

68 Bela Debrida, a scholar working in archaeology and mythology, writes of mythology, "[a]s I learn more of the myths of other cultures, of all periods, I become ever more convinced that all mythology reveals women's power." "Drawing from Mythology in Woman's Quest for Selfhood," *The Politics of Women's Spirituality*, 141.

69 Clare Coss, Sondra Segal, and Roberta Sklar, "Separation and Survival: Mothers, Daughters, Sisters – The Women's Experimental Theater," *The Future of Difference*, eds. Hester Eisenstein and Alice Jardine (Boston: G. K. Hall & Co., 1980) 234.

70 Christ, 83.

71 Adrienne Rich, *Of Woman Born: Motherhood as an Experience and Institution* (New York: W. W. Norton, 1976, 1986) 218.

72 Robin Morgan, ed., *Sisterhood is Powerful: An Anthology of Writings from The Women's Liberation Movement* (New York: Vintage Books, 1970).

73 Rich, 225.

74 Rich, 220.

75 Trinh T. Minh-ha, "Grandma's Story," *Woman, Native, Other: Postcoloniality, Feminism, and Writing* (Bloomington: University of Indiana Press, 1989) 121.

76 Connie Young Woo, "The World of Our Grandmothers," *Making Waves: An Anthology of Writings By and About Asian American Women*, eds. Asian Women United of California (Boston: Beacon Press, 1989) 35.

77 Cherrie Moraga, "La Güera," *This Bridge Called My Back*, 30.

78 At the Foot of the Mountain, "Mission Statement," n.d., n.p.

79 "Our program includes: the creation and performance of collaborative works, the development of experimental methods of acting through workshops, the nurturance of writers, directors, and performers, public research with women in themes relevant to our experience. As the Women's Experimental Theater we are concerned with the evolution of a feminist theater aesthetic. "Statement of Purpose" in the personal files of Roberta Sklar.

80 Clare Coss, Sondra Segal, and Roberta Sklar, *Daughters*, unpublished playscript.
81 Sondra Segal, personal interview, 21 December 1989.
82 Clare Coss, personal interview, 19 December 1989.
83 Bettina Aptheker, *Women's Legacy: Essays on Race, Sex, and Class in American History* (Amherst: University of Massachusetts Press, 1982).
84 Suzanne Messing, "Unmasking Some Female Branches on a Family Tree," *New York Times* 14 September 1980: 27.
85 Martha Boesing, in collaboration with the women At the Foot of the Mountain, "The Story of A Mother: A Ritual Drama," *Women in American Theater*, eds. Helen Krich Chinoy and Linda Walsh Jenkins (New York: Theater Communications Group, 1987) 44.
86 Boesing, 45.
87 Flynn, 189.
88 *Daughters*, 2.
89 The script describes the "totem" thus: "two women perform the roles of the Mother/Daughter totem in several scenes. Each role reflects the overtones of daughterhood at all times." *Daughters*, ii.
90 *Daughters*, 6 and 39.
91 Martha Boesing, and At the Foot of the Mountain Company, *The Story of a Mother*, unpublished playscript, 11.
92 *Story of a Mother*, 22.
93 *Daughters*, 54.
94 Rhode Island Feminist Theater (RIFT), afterword, *Frontiers*, special issue, "Mothers and Daughters," 3.2 (1978): 72.
95 John C. Meyers, "I Want to Wake Up and Be Free," *Rhode Islander* 29 February 1976: 14.
96 RIFT, 61.
97 The afterword described the structure: "The modern-day scenes follow each new action in the myth." RIFT, 73.
98 RIFT, 65.
99 RIFT, 72.
100 Bejarano, "*Teatropoesía*," 79.
101 Bejarano, "*Teatropoesía*," 79.
102 New Cycle Theater membership flyer, n.d., n.p.
103 L. A. Croghan, "A Monster Has Stolen the Sun," *Brooklyn Heights Press* 5 March 1981: n.p.
104 Karen Malpede, *The End of War, A Monster Has Stolen the Sun and Other Plays* (Marlboro, VT: Marlboro Press, 1987) 46.
105 Karen Malpede, "*Rebeccah*: Rehearsal Notes," *Women in American Theater*, 309.
106 Malpede, "*Rebeccah*," 308.
107 Peggy Morgan, "Off the Beaten Trail with New York Theater," *Rutgers Daily Targum* 7 April 1976: n.p.
108 Mel Gussow, "Theater: Women's Work," *New York Times* 30 March 1976: n.p.
109 N.a., n.t., *The Majority Report* 14 July 1975: n.p.
110 Darlene Hoskins Evans, Jo Carney, Rhoda Staley, Ellen Hope Meyer, Marcia Slotkin, and Claire Nicolas White, *Mothers and Daughters*,

unpublished playscript. The script was in the files of the Theater of Light and Shadow in the Sophia Smith Collection (SSC) at Smith College. It was not dated and, other than the names of authors, had no information about the group. Subsequent research has not yielded any reference to them.

111 *Mothers and Daughters*, 1. From the SSC.
112 *Mothers and Daughters*, 1. From the SSC.
113 *Mothers and Daughters*, 3. From the SSC.
114 *Mothers and Daughters*, 7. From the SSC.
115 Linfante, interview.
116 Linfante, interview.
117 Michelle Linfante, *Pizza*, in *West Coast Plays 6*, ed. Rick Foster (Berkeley: California Theater Council, 1980) 27.
118 Linfante, 33.
119 Bejarano, "*Teatropoesía*," 80.
120 Brinson-Pineda, 7.
121 Bejarano, "*Teatropoesía*," 80.
122 Miguel, interview.
123 Spiderwoman, "Our Repertoire," n.d., n.p.
124 Spiderwoman, discussion.
125 Vivian M. Patraka, "*Split Britches* in Split Britches: Performing History, Vaudeville, and the Everyday," *Women and Performance* 4.8 (1989): 59.
126 Anita Mattos, letter to the author, 1 March 1994.
127 Mattos, interview.
128 Mattos, interview.
129 Mattos, interview.
130 Mattos, interview.
131 Mattos, interview. For more information on this festival see Yvonne Yarbro-Bejarano, "The Role of Women in Chicano Theater Organizations," *Revista Literaria del Tecolote* 2.3–4 (1981).
132 Naomi Newman, personal interview, 5 April 1990.
133 Naomi Newman, *Snake Talk: Urgent Messages from the Mother*, program notes.
134 Newman, interview.
135 Naomi Newman, phone conversation, May 1994.
136 Newman, phone conversation.
137 All details about scenic design and performance come from Naomi Newman, *Snake Talk: Urgent Messages From the Mother*, sound recording of live performance, Blake Street Hawkeyes Theater, Berkeley, California, 7 January 1989.
138 Newman, recording.
139 Newman, recording.
140 Newman, recording.
141 Newman, recording.
142 Newman, recording.
143 Newman, phone conversation.
144 Newman, recording.

5 REPRESENTING THE PATRIARCHY AND EXPERIENCE

1 Susan Brownmiller, *Against Our Will: Men, Women, and Rape* (New York: Simon and Schuster, 1975) 8. Emphasis hers.
2 Brownmiller, 9.
3 Brownmiller, 8. Emphasis hers.
4 Brownmiller, 8.
5 Susan Griffin, *Rape: The Politics of Consciousness* (San Francisco: Harper and Row, 1979; third revised edition, 1986) 3.
6 Noreen Connell and Cassandra Wilson, eds., *Rape: The First Sourcebook for Women* (New York: New American Library, 1974) 11 and 17.
7 Anne Koedt, Ellen Levine, and Anita Rapone, eds., *Radical Feminism* (New York: Quadrangle Books, 1973) 63–71.
8 Katie Roiphe, *The Morning After: Sex, Fear, and Feminism on Campus* (Boston: Little, Brown, 1993) 7.
9 Connell and Wilson, 274.
10 Connell and Wilson, i. Emphasis mine.
11 Melanie Kaye, "Women and Violence," *Fight Back: Feminist Resistance to Male Violence*, eds. Frédérique Delacoste and Felice Newman (Minneapolis: Cleis Press, 1981) 161.
12 Brownmiller, 209. Emphasis hers.
13 Connell and Wilson, 3.
14 Del Martin, *Battered Wives* (San Francisco: Glide Publications, 1976) 155.
15 Connell and Wilson, 27.
16 Brownmiller, 311.
17 Connell and Wilson, 173.
18 Barbara Mehrhof and Pamela Kearon, "Rape: An Act of Terror," *Radical Feminism*, 233.
19 Brownmiller, 312.
20 Susan Madden, "Fighting Back with Deadly Force: Women Who Kill in Self Defense," *Fight Back*, 143.
21 Madden, 146.
22 Martin, xiv.
23 See especially Martin, 160.
24 "Take Back the Night Candle Light Vigil," poster, University of Washington, Seattle, Washington, 11 May 1991.
25 Griffin, 93–137.
26 Starhawk, *The Spiral Dance: A Rebirth of the Ancient Religion of the Great Goddess* (San Francisco: Harper, 1979; 10th anniversary edition, 1989) 143.
27 Starhawk, 151.
28 Laura Lederer, introduction, *Take Back the Night: Women on Pornography*, ed. Laura Lederer (New York: William Morrow, 1980) 19.
29 While historically, especially in the 1980s, the critique of pornography has been intertwined with the analysis of violence against women, this work cannot take on the complex enormities of the feminist discourses around pornography. While there is, however, a fluidity between the

two issues I will examine and discuss only those works specifically about violence.

30 Hallie Iglehart, *Womanspirit: A Guide to Women's Wisdom* (San Francisco: Harper and Row, 1983) 168.
31 Iglehart, 134.
32 Lederer, 286; and Starhawk, 143.
33 Lederer, 286.
34 Andrea Dworkin, "Pornography and Grief," *Take Back the Night*, 290.
35 Starhawk, 144.
36 Starhawk, 144. I am unsure what exactly the "canal" was or how it functioned. Hallie Iglehart describes two possibilities in her book. She explains a "birth arch" thus "Two women face one another, holding hands with their arms raised above their heads. Another woman steps between them and they drop their arms around her, saying, 'By a woman you were born into this world; by women you are born into this circle.'" 138–39. The other form Iglehart describes is the birth canal formed by women "standing in a line, one behind the other with your legs apart. Each person takes a turn lying down on her back and being pulled through the canal by others, who chant and sing her name." 139. It is difficult to envision how this was done in a city park for 3,000 women.
37 Starhawk, 144.
38 Starhawk, 144.
39 Starhawk, 145.
40 Starhawk, 145.
41 Lacy would go on to create a Mother's Day Pageant with At the Foot of the Mountain in the 1985–86 season. Linda Walsh Jenkins, "At The Foot of the Mountain," *Women in American Theater*, eds. Helen Krich Chinoy and Linda Walsh Jenkins (New York: Theater Communications Group, 1987) 303.
42 Suzanne Lacy, "Three Weeks in May," *Fight Back*, 276.
43 Sue-Ellen Case, *Feminism and Theater* (London: Methuen, 1988) 57.
44 Suzanne Lacy and Leslie Labowitz, "In Mourning and In Rage . . .," *Fight Back*, 278.
45 Brownmiller, 15. Emphasis hers.
46 Lacy and Labowitz, 278.
47 Melanie Kaye, "Ritual: We Fight Back," *Fight Back*, 334.
48 Kaye, "Ritual," 334.
49 Kaye, "Ritual," 338. Kaye cites the original phrase from Adrienne Rich's *Women and Honor* "When a woman tells the truth, she is creating the possibility for more truth around her."
50 Kaye, "Ritual," 338.
51 Kay Turner, "Contemporary Feminist Rituals," *Heresies*, special issue "The Great Goddess," 2.1 (1978): 26.
52 Dworkin, 291.
53 Dolores Walker, *Abide in Darkness*, unpublished ms. From the Sophia Smith Collection (SSC).
54 Susi Kaplow, "Getting Angry," *Radical Feminism*, 40.
55 Leilani Johnson, Joel Polinsky, Sara Salisbury, Joe Volpe, Aili Singer,

Anne Barclay, David Klein, and Barbara Fleischmann, *How To Make A Woman*, unpublished ms.

56 *How To Make A Woman.*
57 *How To Make A Woman.*
58 *How To Make A Woman.*
59 Linda Killian, "Feminist Theater," *Feminist Art Journal* 3.1 (1974): 23.
60 Killian, 23.
61 Walker, unpublished. From the SSC.
62 Walker, unpublished. From the SSC.
63 Walker, unpublished. From the SSC.
64 Charlotte Rea, "Women's Theater Groups," *Drama Review* 16.2 (1972): 88.
65 Rea, 88.
66 Dinah Luise Leavitt, *Feminist Theater Groups* (Jefferson, NC: McFarland, 1980) 34.
67 Leavitt, 35.
68 See chapter six for further discussion on audiences.
69 Leavitt, 58.
70 Leavitt, 58.
71 At the Foot of The Mountain, "Multi-Year Plan – FY's '86, '87, '88," n.d., 2.
72 Meredith Flynn, "The Feeling Circle, Company Collaboration, and Ritual Drama: Three Conventions Developed by the Women's Theater, At The Foot of the Mountain," diss., Bowling Green State University, Ohio, 1984, 29.
73 Brownmiller, 8.
74 Martha Boesing, "Process and Problems," *Women in American Theater*, 323.
75 Flynn, 31.
76 Flynn, 32.
77 Clare Coss, Sondra Segal, and Roberta Sklar, *Electra Speaks*, unpublished ms.
78 Sondra Segal, personal interview, 21 December 1989.
79 Muriel Miguel, personal interview, 26 April 1990.
80 Jill Nicholls, review of the Spiderwoman Theater Company, *Spare Rib*, n.d.: 36.
81 Spiderwoman Theater, "Spiderwoman Theater Workshop," publicity flyer, n.d.
82 Paula Giddings, *When and Where I Enter: The Impact of Black Women on Race and Sex In America* (New York: Bantam Books, 1984) 281, and chapter xvii.
83 Spiderwoman Theater, "Workshop."
84 Miguel, interview.
85 Miguel, interview.
86 Miguel, interview.
87 Miguel, interview.
88 Miguel, interview.
89 Hellmut Kotschenreuther, "Lysistratissima!" *Der Tagesspiegal* 31 October 1982, trans.: n.p.

90 Eleanor Johnson, "Notes on the Process of Art and Feminism," *Women in Theater: Compassion and Hope*, ed. Karen Malpede (New York: Limelight Editions, 1983) 251. Emphasis hers.

91 Ruth Wolff, "The Aesthetics of Violence: Women Tackle the Rough Stuff" *Ms.* (February 1979): 34.

92 Erika Munk, "False Start, True Art," *Village Voice* 8 May 1978: 8.

93 Val Mehlig, "RIFT Hits Hard with Internal Injury," *NewPaper* 24 May 1978: n.p.

94 Julie Landsman, "Feminist Group Blends Emotion with Politics," *Fresh Fruit* 15 May 1978: n.p.

95 Anita Diamant, "Bruises and Excuses: The Internal Injuries of Domestic Violence," *Equaltimes* vol. 2, no. 40, May 1978. The passage in *Battered Wives* is longer and involves a detailed description of how this thinking develops (Martin, 82).

96 Landsman, n.p.

97 Landsman, n.p.

98 Wolff, 34.

99 Iris Landsberg, personal interview, 7 April 1990.

100 Landsberg, interview.

101 Landsberg, interview; and Adele Prandini, personal interview, 5 April 1990.

102 Bernard Weiner, "A Women's Troupe Looks at Battered Women," *San Francisco Chronicle* 2 May 1980: n.p.

103 Landsberg, interview.

104 Prandini, interview.

105 Theater of Light and Shadow, "A History of TLS in Names, Dates, Places, and Performances," unpublished. From the SSC.

106 Mary Beth Bruno, "Closing the Curtain," *New Haven Advocate* 17 August 1983: 30. From the SSC.

107 Hanna Rubin, "Acting Out Abuse," *Glamour* (October 1991): 102.

108 Rubin, 102.

109 Carolyn Levy, "The Date Rape Play: A Collaborative Process," *Transforming A Rape Culture*, eds. Emilie Buchwald, Pamela R. Fletcher, and Martha Roth (Minneapolis: Milkweed Editions, 1993) 235.

110 Levy, 229.

111 Levy, 230–31.

112 Levy, 232–33.

113 Anne Davis Basting, "The Date Rape Play," *Theater and Social Change Newsletter*, vol. 5, no. 3 (1994): 2.

114 Basting, 2.

115 Theodore Shank, *American Alternative Theater* (New York: St. Martin's Press, 1982) 56.

6 THE COMMUNITY AS AUDIENCE

1 Sondra Segal and Roberta Sklar, "The Women's Experimental Theater," *Women in American Theater*, eds. Helen Krich Chinoy and Linda Walsh Jenkins (New York: Theater Communications Group, 1987) 306.

2 The Living Theater's *Paradise Now* (1969) was intended to incite the audience to revolution by aggressively eliminating the barriers between audience and performer. The various forms of alternative theater – happenings, guerilla theater, and environmental theater – all sought to explore and create new personal and political relations in the audience. Particular groups engaged in this process were the San Francisco Mime Troupe, Schechner's Performance Group, the Open Theater, the Bread and Puppet Theater, and the Free Southern Theater. Many women from these theaters left to found feminist theaters. (See also chapter two.)

3 Sally Banes, *Greenwich Village 1963: Avant-Garde Performance and the Effervescent Body* (Durham NC: Duke University Press, 1993) 115.

4 "Communal consciousness outside of the theater was maintained through ideological commitment to and physical involvement in social change. Both El Teatro Campesino and Spirit House [LeRoi Jones' theater] were participants in greater movements of social change. Their audiences consisted of those equally committed to the cause." Harry J. Elam, Jr., "Ritual Theory and Political Theater," *Theater Journal* 38.4 (1986): 468.

5 Susan Suntree, "Women's Theater: Creating the Dream Now", *Women's Culture: The Women's Renaissance of the Seventies*, ed. Gayle Kimball (Metuchen, NJ: Scarecrow Press, 1981) 111.

6 Suntree, 111–12.

7 Suntree, 110.

8 Sondra Segal, personal interview, 21 December 1989.

9 Rosemary Curb, Phyllis Mael, and Beverley Byers Pevitts, "Catalog of Feminist Theaters – Parts 1 and 2," *Chrysalis* 10 (1979): 65.

10 It is significant that without a feminist theoretical critique of the canon foregrounding the dangers of universalism, feminists replicated some of the patriarchal structures. With hindsight it might have made more sense to reintroduce women historical figures, such as Susan B. Anthony, Elizabeth Cady Stanton, or Ida B. Wells, and evolve a mythos from their experiences. But the predominantly white groups instead reached back to the traditions of their cultural heritages to find their myths. There were certainly plays about historical women; RIFT and Lilith both did history plays centered on women. However, none of these works presented these women as figures upon which to build alternative conceptions of myth and ritual. Instead, they were stories reclaimed as actual occurrences, not as a mythic heritage.

11 Foundation Grant Application, New York State Council on the Arts 1970–71, cited in Karen Malpede Taylor, *People's Theater in Amerika* (New York: Drama Book Specialists, 1973) 326.

12 Georgia Dullea, "Dreams Are What a Feminist Group's Plays Are Made Of," *New York Times* 21 December 1972: n.p.

13 Susan Bennett, *Theater Audiences: A Theory of Production and Reception* (London: Routledge, 1990) 149.

14 Charlotte Rea, "Women for Women," *Drama Review* 18.4 (1974): 79.

15 Jill Dolan, *The Feminist Spectator as Critic* (Ann Arbor: UMI, 1988) 18.

16 Clare Coss, Roberta Sklar, and Sondra Segal "Notes on the Women's

Experimental Theater," *Women in Theater: Compassion and Hope*, ed. Karen Malpede (New York: Limelight, 1987) 238.

17 Clare Coss, personal interview, 19 December 1989.

18 Coss, interview.

19 Segal, interview.

20 Twila Thompson, personal interview, 19 December 1989.

21 Thompson, interview.

22 Barbara Tholfsen, personal interview, 18 January 1990.

23 Lori Hansen and Jan Mandel, "Alive and Trucking Theater," *Women: A Journal of Liberation* 3.2 (1972): 8.

24 Clare Coss, Sondra Segal, and Roberta Sklar, "Separation and Survival: Mothers, Daughters, Sisters – The Women's Experimental Theater," *The Future of Difference*, eds. Hester Eisenstein and Alice Jardine (Boston: G.K. Hall and Co., 1980) 233.

25 Phyllis Mael lists Kate Millet, *Sexual Politics*; Dorothy Dinerstein, *The Mermaid and the Minotaur*; Nancy Chodorow, *The Reproduction of Mothering*; Shulamith Firestone, *The Dialectic of Sex*; Adrienne Rich, *Of Woman Born*; and Mary Daly, *Gyn/Ecology*. Mael states that all these books were mentioned, some more than once, by feminist theater practitioners she interviewed (Curb, Mael, and Byers Pevitts, 52). The first book on Mael's list to be published was *Sexual Politics* in 1969 and the two most recent were *The Reproduction of Mothering* and *Gyn/Ecology* in 1978.

26 Laurie Stone, "'Sister/Sister' – Working It Out Onstage," *Ms.* (November 1978): 40.

27 Segal, interview.

28 Dinah Leavitt, *Feminist Theater Groups* (Jefferson, NC: McFarland, 1980) 102.

29 Val Mehlig, "RIFT Hits Hard With Internal Injury," *NewPaper*, 24 May 1978: n.p.

30 Julie Landsman, "Feminist Group Blends Emotion With Politics," *Fresh Fruit*, 15 May 1978: n.p.

31 Anita Diamant, "Bruises and Excuses: The Internal Injuries of Domestic Violence," *Equaltimes* vol. 2, no. 40, May 1978: n.p.

32 Rhode Island Feminist Theater (RIFT), brochure, 1975–76.

33 Circle of the Witch, "Theater History" n.d., n.p.

34 Mary Catherine Wilkins and Cathleen Schurr, "The Washington Area Feminist Theater", *Women in American Theater*, 291.

35 Leavitt, 23.

36 Elizabeth J. Natalle, *Feminist Theater: A Study in Persuasion* (Metuchen, NJ: Scarecrow Press, 1985) 22.

37 Natalle, 22.

38 Georgia Dullea, n.p.

39 A Bunch of Experimental Theaters of New York, Inc., "The Cutting Edge," press packet, n.d., n.p.

40 In April of 1990, during their run of *Winnetou* in Seattle, Washington, Spiderwoman Theater offered this workshop through the Group Theater and I was one of the participants.

41 Unidentified student, "Women's Collage Theater Comment Book," unpublished n.d., n.p.
42 Meredith Flynn, "The Feeling Circle, Company Collaboration, and Ritual Drama: Three Conventions Developed by the Women's Theater, At the Foot of the Mountain" diss., Bowling Green State University, Ohio, 1984, 26.
43 Michele Linfante, personal interview, 3 April 1990.
44 Joan Mankin, interview with Sue-Ellen Case, 19 February 1989.
45 Bennett, 1.
46 Unidentified artist, "Comment Book," n.d., n.p.
47 N.a., "Comment Book," n.d., n.p.
48 Anne Herbert, "*Snake Talk* and Other Planets That We Make Among Ourselves," unpublished ms.
49 Naomi Newman believes that wisdom is what people find in her play. "Over and over again people said that they felt like I was speaking through them. They also felt very grateful for the wisdom." (Newman, personal interview, 5 April 1990).
50 Herbert, unpublished.
51 Seattle, "Comment Book," 26 March 1979, n.p.
52 N.a., "Comment Book," 26 March 1979, n.p.
53 RIFT, *Persephone's Return Frontiers: A Journal of Women's Studies* 3.2 (1978): 72.
54 RIFT, *Persephone's Return* 72.
55 Letter to the Theater of Light and Shadow, 31 May 1981. From the Sophia Smith Collection (SSC).
56 Letter. From the SSC.
57 Debra Flynn and Nancy Lee Kathan, response to letter, 23 July 1981. From the SSC.
58 Marcia Cohen, *The Sisterhood: The Inside Story of the Women's Movement and the Leaders Who Made It Happen* (New York: Fawcett, 1988) 205.
59 Peta Tait, *Original Women's Theatre: The Melbourne Women's Theatre Group 1974–77* (Melbourne, Australia: Artmoves, 1993) 3.
60 Muriel Miguel, personal interview, 26 April 1990.
61 Miguel, interview. Emphasis hers.
62 Harriet Ellenberger, "The Dream is the Bridge: In Search of Lesbian Theater," *Trivia* 5 (1984): 34.
63 Ellenberger, 35.
64 Ellenberger, 35.
65 Patricia Van Kirk, personal interview, 10 July 1990.
66 Van Kirk, interview.
67 Iris Landsberg, personal interview, 7 April 1990.
68 Landsberg, interview.
69 San Francisco Mime Troupe, *The Independent Female, or A Man Has His Pride, By Popular Demand: Plays and Other Works* (San Francisco: San Francisco Mime Troupe, 1980) 171.
70 *Independent Female*, 175.
71 *Independent Female*, 180.
72 *Independent Female*, 192.

73 *Independent Female*, 193.
74 Joan Holden, personal interview, 6 April 1990.
75 Holden, interview.
76 Holden, interview. Holden also recalls that Judy Grahn, lesbian poet and playwright, was one member of the committee that formed to re-write *Independent Female*. When I asked Grahn if she remembered doing this she said no, but "it sounds like the kind of thing I would have done." (Judy Grahn, personal interview, 9 April 1990).
77 Holden, interview.
78 Holden, interview.
79 Holden, interview.
80 Dolan, 93–94.
81 Dolan, 94.
82 Anna Deavere Smith, "Chlorophyll Postmodernism and the Mother Goddess/ A Conversation," *Women and Performance* 4.2 (1989): 32.
83 Dolan, 94.
84 Dolan, 94.
85 Smith, 33.
86 For further information on the Women and Theater program generally and this event specifically, see the special issue "Celebrating the Women and Theater Program" of *Women and Performance* 4.8 (1989).
87 Bennett, 107.

CONCLUSION

1 Roberta Sklar, personal interview, 20 December 1989.
2 Harriet Schiffer, personal interview, 30 October 1994.
3 Steven M. Buechler, *Women's Movements in the United States: Woman Suffrage, Equal Rights, and Beyond* (New Brunswick, NJ: Rutgers University Press, 1990) 187; and Flora Davis, *Moving the Mountain: The Women's Movement in America Since 1960* (New York: Simon and Schuster, 1991) 472.
4 Davis, 473. For an excellent examination of the impact on women of the characterization of feminism and feminists by mainstream media (from print journalism to made-for-television movies to Hollywood to fashion trends) see Susan Faludi, *Backlash: The Undeclared War Against American Women* (New York: Crown Publishers, 1991).
5 Buechler, 229.
6 "Feminist Theaters Index," *Women in American Theater*, eds. Helen Krich Chinoy and Linda Walsh Jenkins (New York: Theater Communications Group, 1987) 392–95.
7 Davis, 472.
8 Barbara Tholfsen, personal interview, 18 January 1990.
9 Iris Landsberg, personal interview, 7 April 1990.
10 Sklar, interview.
11 Mary Beth Bruno, "Closing the Curtain," *New Haven Advocate* 17 August 1983: 30. From the Sophia Smith Collection.
12 Schiffer, interview.

13 Patricia Van Kirk, personal interview, 10 July 1990.
14 Van Kirk, interview.
15 Joan Mankin, personal interview with Sue-Ellen Case, 19 January 1989.
16 Mankin, interview.
17 Mankin, interview.
18 Mitsuye Yamada, "Asian Pacific American Women and Feminism," *This Bridge Called My Back: Writings By Radical Women of Color,* eds. Cherrie Moraga and Gloria Anzaldua (New York: Kitchen Table: Women of Color Press, 1981) 73.
19 Mankin, interview.
20 Sondra Segal, personal interview, 21 December 1989.
21 Muriel Miguel, personal interview, 26 April 1990.
22 Hilary Harris, rev. of "Anniversary Waltz" by Split Britches Company, *Theater Journal* 42.4 (1990) 484–88.
23 Horizons: Theater From a Woman's Perspective, subscription flyer, n.d., n.p.
24 Mankin, interview.
25 Twila Thompson, personal interview, 19 December 1989.
26 Roberta Uno, "Marga Gomez: Resistance from the Periphery," *Theatre-Forum* 4 (Winter/Spring 1994): 5.
27 Schiffer, interview.
28 Uno, 7.
29 Schiffer, interview.
30 Women's Interart Center, publicity flyer, n.d., n.p.
31 Arthur Sainer, "Interart Walks a Tightrope," *Village Voice* 7 August 1984: 85.
32 Linda Killian, "Feminist Theater," *Feminist Art Journal* 3.1 (1974): 24.
33 Margot Lewitin, personal interview, 14 December 1989. Another example of a liberal organization would be The Women's Project at the American Place Theater. Founded in 1978 by Julia Miles, it is primarily intended to launch women playwrights and directors into commercial theater.
34 Ellen Gavin, personal interview, 9 April 1990.
35 Gavin, interview.
36 For a further discussion of the play and this particular production see Yvonne Yarbro-Bejarano, "Cherrie Moraga's 'Shadow of a Man': Touching the Wound in Order to Heal," *Acting Out: Feminist Performances*, eds. Lynda Hart and Peggy Phelan (Ann Arbor: University of Michigan Press, 1993) 85–104.
37 This figure is computed from the dates provided for theaters in Rosemary Curb, Phyllis Mael, and Beverley Byers Pevitts, "Catalog of Feminist Theater – Parts 1 and 2," *Chrysalis* 10 (1979): 67–75.
38 Adele Prandini, personal interview, 5 April 1990.
39 Bruno, 41.

BIBLIOGRAPHY

BOOKS AND ANTHOLOGIES

Allen, Pam, "Free Space," in *Radical Feminism*, ed. Anne Koedt, Ellen Levine, and Anita Rapone, New York: Quadrangle Books, 1973.

Antonelli, Judith, "Feminist Spirituality: Politics of the Psyche," in *The Politics of Women's Spirituality: Essays on the Rise of Power within the Feminist Movement*, ed. Charlene Spretnak, New York: Doubleday, 1982.

Aptheker, Bettina, *Women's Legacy: Essays on Race, Sex, and Class in American History*, Amherst: University of Massachusetts Press, 1982.

Aronowitz, Stanley, "When the New Left Was New," in *The 60s Without Apology*, ed. Sohnya Sayres, Anders Stephanson, Stanley Aronowitz, and Frederic Jameson, Minneapolis: University of Minnesota Press, 1984.

Austin, Gayle, *Feminist Theories for Dramatic Criticism*, Ann Arbor: University of Michigan Press, 1990.

Banes, Sally, *Greenwich Village 1963: Avant-Garde Performance and the Effervescent Body*, Durham, NC: Duke University Press, 1993.

Barrett, Michèle, "Feminism and the Definition of Cultural Politics," in *Feminism, Culture amd Politics*, ed. Rosalind Brunt and Caroline Rowan, London: Lawrence and Wishart, 1982.

Bennett, Susan, *Theater Audiences: A Theory of Production and Reception*, London: Routledge, 1991.

Bernard, Jessie, (ed.) "Introduction" to *The New Feminist Movement*, Maren Lockwood Carden, New York: Russell Sage Foundation, 1974.

Blumenthal, Eileen, *Joseph Chaiken: Exploring the Boundaries of Theater*, New York: Cambridge University Press, 1984.

Boesing, Martha (in collaboration with the women At the Foot of the Mountain), "The Story of A Mother: A Ritual Drama," in *Women in American Theater*, ed. Helen Krich Chinoy and Linda Walsh Jenkins, New York: Theater Communications Group, 1987.

—— "Process and Problems," in *Women in American Theater*, ed. Helen Krich Chinoy and Linda Walsh Jenkins, New York: Theater Communications Group, 1987.

Brockett, Oscar and Findlay, Robert, *Century of Innovation: A History of*

European and American Theatre and Drama Since 1870, Englewood Cliffs, NJ: Prentice Hall, 1973.

Brown, Janet, *Feminist Drama: Definition and Critical Analysis*, Metuchen, NJ: Scarecrow Press, 1979.

—— *Taking Center Stage: Feminism in Contemporary U.S. Drama*, Metuchen, NJ: Scarecrow Press, 1991.

Brownmiller, Susan, *Against Our Will: Men, Women, and Rape*, New York: Simon and Schuster, 1975.

Brunt, Rosalind and Rowan, Caroline (eds.), *Feminism, Culture, and Politics*, London: Lawrence and Wishart, 1982.

Buchwald, Emilie, Fletcher, Pamela R., and Roth, Martha (eds.), *Transforming a Rape Culture*, Minneapolis: Milkweed Editions, 1993.

Buechler, Steven M., *Women's Movements in the United States: Woman Suffrage, Equal Rights, and Beyond*, New Brunswick, NJ: Rutgers University Press, 1990.

Bunch, Charlotte, *Passionate Politics: Feminist Theory in Action*, New York: St. Martin's Press, 1987.

Carden, Maren Lockwood (ed.), *The New Feminist Movement*, New York: Russell Sage Foundation, 1974.

Carmines, Reverend Al, "The Judson Poets' Theater," in *Eight Plays from Off Off-Broadway*, ed. Michael Smith and Nick Orzel, New York: Bobbs-Merrill, 1966.

Carson, Anne, *Feminist Spirituality and the Feminist Divine: An Annotated Bibliography*, Trumansberg, NY: Crossing Press, 1986.

Case, Sue-Ellen, *Feminism and Theater*, New York: Methuen, 1988.

—— "Toward a Butch-Femme Aesthetic," in *Making a Spectacle: Feminist Essays on Contemporary Women's Theatre*, ed. Lynda Hart, Ann Arbor: University of Michigan Press, 1989.

Chaiken, Joseph, "The Open Theater," in *Eight Plays from Off Off-Broadway*, ed. Michael Smith and Nick Orzel, New York: Bobbs-Merrill, 1966.

—— "Notes on Acting Time and Repetiton," in *The Mutation Show: Three Works by the Open Theatre*, ed. Karen Malpede, New York: Drama Book Specialists, 1974.

Chinoy, Helen Krich and Jenkins, Linda Walsh (eds.), *Women in American Theater*, New York: Theater Communications Group, 1983.

Christ, Carole P., "Why Women Need the Goddess: Phenomenological, Psychological, and Political Reflections," in *The Politics of Women's Spirituality: Essays on the Rise of Power within the Feminist Movement*, ed. Charlene Spretnak, New York: Doubleday, 1982.

Cino, Joe, "Caffe Cino," in *Eight Plays from Off Off-Broadway*, ed. Michael Smith and Nick Orzel, New York: Bobbs-Merrill, 1966.

Cohen, Marcia, *The Sisterhood: The Inside Story of the Women's Movement and the Leaders Who Made it Happen*, New York: Fawcett, 1988.

Connell, Noreen and Wilson, Cassandra (eds.), *Rape: The First Sourcebook for Women*, New York: New American Library, 1974.

Coss, Claire, Segal, Sondra and Sklar, Roberta, "Separation and Survival: Mothers, Daughters, and Sisters – The Women's Experimental Theater", in *The Future of Difference*, ed. Hester Eisenstein and Alice Jardine, Boston: G.K. Hall & Co. 1980.

—— "Notes on the Women's Experimental Theater," in *Women in Theater: Compassion and Hope*, ed. Karen Malpede, New York, Limelight, 1987.

Croyden, Margaret, *Lunatics, Lovers and Poets: The Contemporary Experimental Theater*, New York: McGraw-Hill, 1974.

Davis, Flora, *Moving the Mountain: The Women's Movement in America Since 1960*, New York: Simon and Schuster, 1991.

Davis, R. G., *The San Francisco Mime Troupe: The First Ten Years*, Palo Alto: Ramparts Press, 1975.

Debrida, Bela, "Drawing from Mythology in Woman's Quest for Selfhood," in *The Politics of Women's Spirituality: Essays on the Rise of Power within the Feminist Movement*, ed. Charlene Spretnak, New York: Doubleday, 1982.

Delacoste, Frédérique and Newman, Felice (eds.), *Fight Back: Feminist Resistance to Male Violence*, Minneapolis: Cleis Press, 1981.

Dolan, Jill, *The Feminist Spectator as Critic*, Ann Arbor: UMI Research Press, 1988.

—— *Presence and Desire: Essays on Gender, Sexuality, and Performance*, Ann Arbor: University of Michigan Press, 1993.

Drinker, Sophie, "The Origins of Music: Women's Goddess Worship," in *The Politics of Women's Spirituality: Essays on the Rise of Power within the Feminist Movement*, ed. Charlene Spretnak, New York: Doubleday, 1982.

Dworkin, Andrea, "Pornography and Grief," in *Take Back the Night: Women on Pornography*, ed. Laura Lederer, New York: William Morrow, 1980.

Echols, Alice, *Daring to Be Bad: Radical Feminism in America, 1967–1975*, Minneapolis: University of Minnesota Press, 1989.

Eisenstein, Hester and Jardine, Alice (eds.), *The Future of Difference*, New Brunswick: Rutgers University Press, 1980.

Faludi, Susan, *Backlash: The Undeclared War Against American Women*, New York: Crown Publishers, 1991.

Hinton, William, *Fanshen: A Documentary of Revolution in a Chinese Village*, New York: Vintage Books, 1966.

Feldman, Peter, "Notes for the Open Theater Production," in *Viet Rock, Comings and Goings, Keep Tightly Closed in a Cool Dry Place, and In the Gloaming, Oh My Darling: Four Plays by Megan Terry*, Megan Terry, New York: Simon and Schuster, 1966.

Firestone, Shulasmith, *The Dialectic of Sex: The Case for Feminist Revolution*, New York: Bantam, 1970.

Fletcher, Marilyn Lowen, "A Chant for My Sisters," in *Sisterhood is Powerful: An Anthology of Writings from the Women's Liberation Movement*, ed. Robin Morgan. New York: Vintage Books, 1970.

Giddings, Paula, *When and Where I Enter: The Impact of Black Women on Race and Sex in America*, New York: Bantam Books, 1984.

Gilder, Rosamond, *Enter the Actress: the First Women in the Theater*, New York: Houghton Mifflin, 1931.

Gimbutas, Marija, "Woman and Culture in Goddess Oriented Old Europe," in *The Politics of Women's Spirituality: Essays on the Rise of Power within the Feminist Movement*, ed. Charlene Spretnak, New York: Doubleday, 1982.

Goodman, Lizbeth, *Contemporary Feminist Theatres: To Each Her Own*, London: Routledge, 1993.

Griffin, Susan, *Rape: The Politics of Consciousness*, San Francisco: Harper and Row, 1979 (third revised edition 1986).

Grimstad, Kirsten and Rennie, Susan (eds.), *The New Woman's Survival Catalog*, New York: Coward, McCann, and Geoghegan, 1973.

Hanisch, Carol, "The Liberal Takeover of Women's Liberation," in *Feminist Revolution*, ed. Redstockings (abridged edition), New York: Random House, 1978.

Hart, Lynda and Phelan, Peggy (eds.), *Acting Out: Feminist Performances*, Ann Arbor: University of Michigan Press, 1993.

Hoffman, William, *Gay Plays: The First Collection*, New York: Avon Books, 1979.

Hole, Judith and Levine, Ellen, *Rebirth of Feminism*, New York: Quadrangle Books, 1971.

hooks, bell, *Talking Back: Thinking Feminist, Thinking Black*, Boston: South End Press, 1989.

Iglehart, Hallie, *Womanspirit: A Guide to Women's Wisdom*, San Francisco: Harper and Row, 1983.

Jenkins, Linda Walsh, "Feminist Theater," in *Women in American Theater*, ed. Helen Krich Chinoy and Linda Walsh Jenkins, New York: Theater Communications Group, 1987.

Johnson, Eleanor, "Notes on the Process of Art and Feminism," in *Women in Theater: Compassion and Hope*, ed. Karen Malpede, New York: Limelight Editions, 1983.

Kaye, Melanie, "Ritual: We Fight Back,", in *Fight Back: Feminist Resistance to Male Violence*, ed. Frédérique Delacoste and Felice Newman, Minneapolis: Cleis Press, 1981.

—— "Women and Violence," in *Fight Back: Feminist Resistance to Male Violence*, ed. Frédérique Delacoste and Felice Newman, Minneapolis: Cleis Press, 1981.

Kaplow, Susi, "Getting Angry," in *Radical Feminism*, ed. Anne Koedt, Ellen Levine, and Anita Rapone, New York: Quadrangle Books, 1973.

Keyssar, Helene, *Feminist Theatre: An Introduction to Plays by Contemporary British and American Women*, London: Macmillan, 1984.

Kimball, Gayle (ed.), *Women's Culture: The Women's Renaissance of the Seventies*, Metuchen, NJ: Scarecrow Press, 1981.

Koedt, Anne, "The Myth of the Vaginal Orgasm," in *Radical Feminism*, ed. Anne Keodt, Ellen Levine, and Anita Rapone, New York: Quadrangle Books, 1973.

—— Levine, Ellen and Rapone, Anita (eds.), *Radical Feminism*, New York: Quadrangle Books, 1973.

Koppelman, Susan (ed.), *Images of Women in Fiction*, Bowling Green: Bowling Green University Popular Press, 1972.

Lacy, Suzanne, "Three Weeeks in May," in *Fight Back: Feminist Resistance to Male Violence*, ed. Frédérique Delacoste and Felice Newman, Minneapolis: Cleis Press, 1981.

—— and Labowitz, Leslie, "In Mourning and in Rage," in *Fight Back: Feminist Resistance to Male Violence*, ed. Frédérique Delacoste and Felice Newman, Minneapolis: Cleis Press, 1981.

Leavitt, Dinah Luise, *Feminist Theater Groups*, Jefferson, N.C.: McFarland, 1980.

Lederer, Laura (ed.), *Take Back the Night: Women on Pornography*, New York: William Morrow, 1980.

Lerner, Gerda, *The Majority Finds Its Past*, New York: Oxford University Press, 1979.

Levy, Carolyn, "The Date Rape Play: A Collaborative Process," in *Transforming a Rape Culture*, ed. Emilie Buchwald, Pamela R. Fletcher, and Martha Roth, Minneapolis: Milkweed Editions, 1993.

Linfante, Michele, *Pizza*, in *West Coast Plays 6*, ed. Rick Foster, Berkeley: California Theater Council, 1980.

Lorde, Audre, *Sister Outsider*, Trumansburg, NY: The Crossing Press, 1984.

Madden, Susan, "Fighting Back with Deadly Force: Women who Kill in Self Defense," in *Fight Back: Feminist Resistance to Male Violence*, ed. Frédérique Delacoste and Felice Newman, Minneapolis: Cleis Press, 1981.

Malpede, Karen, (ed.), *Women in Theater: Compassion and Hope*, New York: Limelight Editions, 1983.

—— *The End of War, A Monster Has Stolen the Sun and Other Plays*, Marlboro, VT: Marlboro Press, 1987.

—— "*Rebeccah*: Rehearsal Notes," in *Women in American Theater*, ed. Helen Krich Chinoy and Linda Walsh Jenkins, New York: Theater Communications Group, 1987.

Malnig, Julie and Rosenthal, Judy C., "The Women's Experimental Theater: Transforming Family Stories into Feminist Questions," in *Acting Out: Feminist Performances*, ed. Lynda Hart and Peggy Phelan, Ann Arbor: University of Michigan Press, 1993.

Martin, Del, *Battered Wives*, San Francisco: Glide Publications, 1976.

Mehrhof, Barbara and Kearon, Pamela, "Rape: An Act of Terror," in *Radical Feminism*, ed. Anne Koedt, Ellen Levine, and Anita Rapone, New York: Quadrangle Books, 1973.

Miller, James, *Democracy is in the Streets: From Port Huron to the Siege of Chicago*, New York: Simon and Schuster, 1987.

Millet, Kate, *Sexual Politics*, Garden City, NY: Doubleday, 1970.

Minh-ha, Trinh T., *Woman, Native, Other: Postcoloniality, Feminism, and Writing*, Bloomington: University of Indiana Press, 1989.

Moraga, Cherrie, "La Güera," in *This Bridge Called My Back: Writings By Radical Women of Color*, ed. Cherrie Moraga and Gloria Anzaldua, New York: Kitchen Table: Women of Color Press, 1981.

Moraga, Cherrie and Anzaldua, Gloria (eds.), *This Bridge Called My Back: Writings By Radical Women of Color*, New York: Kitchen Table: Women of Color Press, 1981.

Morgan, Robin (ed.), *Sisterhood is Powerful: An Anthology of Writings from The Women's Liberation Movement*, New York: Vintage Books, 1970.

—— *Going Too Far: the Personal Chronicle of a Feminist*, New York: Vintage Books, 1978.

Natalle, Elizabeth J., *Feminist Theater: A Study in Persuasion*, Metuchen, NJ: Scarecrow Press, 1985.

Open Theater Ensemble, *The Mutation Show: Three Works by the Open Theater*, ed. Karen Malpede, New York: Drama Book Specialists, 1974.

Pasolli, Robert, *A Book on the Open Theater*, New York: Avon Books, 1970.

Podos, Batya, "Feeding the Feminist Psyche Through Ritual Theater," in *The Politics of Women's Spirituality: Essays on the Rise of Power within the Feminist Movement*, ed. Charlene Spretnak, New York: Doubleday, 1982.

Poggi, Jack, *Theater in America: Impact of Economic Forces, 1870–1967*, Ithaca: Cornell University Press, 1968.

Reagon, Berenice Johnson, "Coalition Politics: Turning the Century," in *Home Girls: A Black Feminist Anthology*, ed. Barbara Smith, New York: Kitchen Table: Women of Color Press, 1983.

Redmond, Michael (ed.), *Themes in Drama: Women in Theater*, Cambridge: Cambridge University Press, 1989.

Redstockings (ed.), *Feminist Revolution* (abridged edition), New York: Random House, 1978.

Rich, Adrienne, *Of Woman Born: Motherhood as an Experience and Institution*, New York: W. W. Norton, 1976/1986.

Roiphe, Katie, *The Morning After: Sex, Fear, and Feminism on Campus*, Boston: Little, Brown, 1993.

Russ, Joanna, "Why Women Can't Write," in *Images of Women in Fiction*, ed. Susan Koppelman, Bowling Green, Ohio: Bowling Green University Popular Press, 1972.

Sainer, Arthur, *The Radical Theater Notebook*, New York: Avon Books, 1975.

San Francisco Mime Troupe, *The Independent Female, or A Man Has His Pride*, in *By Popular Demand: Plays and Other Works*, San Francisco: San Francisco Mime Troupe, 1980.

Sarachild, Kathie, "Consciousness-Raising: A Radical Weapon," in *Feminist Revolution*, ed. Redstockings (abridged edition), New York: Random House, 1978.

Sayres, Sohnya, Stephanson, Anders, Aronowitz, Stanley, and Jameson, Frederic (eds.), *The 60s Without Apology*, Minneapolis: University of Minnesota Press, 1984.

Scott, Joan Wallach, *Gender and the Politics of History*, New York: Columbia University Press, 1988.

Segal, Sondra and Sklar, Roberta, "The Women's Experimental Theater," in *Women in American Theater*, ed. Helen Krich Chinoy and Linda Walsh Jenkins, New York: Theater Communications Group, 1987.

Shank, Theodore, *American Alternative Theater*, New York: St. Martin's Press, 1982.

Sklar, Roberta, "Reflections," in *Women in American Theater*, ed. Helen Krich Chinoy and Linda Walsh Jenkins, New York: Theater Communications Group, 1987.

Smith, Barbara (ed.), *Home Girls: A Black Feminist Anthology*, New York: Kitchen Table: Women of Color Press, 1983.

Smith, Michael and Orzel, Nick (eds.), *Eight Plays from Off Off-Broadway*, New York: Bobbs-Merrill, 1966.

Smith-Rosenberg, Carroll, *Disorderly Conduct: Visions of Gender in Victorian America*, New York: A. A. Knopf, 1985.

Spolin, Viola, *Improvisation for the Theater: A Handbook of Teaching and Directing Techniques*, Evanston, IL: Northwestern University Press, 1963.

Spretnak, Charlene (ed.), *The Politics of Women's Spirituality: Essays on the Rise of Power within the Feminist Movement*, New York: Doubleday, 1982.

Starhawk, *The Spiritual Dance: A Rebirth of the Ancient Religion of the Great Goddess*, San Francisco: Harper, 1979 (10th anniversary edition, 1989).

Stewart, Ellen, "La Mama Experimental Theater Club," in *Eight Plays from Off Off-Broadway*, ed. Michael Smith and Nick Orzel, New York: Bobbs-Merrill, 1966.

Stone, Merlin, *When God Was a Woman*, New York: Dial Press, 1976.

Suntree, Susan, "Women's Theater: Creating the Dream Now," in *Women's Culture: The Women's Renaissance of the Seventies*, ed. Gayle Kimball, Metuchen, NJ: Scarecrow Press, 1981.

Tait, Peta, *Original Women's Theater: The Melbourne Women's Theater Group 1974–77*, Melbourne, Australia: Artmoves, 1993.

Taylor, Karen Malpede, *People's Theater in Amerika*, New York: Drama Book Specialists, 1973.

Terry, Megan, *Viet Rock, Comings and Goings, Keep Tightly Closed in a Cool Dry Place, and In the Gloaming, Oh My Darling: Four Plays by Megan Terry*, New York: Simon and Schuster, 1966.

Thompson, Paul, *The Voice of the Past: Oral History*, Oxford: Oxford University Press, 1988.

Viorst, Milton, *Fire in the Streets: America in the 1960s*, New York: Simon and Schuster, 1979.

Walter, Sidney S., "Notes for the Firehouse Theater Production," in *Viet Rock, Comings and Goings, Keep Tightly Closed in a Cool Dry Place, and In the Gloaming, Oh My Darling: Four Plays by Megan Terry*, Megan Terry, New York: Simon and Schuster, 1966.

Wandor, Michelene, *Carry on, Understudies: Theatre and Sexual Politics*, New York: Routledge and Kegan Paul, 1986.

Weedon, Chris, *Feminist Practice and Poststructuralist Theory*, Oxford: Basil Blackwell, 1987.

Wetzsteon, Ross (ed.), *The Obie Winners: the Best of Off-Broadway*, Garden City, New York: Doubleday, 1980.

Wilkerson, Margaret (ed.), *Nine Plays by Black Women*, New York: New American Library, 1986.

Wilkins, Mary Catherine and Schurr, Cathleen, "The Washington Area Feminist Theater," in *Women in American Theater*, ed. Helen Krich Chinoy and Linda Walsh Jenkins, New York: Theater Communications Group, 1987.

Woo, Connie Young "The World of Our Grandmothers," in *Making Waves: An Anthology of Writings By and About Asian American Women*, ed. Asian Women United of California, Boston: Beacon Press, 1989.

Yamada, Mitsuye, "Asian Pacific American Women and Feminism," in *This Bridge Called My Back: Writings By Radical Women of Color*, ed. Cherrie Moraga and Gloria Anzaldua, New York: Kitchen Table: Women of Color Press, 1981.

Yarbro-Bejarno, Yvonne, "*Teatropoesía* by Chicanas in the Bay Area," in *Mexican American Theater: Then and Now*, ed. Nicolás Kanellos, Houston: Arte Publico Press, 1983.

—— "Cherrie Moraga's 'Shadow of a Man': Touching the Wound in Order to Heal", in *Acting Out: Feminist Performances*, ed. Lynda Hart and Peggy Phelan, Ann Arbor: University of Michigan Press, 1993.

Zivanovic, Judith, "The Rhetorical and Political Foundations of Women's Collaborative Theatre," in *Themes in Drama: Women in Theater*, ed. Michael Redmond, Cambridge: Cambridge University Press, 1989.

ARTICLES

Anderson, Katheryn, Armitage, Susan, Jack, Dana, and Wittner, Judith, "Beginning Where We Are: Feminist Methodology in Oral History," *Oral History Review*, no. 15, 1987.

Armitage, Susan, "The Next Step," *Frontiers* special issue, "Women's Oral History Two," vol. 7, no. 1, 1983.

Bassnett, Susan, "Struggling With the Past: Women's Theater in Search of History," *New Theater Quarterly*, vol. 5, no. 18, 1989.

Basting, Anne Davis, "The Date Rape Play," *Theater and Social Culture*, vol. 5, no. 3, 1994.

Brinson-Pineda, Barbara, "Voz de la Mujer," *El Tecolote Literary Magazine*, vol. 23, no. 4, 1981.

Brown, Kenneth, "Oral Tradition into History: Put it into Writing!," *Social Analysis*, no. 4, 1980.

Brunner, Cornelia, "Roberta Sklar: Toward Creating a Women's Theater", *Drama Review*, vol. 24, no. 2, June 1980.

Bruno, Mary Beth, "Closing the Curtain," *New Haven Advocate*, 17 August 1983.

Campbell, Karlyn Kors, "The Rhetoric of Women's Liberation: An Oxymoron," *Quarterly Journal of Speech*, vol. 59, no. 1, 1973.

Case, Sue-Ellen, "Judy Grahn's Gynopoetics: *The Queen of Swords*," *Studies in the Literary Imagination*, vol. 21, no. 2, 1988.

Collins, Robert, "A Feminist Theater in Transition," *American Theater*, vol. 4, no. 11, 1988.

Coss, Clare, "From Daughter of Alistine Melpomene Thalia: a Play within a Play," *Chrysalis: A Magazine of Women's Culture*, no. 5, 1977.

Curb, Rosemary, Mael, Phyllis, and Byers Pevitts, Beverley, "Catalog of Feminist Theater – Parts 1 and 2," *Chrysalis*, no. 10, 1979.

Dolan, Jill, "In Defense of Discourse: Materialist Feminism, Postmodernism, Poststructuralism . . . and Theory," *Drama Review*, vol. 33, no. 3, 1989.

Elam, Jr., Harry J., "Ritual Theory and Political Theater," *Theater Journal*, vol. 38, no. 4, 1986.

Ellenberger, Harriet, "The Dream is the Bridge: In Search of Lesbian Theater," *Trivia*, no. 5, 1984.

Feingold, Michael, "Caffe Cino, 20 Years After Magic Time," *Village Voice*, 14 May 1985.

Gillespie, Patti, "Feminist Theater: A Rhetorical Phenomenon," *Quarterly Journal of Speech*, no. 64, 1978.

Gussow, Mel, "Theater: Women's Work," *New York Times*, 30 March 1976.

Hahn, Roger, "Profile: K. D. Codish," *New Haven Register*, October 1983.

Hall, Trish, "Reaching Beyond Rhetoric," *New Haven Advocate*, 28 November 1979.

Hansen, Lori and Mansel, Jan, "Alive and Trucking Theater," *Women: A Journal of Liberation*, vol. 3, no. 2, 1972.

Hoff, Joan, "The Pernicious Effects of Poststructuralism on Women's History," *The Chronicle of Higher Education*, 20 October 1993.

House, Jane, "Interview with Dacia Maraini," *Western European Stages*, vol. 1, no. 1, 1989.

Killian, Linda, "Feminist Theater," *Feminist Art Journal*, vol. 3, no. 1, 1974.

Koonz, Claudia, "Post Scripts," *Women's Review of Books*, vol. 6, no. 4, January 1989.

Kruger, Loren, "The Dis-Play's the Thing: Gender and Public Sphere in Contemporary British Theater," *Theatre Journal*, vol. 42, no. 1, March 1990.

Lowell, Sondra, "Art Comes to the Elevator: Women's Guerilla Theater," *Women: A Journal of Liberation*, vol. 2, no. 1, 1970.

—— "New Feminist Theater," *Ms.*, August 1972.

Messing, Suzanne, "Unmasking Some Female Branches on a Family Tree," *New York Times*, 14 September 1980.

Meyers, John C., "I Want to Wake up and be Free," *Rhode Islander*, 29 February 1976.

Moore, Honor, "Theater Will Never Be the Same," *Ms.*, Dec. 1977.

Neff, Renfreu, "Spiderwoman Theater," *Other Stages*, 5 May 1983.

Patraka, Vivian M., "Split Britches in *Split Britches*: Performing History, Vaudeville, and the Everyday," *Women and Performance*, vol. 4, no. 8, 1989.

Perinciolo, Lillian, "Feminist Theaters: They're Playing in Peoria," *Ms.*, October 1975.

Rea, Charlotte, "Women for Women," *Drama Review*, vol. 18, no. 4, 1974.

—— "Women's Theater Groups," *Drama Review*, vol. 16, no. 2, 1972.

Rhode Island Feminist Theater, *Persephone's Return*, in *Frontiers: A Journal of Women's Studies*, Special issue "Mothers and Daughters," vol. 3, no. 2, 1978.

Rosaldo, Renato, "Doing Oral History," *Social Analysis*, no. 4, 1980.

Rubin, Hanna, "Acting Out Abuse," *Glamour*, October 1991.

Sainer, Arthur, "Interart Walks a Tightrope," *Village Voice*, 7 August 1984.

Scott, Adrienne and Mirviss, Sophia, "The Incredible Spiderwoman," *Womannews*, April 1980.

Scott, Joan W., "Response to Linda Gordon's rev. of *Gender and the Politics of History*," *Signs*, vol. 15. no. 4, 1990.

Shank, Ted, "Collective Creation," *Drama Review*, vol. 16, no. 2, 1972.

Sisley, Emily, "Notes on Lesbian Theater," *Drama Review*, vol. 18, no. 1, 1981.

Sklar, Roberta, "'Sisters or Never Trust Anyone Outside the Family,' *Women and Performance*, vol. 1, no. 1, 1983.

Smith, Anna Deavere, "Chlorophyll, Postmodernism, And the Mother Goddess/A Conversation," *Women and Performance*, vol. 4, no. 8, 1989.

Solomon, Alisa, "The WOW Cafe," *Drama Review*, vol. 29, no. 1, 1985.

Tsui, Kitty, "Lilith and the Hired Help," *Heresies*, vol. 5, no. 1, 1984.

Turner, Kay, "Contemporary Feminist Rituals," *Heresies*, Special issue "The Great Goddess", vol. 2, no. 1, 1978.

Uno, Roberta, "Marga Gomez: Resistance From the Periphery," *Theatre Forum*, vol. 4, Winter Spring 1994: 4–100.

Weinberg, Grazia Sumeli, "Women's Theater: Teatro La Maddalena and the Work of Dacia Maraini," *Western European Stages*, vol. 1, no. 1, 1989.

Wolff, Ruth, "The Aesthetics of Violence: Women Tackle the Rough Stuff," *Ms.*, February 1979.

Yarbro-Bejarano, Yvonne, "Chicanas in Theater," *Women and Performance*, vol. 2, no. 2, 1985.

—— "The Role of Women in Chicano Theater Organizations," *Revista Literaria del Tecolote*, vol. 2, no. 3–4, 1981.

REVIEWS

Adcock, Joe, "The Wackiness Shines Through This Up-to-Date 'Lysistrata'", *Seattle Post-Intelligencer*, 24 February 1983.

Blumenthal, Eileen, "Spinning Free," *Village Voice*, 18 February 1980.

Brown, Rebecca, "Type for Adventure," *Lights*, 30 September–13 October n.y.

Chevigny, Bell Gale, review of *Cycles*, *University Review*, December 1973.

Croghan, L. A., review of *A Monster Has Stolen the Sun*, *Brooklyn Heights Press*, 5 March 1981.

Davies, Christopher V., "Spiderwoman Spins a Delightful Web of Entertainment Overseas," *New York City Tribune*, 30 December 1987.

Diamant, Anita, "Bruises and Excuses: The Internal Injuries of Domestic Violence," *Equaltimes*, vol. 2, no. 40, May 1978.

Dullea, Georgia, "Dreams Are What a Feminist Group's Plays Are Made Of," *New York Times*, 21 December 1972.

Gaar, Gillian G., "Summertime When the Livin' is Easy," *Washington Cascade Voice*, 25 January 1985.

Garnett, Julia, "A National Women's Festival in Santa Cruz," *San Francisco Chronicle Datebook*, 15 May 1983.

Gruber, Ira, review of *In Search of the Hammer*, *Northwest Passage*, November 1983.

Harris, Hilary, review of Split Britches Company "Anniversary Waltz," *Theatre Journal*, vol. 42, no. 4, 1990.

Kelly, Tom W., "Cove 'Beneficial to Gay Image' Not to Be Missed," *Seattle Gay News*, 25 January 1985.

Kotschenreuther, Hellmut, "Lysistratissima!," *Der Tagesspiegel*, 31 October 1982.

Landsman, Julie, "Feminist Group Blends Emotion With Politics," *Fresh Fruit*, 15 May 1978.

Mehlig, Val, "RIFT Hits Hard With Internal Injury," *NewPaper*, 24 May 1978.

Michener, Marian, "*Return of the Hammer* in Rehearsal at Front Room Theater," *Seattle Gay News*, 3 May 1985.

Morgan, Peggy, "Off the Beaten Trail with New York Theater," *Rutgers Daily Targum*, 7 April 1976.

Munk, Erika, "False Start, True Art," *Village Voice*, 8 May 1978: 8.

Nicholls, Jill, review of Spiderwoman Theater Company, *Spare Rib*, n.d.

Solomon, Alisa, "Tangled Web," *Village Voice*, 19 March 1985.

Spedding, Carole, "Words *Plus* Texture," n.d.

Stone, Laurie, "'Sister/Sister'–Working It Out Onstage," *Ms.*, November 1978.

Weiner, Bernard, "A Women's Troupe Looks at Battered Women," *San Francisco Chronicle*, 2 May 1980.

NEWSLETTERS/THEATER-GENERATED MATERIALS

At the Foot of The Mountain, *Newsletters*, spring 1985 – fall 1989.

Circle of the Witch, "Theater History", n.d.

The Cutting Edge, press materials, 1976.

Front Room Theater, *Newsletters*, fall 1984 – fall 1985.

In Search of the Hammer: the First Adventures of the the Three Mustbequeers program.

Rhode Island Feminist Theater, publicity material, 1975–76.

Spiderwoman Theater, "Our Source," publicity materials, n.d.

Women and Theater Program, *Newsletters*, 1978–91.

Women's Interart Theater, publicity materials, n.d.

UNPUBLISHED MATERIALS

Baum, Terry, Meyers, Carolyn, Linfante, Michele, and Winter, Resnais, *Sacrifices: A Fable of the Women's Movement*, unpublished playscript, 1978.

Boesing, Martha, in collaboration with the company At the Foot of the Mountain, *The Story of a Mother: An Ensemble Work*, unpublished playscript, 1978 (revised 1987).

Coss, Clare, Segal, Sondra and Sklar, Roberta, *Electra Speaks*, unpublished playscript, 1980.

Flynn, Debra and Kathan, Nancy Lee, response to letter, 23 July 1981.

Flynn, Meredith, "The Feeling Circle, Company Collaboration, and Ritual Drama: Three Conventions Developed by the Women's Theater, At the Foot of the Mountain," diss., Bowling Green State University, 1984.

Herbert, Anne, "*Snake Talk* and Other Planets That We Make Among Ourselves," unpublished essay, 1989.

Johnson, Leilani, Polinsky, Joel, Salisbury, Sara, Singer, Aili, Barclay, Anne, Klein, David, and Fleishman, Barbara, *How to Make a Woman*, unpublished m.s.

Odeen, Diane, "A Cultural Feminist Theater: The *Stories* Change with the Times," unpublished paper presented at the Association for Theater in Higher Education Conference, Chicago, Illinois, 10 August 1990.

Phelan, Peggy, remarks on the keynote panel "Making Feminism/Making Comedy," Women and Theater Program Conference of the Association for Theater in Higher Education 1–3 August 1993.

Letter to the Theater of Light and Shadow, 31 May 1981.

Walker, Dolores, *Abide in Darkness*, unpublished ms., n.d.

Women's Collage Theater, "Women's Collage Theater Comment Book," unpublished audience comment book, 1979–81.

SOUND RECORDINGS

Newman, Naomi, *Snake Talk: Urgent Messages From the Mother*, sound recording, Blake Street Hawkeyes Theater, Berkeley, California, 7 January 1989.

Pickett, Phrin and Kotz, Cappy, *In Search of the Hammer* and *Return of the Hammer*, sound recording, 1985.

INDEX

271

Printed in the United States
35528LVS00002B/41